An important 2-volume collection of essays by one of the "most-renowned authorities in the field" —Library of Special Education

LITIES

CONCEPTS IN LEARNING DISABILITIES

SELECTED WRITINGS   VOLUME 2

WILLIAM M. CRUICKSHANK
Foreword by William H. Gaddes, University of Victoria, British Columbia

"THE PUBLICATION of selected writings by William M. Cruickshank is certain to be welcomed by special educators, psychologists, parents, and others interested in the complex developmental problems of learning disabilities. . . . [It] should be read with grateful satisfaction because of his clarity of statement and the logical development of his theoretical model. . . . For those interested in the problems of learning disabilities who have never read William Cruickshank's publications, this selection will provide an unexpected delight; for those who have had some familiarity with his work, this selection will provide a memorable survey of his essential views."—from the *Foreword*

CONCEPTS IN LEARNING DISABILITIES

Selected Writings

Volume 2

WILLIAM M. CRUICKSHANK

SYRACUSE UNIVERSITY PRESS

1981

FOREWORD

*T*HIS PUBLICATION of selected writings by William M. Cruickshank is certain to be welcomed by special educators, psychologists, parents, and others interested in the complex developmental problems of learning disabilities. Because no other area of special education has generated so much enthusiastic interest and at the same time so much confusion and controversy, Dr. Cruickshank's volume should be read with grateful satisfaction because of his clarity of statement and the logical development of his theoretical model. In a professional area which is still in its infancy and is inadequately researched, his lucid analyses and commanding knowledge will provide a helpful direction and assurance to the uninitiated or poorly informed professional and to the concerned parent looking for help for his or her child.

The problems of academic underachievement have been with us since the establishment of the first school, but the history of learning disabilities, as they are currently professionally conceived, began formally in 1963. As will be made clear in several of the papers in this collection, many educators and others are not aware of this distinction because of an ignorance of the history of ideas leading up to the most definitive current thinking. But Dr. Cruickshank has been a part of that history since 1945, and still is an active participant in molding present-day knowledge about and attitudes toward the concept of learning disabilities.

Modern theories and methods for teaching the chronically learning disabled person have grown out of the many aphasia studies in neurological clinics during the nineteenth century, and from those writers since the early part of this century who have attempted to integrate neurological, psychological, and educational knowledge. By 1950 neuropsychological research was beginning to reveal exciting new insights into perception, cognition, motor response, and language function, and their correlations with known brain functions, but most of these investigations at that time were with adults. One person who was studying these problems in children was Alfred Strauss at the Wayne County Training School in Michigan. By the early 1940s he had developed an experimental clinical program with mentally handicapped children which was breaking new ground, and in 1947 he and his junior colleague, Laura Lehtinen, published their ideas in a book, *Psychopathology and Education of the Brain-Injured Child,* which was to have a major influence on future ideas and practices in special education. A number of bright young scholars were attracted to this center and were influenced profoundly by Strauss's work. Among them, in addition to Laura Lehtinen, were Newell Kephart, Samuel Kirk, and William M. Cruickshank, all of whom have made major contributions to the field of child development in general and learning disabilities in particular.

Any reader of Dr. Cruickshank's many writings, of which the present selection is but a small sample, will be aware of his breadth of understanding of child development and his competence in clinical assessment. Also, one is soon apprised of his familiarity with the attitudes of parents and their participation in parent organizations, and his over-riding humanity that reflects a genuine concern for the problems of learning disabled children and the frustrations of their parents.

Recurring themes in his writings include the need for more and better research in the development of educational practices; the need for high-quality special education treatment programs: the need for expert teacher training programs for special education teachers; the need to understand and recognize the neurological origins of the behavior of the learning disabled child; the importance of identifying subgroups of children with special needs, and the dangers and invalidity of recommending mainstreaming unselectively for all underachievers; the necessity of administrators, as well as special teachers, to understand the problems of learning disabilities; and the value of using medical, psychological, and educational knowledge in diagnosis, but primarily educational knowledge and procedures in treating the learning disabled child. At all times throughout these papers, the discussions are child-centered.

Frequently the critics of organized education hesitate or are afraid to do anything to correct its weaknesses. Dr. Cruickshank is not one of these. He is quick to attack any mediocre established educational practices, and he makes no defense for ineffectual school programs, and advises replacing their pretense of expertise with scholarly understanding and tested treatment procedures. His analyses are direct and his proposed corrective measures logical, detailed, constructive and practical.

Dr. Cruickshank has consistently stressed the importance of recog-

Volume 2 covers the specific area of learning disabilities in 18 essays, from general overviews and issues of definition to precise teaching and curriculum at all age levels.

Some of the essays included are:

Rehabilitation—Toward a Broader Spectrum

Education for All Children in a Democracy

Perceptual and Learning Disability: Overview of the Problem

Special Education, the Community, and Constitutional Issues

Integration: A Conceptual Model

Learning Disabilities and the Special School

Hyperactive Children: Their Needs and Curriculum

Myths and Realities in Learning Disabilities

Learning Disabilities: A Charter for Excellence

Adolescents with Learning Disabilities

ites of cognitive defi-
Strauss and Werner,
stic concept of brain
ieless, he has always
iowledge. In 1966 he
ie excuse for lack of
ren is that too little is
is not true. Much is
lucators cannot await
; to assemble the puz-

iing disabilities who
nis selection will pro-
ie familiarity with his
of his essential views.

William H. Gaddes

WILLIAM M. CRUICKSHANK has always been an ardent defender of quality in special education and an outspoken critic of mediocrity in the education of exceptional children. He has published widely in many fields of special education. His most recent book is *Learning Disabilities: The Struggle from Adolescence toward Adulthood,* with William C. Morse and Jeannie Johns. Dr. Cruickshank is presently Professor of Child and Family Health, University of Michigan, and currently serves as the President of the International Academy for Research in Learning Disabilities.

CONTENTS

11   Learning Disabilities and the Special School   156

12   Hyperactive Children: Their Needs and Curriculum   165

13   Problems in the Education of Children with
     Learning Disabilities and Some Practical Solutions   181

PART V: **ISSUES AND MYTHS**

14   Some Issues Facing the Field of Learning Disability   198

15   Myths and Realities in Learning Disabilities   212

16   Learning Disabilities: A Charter for Excellence   223

17   Adolescents with Learning Disabilities   239

PART VI: **THE FUTURE**

18   A Time to Review in Time to Act   254

     BIBLIOGRAPHY, 1966–81   273

     CONTENTS, Volume 1   279

PREFACE

*I*N THE PREFACE TO VOLUME 1 of these *Selected Papers,* I used the year 1965 as the point between two major writing foci of mine. Prior to 1965, my writing was inclusive of several aspects of the education and psychology of many different types of exceptional children: journal articles, books, and speeches. Since 1965, professional concern has been almost solely in the direction of children with learning disabilities, or, as I prefer to speak of them, children with perceptual processing deficits. With respect to the latter, the year 1965 is not entirely accurate.

In 1938, I began a long association with Heinz Werner and Alfred A. Strauss, both direct daily contact and later, when they both moved from Michigan, a rewarding correspondence and a much less frequent opportunity to visit: Werner at Clark University and Strauss at his Cove School in Racine, Wisconsin. The stimulus for a lifetime interest in and concern for the neurologically handicapped child began at that time.

In the 1950s as an outgrowth of her excellent doctoral dissertation at Syracuse University, I published with Dr. Jane E. Dolphin-Courtney a replication of most of the work of Strauss and Werner (see Volume 1), but with intellectually normal cerebral palsy children instead of mentally retarded youth, as had been the area of interest of Strauss and Werner. From this, a large foundation-funded study of *Perception and Cerebral Palsy* (Syracuse University Press, 1957 and 1965) was undertaken and completed in two editions with Drs. Harry V. Bice of New Jersey Crippled Children's Commission, Norman E. Wallen, and Ms. Karen S. Lynch, the latter two then graduate students. The results of these investigations led to an experimental study-demonstration of a teaching method for brain-injured and hyperactive children which appeared in 1961. Thus, the groundwork was laid, both in my thinking and clinical work, for what since 1965 has consumed my time and efforts until today. My interests in other areas of exceptionality in children, youth, and adults ceased, because in contrast to the earlier years, there are now many who are far more experienced than I in other fields, and it is now better to leave those alone!

It needs to be pointed out further that individuals of my generation never had the privilege of working in a research setting on a full-time basis. This is not a complaint, but a statement of fact. As with Drs. Frostig, Kirk, and Kephart, among others, whatever writing or research I have done in my professional life until 1980 has been completed as an adjunct to administrative duties and teaching. Universities rarely are sufficiently well financed to be able to afford a cadre of research professors. It is often a wonder to me that knowledge has expanded as much as it has in the face of the multiple responsibilities which the leaders in the education and psychology of exceptional children have carried throughout their careers.

This volume then will be concerned solely with publications regarding so-called learning disability children and youth. My interests in this field have turned more to books than articles, and, thus, what appears here must be supplemented by reference to my books in order to obtain a complete picture of my contributions. These are included in bibliographies which appear at the end of each volume.

I hold a very firm position with respect to children with learning disabilities. I believe that all learning is conditioning, and this fundamental position in turn conditions my total approach to the clinical psychology and clinical education of this large and varied group of children with perceptual processing deficits. A high degree of individualization in the educational approach to these children is required, and as such, I find myself in full agreement with L. J. Peter's concept of prescriptive teaching in *Prescriptive Teaching,* based on extraordinarily complete diagnostic procedures. I also believe that because of the extreme nature of individual differences among children with perceptual processing deficits, controlled research is well nigh impossible to undertake with profit. Most research which has been completed and published involving so-called groups of learning disabled children leaves much to be desired. We learn little from this approach. On the other hand, clinical research and direct observation is essential and exceedingly valuable. The single-subject approach in research has a worth far beyond what has yet been widely demonstrated. From intensive observation of children with perceptual processing deficits coupled with more intense interdisciplinary diagnostic data than is customarily available, or at least utilized, it is possible to make many generalizations which cautiously can be applied to other children who appear to have the same problems. It is impossible to control the many variables which characterize these children when studied in groups so as to be able to generalize meaningfully. The single-subject approach coupled with the controls of conditioning when appropriately utilized can and does go far in both understanding fully the nature and needs of a child and placing that child on a road which most often ends in positive adult adjustment. I have said elsewhere that there is a germ in every youth which when nurtured appropriately, results in a fine man or woman. The responsibility of the professional person is to know the child so well, to learn his or her eccentricities so thoroughly, and to pit these against known learning theory so that progress is insured and a socially positive outcome is insured. This does not mean a forty-five-minute standardized intelligence test administered by a school psychologist. It means a personal investment of much time on a continuous basis over many days in order to understand the dynamics of a given child. On one occasion, perhaps the most extreme in my professional life, a child lived in my home for eight weeks as we worked together to try to understand one another to his benefit. The approach is not unique with me; follow-up studies based on this approach by others, as well as my own, have demonstrated the efficacy of the concept on more than one occasion. Hundreds of children with perceptual processing deficits who, as individuals, have worked with me during the past four decades, have progressed and are functioning as well-adjusted adults. A few of these have been reported in the literature not included here (*Learning Disabilities: The Struggle from Adolescence toward Adulthood,* Syracuse University Press, 1980, with W. M. Morse and J. Johns).

From chapter to chapter in this volume, each originally an independent article or address, a certain amount of repetition occurs, particularly with reference to issues of integration of handicapped children into the regular grades and to the characteristics of accurately defined learning disabled children. The papers in this volume begin around the year 1965. Actually, in 1939 I first wrote about the issue of integrating some exceptional children into the regular grades of the school systems. Thereafter in each decade until 1980 one or more articles appeared under my name which referred to these two issues. The reader who carefully examines these articles which appeared over a forty-year span will observe that a common point of view exists throughout, but that simultaneously there is a maturation in point of view and a blending of ideas in terms of the current professional thought of the time. Undoubtedly this will continue into the future as social, political, and professional developments occur, particularly with respect to learning disabilities.

Ann Arbor, Michigan   William M. Cruickshank
Fall 1980

PART I

INTRODUCTION

1

REHABILITATION —
TOWARD A BROADER SPECTRUM

SOME PSYCHOLOGISTS have been interested in the disabled for many years. The field of rehabilitation psychology as a professional entity, however, is still in its youth. The late Dr. Edgar Doll was a forerunner in bringing the attention of psychologists to the disabled, particularly to the mentally retarded. Dr. T. Ernest Newland has for many years called the attention of psychologists to the oftentimes peculiar needs of the handicapped particularly as these have been a concern of special educators. His recent writings in this area have been and continue to be significant. To these men's names could be added many others. The conference on rehabilitation psychology held in Princeton in 1958, in large measure the handiwork of Dr. Beatrice Wright, was a significant milestone in the formulation of a professional concern. We approach the national conference now being planned for the fall of 1970 in Asilomar, California, where the conference planners under the leadership of Dr. Walter Neff, anticipate that another important step in the maturation of a profession will take place. This conference, sponsored by funds from the Social and Rehabilitation Service of the United States Department of Health, Education, and Welfare, should indeed be the second in a series of conferences scheduled a decade apart as a planned program to keep rehabilitation psychology, its practice and its training, current to the changing demands of its consumers and the society it purports to serve. Only by a continuous program of careful professional assessment and intelligent projection can the profession appropriately monitor its training programs, its products, and the efficiency of its members in seeking and obtaining solutions to

Presidential address, Division 22 meeting of the American Psychological Association, September 1970. Reprinted from *Psychological Aspects of Disability* 17, no. 3 (1970): 149–58, by permission.

the problems of the disability groups found in society in the United States.

A simplistic statement characterizing rehabilitation psychology prior to 1960 finds it essentially a matter of intellectual and sometimes personality diagnosis and evaluation. Important exceptions to this statement can be made, but in the interest of brevity, the sentence can stand. One wonders how many intelligence tests have been administered over the years to institutionalized mentally retarded residents in the United States. For the purpose of classification and placement within the institution, practically every new patient-resident received at least one of the famous intelligence tests and occupied a psychologist's time. When any sort of research was undertaken in institutions new batteries of tests were administered, again assessing the status quo of the resident at that moment.

The public school psychologists, likewise, tested for classification purposes. Assessment and evaluation are important elements in the total spectrum, but they are not the end nor are they the total program. A careful examination of the school psychological programs in many communities of this nation will, however, illustrate that in 1970 the profession has not moved much from the level it was at in 1950 or even earlier. We still test and file, and little else is accomplished. The more unfortunate statement is that psychologists with inadequate training with the disabled still test handicapped children utilizing instruments which have little in them appropriate to the disability characteristic of the child. How else, in New York State could a recent study indicate that thirty percent of all blind children in the state are mentally retarded? When the tests utilized for this population were ascertained, few were listed which had ever been developed specifically for the blind.

Subsequent to 1950, our first point of departure in this statement, the significant writings of Lee Meyerson, Beatrice Wright, Roger Barker, and others began to filter into the thinking of rehabilitation psychologists. Dynamics of disability in addition to status quo became a central issue for the leadership in the field, although the extent to which these concepts settled into the thinking of practitioners at the service level is considered to be minimal. The dynamism of introspective psychology; the significant issues of both psychosomatic and somatopsychological view points; the spin-off from the Rorschach schools and the writings of Herman Rorschach himself, of Samuel J. Beck, Bruno Klopfer, and their associates; the efforts of Dr. Lauretta Bender in relating psychological function to organicity; and the wide reception of the earlier works of Kurt Goldstein — each of these factors in its own way served to deepen a professional understanding of the impact of disability on total adjustment and each became a force to be reckoned with by students in the significant training programs of this nation.

As the profession moves into the decade 1970 and as we hopefully view the forthcoming national conference as a hallmark for the profession significant questions arise. What are some of the issues which must be faced and which in their solution can result in a furtherance of the field of rehabilitation psychology? In this paper we will speak briefly to five issues.

CHRONOLOGICAL AGE LIMITATION

Federal and state government, whether by accident or design, have molded rehabilitation psychology in an unfortunate way and have directly affected training programs throughout the country. An example or two will indicate my thinking. In New York State, blind children, from birth to the early school years, are the legal responsibility of the New York State Commission for the Blind. During school years, they become the responsibility of the New York State Department of Education. Technically, at sixteen years they become the responsibility of the Division of Vocational Rehabilitation which is at least housed within the Department of Education, but practically they are the functional responsibility again of the Commission for the Blind in the Department of Social Welfare. What has been described here is typical of most of the fifty states. With the deaf, there are fewer special commissions as are unfortunately so typical of the blind. With the crippled and neurological disabled, there are even fewer specialized legal state organizations. However, in all states as at the federal level, by law, rehabilitation as a formal professional thrust in behalf of the disabled, begins to make itself felt when the client reaches sixteen years of age. For a child who has been disabled from birth even the term *rehabilitation* is inappropriate; for the most part these are individuals for whom a program of continued habilitation is required. To this adolescent population, however, is brought the concepts of adult rehabilitation oftentimes with little thought on the part of the rehabilitation psychologists or counselor as to the appropriateness of the philosophy.

The arbitrary age of sixteen at which rehabilitation psychology can legally begin to play a part is in and of itself an outmoded time frame. Years ago sixteen was an age when children left school to assume a work role. Then sixteen might have been appropriate as a dividing point. Today, most states yet use this age as a time when children may legally drop out of school but the labor market represented by both the employer and the unions, however, encourages initial employment at a much later age level. Sixteen continues to be the age when divisions of rehabilitation can bring their training funds, medical and service funds to play a part in the further development of the disabled. An in-depth study of the appropriateness of this arbitrary time point should be made. The Social and Rehabilitation Service could change the image of rehabilitation services in the United States by a re-structuring of the chronological age base on which services are rendered. Of what this re-structuring should consist and the age groups it should encompass, should be the basis of a significant national study. The present agency territoriality based on the chronological age of the disabled individual and all too often also on medical stereotypes, confuses the consumer of services, makes train-ing programs in universities unrelated to the need, and perpetuates a serious degree of administrative arbitrariness which results in duplication of efforts, unfilled service gaps, and programmatic artificiality.

Service is not the only issue governed and subtly controlled by arbi-trary age levels. The legal ages within which services can be provided have also been extended to the age levels toward which training can be directed. We are deeply concerned that many students engaged in training in rehabili-tation psychology receive little experience with children below the adolescent years. This restriction is often justified by faculty members on the basis of that fact that the funding agency does not permit training dollars to be spent below a certain chronological age — whether state or federal agency is of no concern at this time. The fact of the matter is that students who have had lit-tle or no pre-service graduate training in rehabilitation psychology with in-fant, early childhood, and pre-adolescent populations of disabled persons do not possess an essential element in their professional armamentarium to provide high quality service to and where the client is.

At sixteen years of age the deaf, the blind, the cerebral palsied, and the mentally retarded do not just suddenly appear. These developmental problems most often have at least a perinatal genesis. Certainly the epigene-sis of the impact of a disability in the life of a given child, together with the positive and negative psychological spin-offs, is a matter of accumulation and years of growth. To look on the disabled individual at sixteen years of age as a new being simply because hc has reached a legislatively determined point in his maturation, is less than professionally mature. In a major uni-versity, doctoral students in clinical psychology who have achieved their aca-demic goal have done so with no experience at any time with children. It is my considered opinion that not to provide students in training with indepth experience with all age levels of clients to be served is not only to deprive dis-abled individuals of high-quality service, but to mislead students as to what rehabilitation psychology is.

LIMITED SCOPE OF REHABILITATION TRAINING

The age spectrum is only one part of a double-edged issue, however. We have graduate training programs in rehabilitation psychology which are essentially limited to students experience with a single type of disability—the deaf, speech problems or other medical clinical categories. For an institution of higher education to select a clinical problem as a single focus to faculty or department research cannot be criticized. When, however, students in training are limited in their experience to a single disability group, when they leave the university and apply such a focus to the breadth of rehabilitation problems, the consumer suffers. The problems of cerebral palsy are not those of the deaf. Certainly those of hearing and speech are not those of most other disability groups.

    The perpetuation of this unidisability emphasis in training centers should be discouraged, and a greater breadth of pre-service experience should be provided. As a matter of fact, we would go one step further as we have been recommending for a number of years to educators. Is it not possible to conceptualize programs of training in rehabilitation psychology which are divorced entirely from medical and clinical categories? In education, what is so unique (except for teaching of a code for reading to the blind) to warrant a total system of education for the blind? What is so unique to children with muscular dystrophy, cerebral palsy, cardiac conditions, or other medical diagnoses to warrant special schools or special classes solely for these clinical problems. The issue may constitute a clinical problem to medicine, and for that we have no quarrel. The medical category and all it implies medically has no place in education or in psychology. The profession of rehabilitation psychology would be far advanced if it dropped all medical clinical categories as systems of organization of thinking, and developed for itself systems of training, treatment and service based on that which is unique to psychology, namely, the psychopathology inherent in, and the result of, disability. There are few psychological problems solely germane to cerebral palsy. To develop a training program in rehabilitation psychology around cerebral palsy is inappropriate. Cerebral palsy individuals are often characterized by psychopathological attributes which also are found in kind or in a different order in individuals who are deaf, blind, emotionally disturbed, or mentally retarded. A student who is provided with an indepth understanding of psychopathology related to organicity, among other things, is much more valuable to the profession than is one whose training has been based on a clinical model of deafness or other clinical category. It would be to the credit of state and federal funding agencies and certainly to the credit of a university faculty discontent with the status quo, to conceptualize and implement for a period of years a graduate training program in rehabilitation psychology which was first, premised on developmental psychology concepts to include the age frame of prenatal life to old age, and second, which was based on the generic psychopathological and sociopathological problems of disability. A program which disregarded artificial chronological age points and which essentially disregarded the traditional stereotypes of the medical model would go far in bringing rehabilitation psychology into this decade as a leadership profession. I do not see it as such now.

REHABILITATION AND DISADVANTAGE

A second issue to which the attention of the profession must be directed deals with the broad issue of disadvantage as a disability. Persons concerned with rehabilitation have had a long history of experience with disability. Much which is known about the psychological aspects of disability relating to physical problems is applicable to disability created by environmental problems. An illustration from a related field is germane. For years — more than 100 — special educators have been working with the mentally retarded and have been developing techniques which are appropriate for children and adults whose problems of social, economic, and emotional adjustment are related to intellectual disability. For almost as many years professional antagonisms have existed between general elementary and secondary educators and special educators, for reasons which are not always easy to understand. In the late 1940s and 1950s, the significance of environmental deprivation on learning began to be understood by educators. Oftentimes general educators in their haste to stake out this area of education as their own moved in with programs of education which completely ignored the long years of experience which special educators have had with almost completely similar types of learning problems. It is hard to estimate the number of dollars and manhours which have been wasted by general educators who have refused to call on special education expertise in the solution of a major educational problem. Only recently as failure compounds failure have general educators turned to special education literature and authority for suggestions which are now found practical for the problem. Such is not to say nor imply that all children reared under conditions of poverty or environmental deprivation are mentally retarded. The dynamics of the issue of children reared in poverty and social neglect are closely related to the dynamics of mental retardation, and as such there are similarities insofar as educational methodology and social solution are concerned.

Furthermore, the early work of Skeels and Dye which Skodak and Skeels recently brought to a conclusion, indicates the impact of deprivation on the growth of intellectual function. The films and writings of René Spitz and the writings of others confirm what the earlier work has suggested but which has been essentially ignored for three decades. Mental retardation the result of deprivation can be created, and its reversability under later conditions of social stimulation is negligible.

It was earlier stated that rehabilitation psychology has had a long interest and concern for disability. Rehabilitation psychologists must be quick to bring their expertise to the related disability of deprivation in all its numerous and insidious forms. Furthermore, what social psychologists have learned regarding the psychology of minority groups can be assimilated by rehabilitation psychologists and applied to the minority group of the physically and mentally disabled. The two fields have much to bring to one another. The point we here make has meaning for the nation's rehabilitation psychology training programs. The student concerns are for honesty in the profession, relevancy in their classroom and practicum experiences, and for issues germane to the confrontation and solution of significant social problems of our time. In the early 1960s, the Social and Rehabilitation Services initiated at Syracuse University under the leadership of Julius S. Cohen both in-service and pre-service training which related rehabilitation counseling and poverty. Rehabilitation counselor trainees began having instructional field experiences in community social agencies, in a county penitentiary, in black-action programs, and in economic opportunity programs. In that university, through federal funds, the concept of rehabilitation counseling was significantly broadened.

The experience reported here is not, however, characteristic of a national thrust in the direction of broadening the total base of either rehabilitation counseling or rehabilitation psychology. Course instruction must be examined and its base broadened. We must give serious attention to the evaluation of course content. The impact of environmental and social deprivation as an aspect of disability must be given full treatment in our training programs. If this can be done along side or as a part of the traditional medical model, then all well and good. If it cannot be, then a rigorous wrenching will be required to bring rehabilitation psychology and all other related programs in psychology, counseling, and education into line with the pressures of current society and liberal view point. In this considered opinion time is an element of which we have little supply. Neither the problems which demand solution, nor the consumers who fervently seek to utilize the solutions, nor the students being trained in the art of searching for solutions will permit colleges and university faculties a much longer time to bring training programs into close harmony with the most pressing social and economic issues this nation may ever face. The question before us is whether or not we continue the cafeteria approach to rehabilitation psychology training which we have followed for too many years, or move at once to a major re-structuring of our total training concept. Do courses, for example, in medical problems in rehabilitation, which are at best the height of superficiality, continue to receive major attention in graduate programs, or are these awarded their rightful non-credit status, and in their place in-depth studies initiated which relate rehabilitation psychology to the turbulent and pressing problems of the century?

REHABILITATION AND LEARNING DISABILITIES

A third issue which I wish to discuss is one concerning which I have had more than thirty years of close and intimate relation. We write now of the issue of children and adults with learning disabilities. It is my considered opinion that this aspect of disability is today in a crisis state. Parents are demanding services for their children. The Association for Learning Disabilities, a parent group, fails to recognize its historical dependency on research in the area of mental retardation and has little dialogue with the National Association for Retarded Children. The result is that mentally retarded children with learning disabilities, the original point of research focus, are ignored and do not receive their birth right. Research is lacking in this area in every component from terminology to educational and psychological methodology. Teachers and psychologists are being trained by professors who themselves have little training, but who term themselves experts: directors of programs for learning disability.

Rehabilitation psychology must take a serious look at this problem, not only within the earlier stated position in this paper to the effect that psychologists concerned with rehabilitation need to attend to the needs of children as well as of adults, but because children with learning disabilities who are inadequately served as children will become the responsibility of the profession as adults.

In large part, the problems of this aspect of disability come from terminology itself. The efforts to define "learning disability" are often humorous. They have occupied an inordinate amount of time for too many people for too long. The term is so inclusive that definitions essentially must be followed by paragraphs of exclusions or explanations. Learning disabilities are based essentially on neurological factors and their concomitant perceptual disorders. Professional personnel cannot service adequately the individual child without a fundamental understanding of perception, the

psychopathological issues of perceptual-motor disturbances, the interrelationship between these problems and emotional concomitants, and techniques of relating perceptual-motor dysfunctions to methods of educational,
physical, and social development. From this point of view, the terms children with cerebral dysfunction or children with specific learning disabilities
are far more appropriate to the real situation. Even more functional and specific is the term used in Michigan, i.e., perceptual disabilities. This writer has
continuously utilized the term brain injured in discussing these children, but
if a more functional term, if often less accurate, is desired, then those mentioned here are far more helpful than the nebulous term of learning disabilities which can mean any and all things and fails to provide quickly a meeting
of the minds among those who work with such children.

        Our problem, however, is not to argue the issue of vocabulary, but
to point out that this is a disability group which rehabilitation psychologists
generally have ignored both in training programs and in practice. It is a vast
group of children sometimes estimated to be greater than or at least equal in
size to the total field of the disabled as the latter traditionally has been defined. No longitudinal studies of this population exist, so that the epigenesis
of the problem is ill-defined and its impact on adult adjustment is unknown.
Studies of children with specific learning disabilities, beginning in childhood
and continuing through the early years of adulthood, are needed and are
ideal vehicles for interdisciplinary training and research in rehabilitation
psychology. Equally as fundamental, however, for training is the need in rehabilitation psychology for a basic understanding by the student of the elements of neuropsychological disorder which exist in all of these children and
the relationship between these elements and their counterparts in the psychoeducational program provided for the children, unless the psychologist understands the essential pieces in the psychological mosaic, he is ineffectual in
his obligation to help educators assemble an appropriate educational blueprint for the child.

INTERDISCIPLINARY ROLE

A fourth matter needs the serious attention of rehabilitation psychologists as
it should have the attention of all other disciplines. For years professional
persons have chanted refrains relating to interdisciplinary action. It is indeed
rare after several decades to see an interdisciplinary program in action which
is successful. We, as professionals, are still too egocentric and oftentimes

professionally too selfish to take the time or to make the effort to produce a working interdisciplinary model. The model of the University Affiliated Centers for interdisciplinary training in mental retardation established in approximately twenty universities in the United States, offers again an opportunity to establish leadership in the direction of which we now write. Some of these are proving successful; others may be too entrenched within a medical model to be able to break through creatively. Regardless, the intent of the legislation which made possible these Centers was to provide a setting for interdisciplinary training, service, and research. The concept of interdisciplinary function requires an intellectual as well as emotional acceptance of the dictum that all professionals are equals among equals. It requires all professions to recognize that there are certain legal responsibilities which are invested in certain professions. It requires persons trained in the art of sublimating personal and disciplinary status for the greater status and professional function of joint disciplinary attack on human problems. Interdisciplinary function is not an innate characteristic of professional people. It is learned and can be learned in the proper setting.

In the facility represented by this writer, the ultimate goal is the creation of a center for manpower development which will involve more than twenty disciplines working together under one roof in the solution of problems of disability. Already functioning effectively together are representatives of psychology, pediatrics, dentistry, occupational therapy, social work, nutrition, rehabilitation counseling, special education, speech and language pathology, higher education, and administration. Soon will be added the disciplines of child psychiatry, child neurology, physical therapy, electroencephalography, audiology, cost benefit economists, media personnel, and epidemiology. In the future it is planned that there be added to the program the disciplines of law, personnel administration, library science, sociology, health education, and possibly others. These are not separate departments within an Institute. No duplication of disciplinary training programs are to be found in the Institute. Everything which takes place in this all-university agency must have and does have an interdisciplinary character. Never — even on such relatively mundane activities as personnel search committees — do disciplines act unilaterally. Multilateral action is required in all things. Students exposed to and participating in such interrelated activities in training, in services, and in research cannot help but leave the experience with a broader functional point of view than when they started. Rehabilitation psychologists who are often the persons in the agency or community who provide the integrating force for effective action must, during their training, have opportunities of working as equals with other professions. Rehabilitation psychology cannot be insular in its approach or perspective. Neither indeed can any other profession or discipline.

ECOLOGICAL TRAINING

A final point will deal with what may be a much over-worked term, namely, the need in rehabilitation psychology training for the student to be exposed to a total ecological concept. Overworked or not, the term has important meaning to us. The principles of a biology which deal with the mutual relationships between organisms and their environment have implications and applications to psychology as a generic concept and to rehabilitation psychology as a specific. Students moulded in the interdisciplinary mode will have a greater opportunity of understanding a total life system than are those whose training has been restricted essentially to the specific knowledge of a discipline. Many of the problems seen by thoughtful leaders in medicine, in dentistry, and in engineering relate to the professional tunnel vision which has been so characteristic of these disciplines over the years. No discipline is completely free of this charge. The results of disciplinary isolationism are to be seen in any community agency and in the pulling and hauling between disciplines in almost every community of this nation. This unfortunate situation, resulting in minimally effective services to consumers, will continue until disciplinary egocentricism is replaced by disciplinary allocentricism. When students are given a theoretical and functional opportunity to view and to participate in a total community structure then a different service model will be created. When students view what they do in the light of its impact on a total social structure and within a total social structure, then and only then will new and reality based dimensions be added to the concept of social service.

If ecological concepts are to have meaning and to become significant guidelines for personal and societal planning, then the spectrum must be broadened in the university training centers through which young men and women can experience the meaning of these concepts and can integrate them into their practice and way of life.

Rehabilitation psychology cannot be content with the model it now has. As a young and maturing profession, it cannot afford to be satisfied with the status quo. Unless the student can bring himself and his professional preparation into apposition with the broad needs of the society in which he functions, he cannot truly participate in that society or assist in it realizing its ultimate goal. The concepts of both habilitation and rehabilitation in their best sense require a new confrontation and a broadening of their structures.

REFERENCES

Barker, R. G.; Wright, B. A.; Meyerson, L.; & Gonick, M. R., *Adjustment to Physical Handicap and Illness; A Survey of the Social Psychology of Physique and Disability.* Social Science Research Council, 1953.

Beck, S. J., *Rorschach's Test: I. Basic Processes.* New York: Grune & Stratton, 1950.

Bender, L., *A Visual motor gestalt test and its clinical use.* New York: American Orthopsychiatric Association, Research Monographs No. 3, 1938.

Feinberg, L. B., & Cohen, J. S., *Rehabilitation and Poverty: Bridging the Gap.* Syracuse University, 1969.

Goldstein, K., *The Organism.* New York: American Book, 1939.

Klopfer, B., & Kelley, D. M., *The Rorschach Technique.* New York: World Book, 1942.

Rorschach, H., *Psychodiagnostics.* New York: Grune & Stratton, 1942.

Skeels, H. M., "Adult Status of Children with Contrasting Early Life Experiences. *"Monographs of the Society for Research in Child Development,"* 31 (1966): 1–65.

Skeels, H. M., & Dye, H. B., A study of the effects of differential stimulation on mentally retarded children. *Convention Proceedings American Association on Mental Deficiency* 44 (1939): 114–36.

2

EDUCATION FOR ALL CHILDREN
IN A DEMOCRACY

*F*OR MANY YEARS in American education, professors in our institutions of higher learning have been urging their students to consider the desiratum: education for all children. For many years the United States has prided itself in providing a system of education for all children. Teachers in the schools of the Nation have for a long while said they were planning for the education of all American children and such planning was to be found the roots of democratic thinking, action, and life.

Without question, many of those professors of education believed sincerely that in *speaking* the idea of a completely universal education would spring into an observable reality. Without question many in this country feel that we *have* an educational system equal to all children. Superintendents without fear of opposition are proud of the educational facilities which they provide to all of the children of their communities. Teachers enthusiastically agree that each child in their classrooms has an equal opportunity for an education under their guidance and leadership.

MISUNDERSTANDING OF CONCEPT —
EDUCATION FOR ALL CHILDREN IN A DEMOCRACY

There is in American education today probably no more frequently mouthed phrase than that of the title of today's address, i.e., "Education for All Children in a Democracy." There is today in American education probably no

Reprinted from *Rhode Island College Journal* (March 1960): 43–49, by permission.

more frequently misunderstood statement. There is today in American education no more misleading a statement, a statement which so clouds the picture or lulls us into a sense of false peace with ourselves. There is no statement behind which we as educators can take such comfort or in which we can find such security from the actual realities of American education in the mid-twentieth century.

I do not doubt the fact that within the four walls of our school houses we include by far the great majority, if not all, of the children in the United States. I do not question the fact that the little red school house and its modern offspring, the central school, is a phenomenon of American culture and that their effects have been widespread. I do not question that our teachers are among the best trained in the world, that our schools are the warmest, that we have more free text books, that we have the children under our guidance longer than any other country, that we spend more for education than any civilized world nation. These facts are all undoubtedly true, and if not, it is of little consequence. They are true, however, but in spite of these statements we do not have an educational system for all children.

We house children; we keep children warm, if not overheated; we feed many of them; we keep records on all children between five and sixteen; we have goals of education; we mouth education principles. We do not, however, educate or provide for the basic needs of all children by any stretch of the imagination. What I say is true of the smallest and the largest school programs in America. By law we have all children within the grasp of education, but by lack of understanding, by lack of knowledge, and even by lack of interest we do not educate these children. We have invented the phenomenon of the normal curve which embraces all children, but in reality on any basis of measurement we concern ourselves educationally today with only that center group of children who are most nearly like ourselves and which we can easily best understand. To these children American education feeds techniques of living and on these children we practice methods of education. It is often education without spirit. It is robot.

Charles A. Lindbergh recounts in his book, *Of Flight and Life,* an interesting incident among others. He writes in his early pages about an experience in which he narrowly escaped death as a test pilot during the last war. He says, following the incident, "Returning from the border of death always makes one more aware of life. Relationships take on a higher value and the senses penetrate to new depth with a new perspective. I brought life rather than an airplane back to ground." The intangible line which Lindbergh has seen between life and the return of an airplane is similar to the line which lies between an education which encompasses all children equally in terms of the goals of democratic citizenship and an education, and one which, living among all children, teaches techniques to only a few. It is an understanding of life and the value of an individual life which makes teaching dynamic and an art and which will eventually make education a reality for a large segment of our child population who can now only say "hope is our stronghold."

CRITICISMS AND REASONS

I do not criticize without reason or without basis for my criticisms. I referred a moment ago to the phenomenon of the normal curve. On such a curve any dimension of human activity can be conceived and plotted. Thus we have seen height, weight, strength, and so on traditionally illustrated in our psychology and education textbooks. We can also plot on such a normal curve other traits of children. There is a normal curve for vision, for hearing, for intelligence, for electrical energy emanating from the cortex of the brain, for physical perfection, for cardiological status, and the like. I stated further that on any basis of measurement we as educators are prone to concern ourselves with the center of the distribution, i.e., with those individuals who are most nearly like ourselves in terms of the measured trait. Thus our efforts in this game of education for all American children are directed at *all* of the children who by sheer-luck find themselves included in the center of the normal curve. I am not certain that educators even know how to provide adequately for this group, but I am absolutely certain that the majority of public school educators and professors of higher education do not know how to provide for the large group of children who deviate from the norm by as much as one standard deviation or more on any of the bases of measurement which we have mentioned. Furthermore, I am aware that many of our outstanding university professors, public school superintendents, principals, and teachers, in general, not only do nothing for this latter group, but are in many instances not interested in these children and in many others are even hostile to the deviating child because that child does not fit into the neat frame of reference which was pronounced by some educational oracle.

     If we as educators are to keep faith with the communities we serve, if we are to meet the needs of children in a realistic way, if we are to be honest with ourselves we must begin to be aware of the fifth of our school population which serves to make up the periphery of our normal curves. In recent years we have seen in the United States parent groups organized which have often forced the school authorities to recognize certain of these groups of children and be compelled to provide for the needs of these children. I am afraid that if educators do not shortly see the light we are going to see many more of these local groups which are now organized into state and national groups come to play an important dictating role in many school systems. I am not afraid of pressure groups. I think, however, that it should be the educator who is the community leader and not the follower of parent leadership. I am speaking of the groups of parents of cerebral palsied children. Similar, but equally vocal groups of parents of mentally retarded and epileptic children have organized. I don't blame them for they are right that their children were and are meeting a poor attitude from the public and private schools of the nation and are being turned away from the doors of public schools as an inferior product socially and vocationally.

The problem of rectifying this situation falls largely on educational leaders, such as yourselves, who are in a position to understand and interpret the facts as they are to those who are learning from you or who are under your supervision.

I could speak in terms of thousands and millions of children in America, and I would be speaking with accuracy. I could tell you that the problem which we face is approximately one out of ten or twelve children in the United States. I could tell you that there are more than one million children of school age who have impaired hearing. There are over 300,000 children in the United States who are physically crippled. We have recently become aware that approximately 700,000 epileptic persons live within the geographical borders of the United States. There are far more than the 450,000 children in our elementary schools who have retarded mental development. I do not wish to bore you with statistics. It suffices to say that recent estimates show that of these and other children whom I might mention, better than 70 percent are not in any way receiving specialized educational care, treatment, or training which their physical or mental condition necessitates in order to bring them to the maximum of their capacity by the time they leave the formal educational experience. These children, among others, constitute the first, second, and third standard deviations of the population against whom we so often and so blithely turn our backs. Some of these children are included in our so-called special education classes, which for the most part are neither *special* nor *educational*, but which, are purely custodial. These are the children included in our so-called opportunity rooms, which are in many instances not opportunities for anyone.

I have criticized and I have been extremely direct in my criticism. The situation, however, is true and I have realistically reflected it. It exists in practically every school center in the United States. What is the answer? I think that there are six or seven answers and I should like to take the remainder of my time this evening to discuss these answers. We shall not discuss them in the order of their importance. Each is important and necessary.

EARLY DISCOVERY

The first of these is what I shall term *early discovery.* At the present time, the great majority of the school laws in the United States provide that children may enter school in September or in February if they are within six months of having reached their fifth year. In some instances, entrance is delayed until the sixth year. This seems adequate for the majority of children coming into the American schools, but for a large segment of our child population it is inadequate. As a matter of fact, some children may, by the very fact of the delay in treatment until even the fifth year, be so seriously retarded, physically or educationally, that they will never be able to take their place as functioning citizens in society. I refer, for instance, to the infant and young child who is deaf or who is hard of hearing, the young child who is afflicted by cerebral palsy, the young child who has epilepsy, the young child who has profoundly defective vision, and the like. The practice of educators to delay special class placement of children with retarded mental development until the eighth or tenth chronological year likewise works to the disadvantage of such children. Private clinics and private parent groups cannot be expected to assume the entire bill for the education of young children prior to the time they reach school age. If early educational programs are needed by certain groups of children in contra-distinction to the larger groups, then this obligation must be assumed by the state. The downward extension of our educational age limit is imperative. If a deaf baby, for example, is exposed to speech training at a time when his natural babbling sounds can be exploited and if specific attention can be given to his early development of speech and lip-reading abilities, then by the time the child is ready for school much will have been accomplished to assist him to take his place among children with more normal hearing acuity. Similarly, if physio-therapy, occupational therapy, and speech therapy are not early brought to the child who has at birth suffered from cerebral palsy, frequently he never will be a physically functioning citizen. When educators have it within their power to make a child more nearly physically normal as opposed to one who all his life will be a social and physical dependant, it behooves us to use every mechanism at our command to bring this about. If this demands the lowering of the educational age limit, then that educational age limit must be lowered. Further, the public must not be lulled into a sense of false understanding. They must not think because isolated private clinics, such as the John Tracy Clinic in Los Angeles, and others are doing something for the young deaf child that all children are thereby being treated. This is a thoroughly misleading concept and one which tends to cloud the issue. The fact that a few, a very small minority of children, are receiving some care in private clinics does not mean that American education has faced this responsibility realistically.

HONEST DIAGNOSIS

The second factor or answer to the problem which I have posed this evening is that of *honest diagnosis*. In considering the problem of diagnosis, I mean honest diagnosis both psychologically and physiologically. In considering the latter problem, accurate evaluation of a child's physical status cannot be made in terms of the usual routine physical examination which is given on a mass production basis by local school physicians and public school nurses. Careful physical examinations must be available to all children in the public schools and when physical defects are noted, these must be brought to the attention of highly trained specialists who are in a position to evaluate accurately the physical abilities of the child. Secondly, and more within our own field and responsibility, is the problem of psychological diagnosis. The inaccuracy of our understanding of the psychological abilities of children is appalling. The frequency with which local school systems use poor objective measures for the evaluation of their children is frightening. Psychologists do have at their fingertips adequate instruments by which careful evaluation can be made of the mental ability of children in public schools. These must be brought to the attention of the local school and they must be placed into use.

HONEST PROGNOSIS

Going along closely with the concept of honest diagnosis is that of *honest prognosis*. We will gain the respect of parents if we tell them honestly and to the extent of our best present understanding, what the limitations of their children are, limitations of a negative as well as of a positive point of view. We cannot expect parents' cooperation without adequate understanding. When we refer to honest prognosis, we are throwing a challenge to both the medical and the psycho-educational personnel who deal in the evaluation of children. Too frequently, parents come to my office with a child who is obviously mentally retarded and we say to them, "Why did you wait so long before getting assistance? Your child is 12 years old. You must have known prior to this time that he was not developing normally." And the parents say, "We did suspect that he was not developing properly. He didn't walk when he should have, and he didn't talk when he should have. We went to our family doctor and asked for his information and advice. And the reply was, "Don't worry. Wait until your child is 16 years of age, and you will never be able to tell him from a normal child." That type of information is inaccurate. Too many of our general practitioners and, in some instances, pediatricians, are not giving parents honest information regarding the prognosis of their child. This may be due either to a lack of understanding on the part of the medical practitioner himself, or his inability to face realistically the parents who come to him for advice. The problem is not purely one which the medical profession frequently meets unrealistically. It is a problem which more frequently is unrealistically met by educators. Too frequently we fail to be honest with parents. Too frequently we say, "Let us have your child for a year or so. Allow us to place him in our special class, and after that we will return him to the regular grade where he will be able to do as well as the next child." If we are speaking in terms of the mentally retarded child, this is nothing but an outright falsehood. We do not have any method yet whereby either educationally or medically we can cure such a condition as mental retardation. Returning the child to the regular classroom implies that educationally we are going to make him normal. That is an impossibility. We can, however, if we are honest educators, provide a method of education for these children which will help them to become socially and vocationally as nearly independent as they can within the limits of their mental ability. This and only this can an honest educator promise a parent. However, if this promise is given, and if it is faithfully carried through, public support will be universal behind the honest educator.

RECONSIDERATION OF THE STATES' CERTIFICATION

A fourth factor which is imperative in solving the problem which we are considering this evening is a *general reconsideration of the states' certification and reimbursement provisions for programs of education for exceptional children.* The education of exceptional children both in public day school programs and in residential school programs is expensive. If we really believe in the concept of meeting the individual needs of children, cost will assume its relative position in terms of the life span consideration of the individual. While costly in terms of general education, not to spend adequate sums of money on exceptional children will mean greater costs will have to be assumed by society when these children are adults. Adequately financed programs of special education for children in elementary and secondary schools will mean independent community living for many children and semi-independent living for many more children who otherwise might require life-span subsidization by the community. In this light, costs of the childhood investment immediately become minimized in any measure which may be applied. State fiscal programs are slow to respond to this urgent need in spite of the pressure of parent groups, forward looking educators, and the increasing number of exceptional children of school age in the United States.

Of equal concern, certainly, is the laggard situation with regard to the certification of specialist teachers of exceptional children. Several states are upgrading their certification requirements in the light of contemporary thinking and research. Too many states have certification programs for teachers of exceptional children which reflect outmoded thinking and the status quo. The profession can be upgraded to high standards of competence and performance through more adequate certification procedures. College and university programs whether we like it or not are and will continue to be reflections of minimum state certification standards. Until these minimums are courageously examined, revised, and publicized, the preparation of specialized personnel for classes of exceptional children will not be able to produce educational leaders on anything like a national scale.

EDUCATING THE TEACHER AND ADMINISTRATOR TO NEEDS OF THE EXCEPTIONAL CHILD

A fifth factor which, if all others were impossible to obtain, would go a long way towards the solution of our problem, is the *education of the general classroom teacher and school administrator to the needs of the exceptional child*. As I travel throughout the country talking with both special and regular classroom teachers, one of the questions which is most frequently asked of me comes from the regular teacher who says, "What do I do with this child who has such-and-such a characteristic?" In almost every instance, the child is one with retarded mental development, is one with impaired hearing, is one who needs special equipment in terms of visual impairment, or one who has some other physical, emotional, or social problem. Our teacher preparation institutions throughout the United States are not preparing teachers to meet the needs of any but those children who fall, as I have earlier said, within the center of the normal curve. Nowhere are teachers becoming familiar with the child who deviates. If we can make teachers and administrators aware of the needs of these children, if we can make them aware of places wherein assistance can be gained, if we can help them to differentiate between those children who logically should be in a special class and those who logically should be incorporated within the regular classroom situation, then we have gone a long way in helping the 10 or 12 million children in America who fall within the classification, "exceptional."

PARENT EDUCATION

A sixth factor which I should like to mention this evening is that of *parent education*. We have for years and years in America talked about parent education, and we have attempted, in numerous ways, to bring parents to a fuller understanding of the needs of their children. For the most part, these efforts have been directed towards parents whose children were physically or mentally normal children. If the parent of a child who is physically and mentally normal needs assistance, how much more does the parent of a child who is physically handicapped or mentally handicapped in some way need understanding in handling and providing for the needs of such a child. The impact of a physical handicap on the adjustment of a child in a family situation and the impact of a physical handicap in one member of a family situation upon the adjustment of the entire family is something that is almost impossible for you to understand and sympathize with unless you have been so unfortunate as to have had this situation arise in your own family. The problems of a physical handicap, however, need not be an insurmountable factor in healthy family adjustment providing the members of that family understand how to assimilate the handicap and the relative importance of the handicap in the light of the child who presents it. The emotional impact on a parent who has just learned that his baby is deaf is terrific. The traumatic experience of a parent who has just been told that his child may never walk is something that you and I have not to date experienced and thus cannot adequately understand. Such information, however, is being received by parents every hour of the day in the United States. These parents need assistance. They need assistance from people who can be honest with them and who give them guidance and understanding as *they* attempt to meet the needs of these children who are deaf and who may never walk. Carefully planned parent education experiences are a requisite to the meeting of the needs of deviating children on the part of the school system in the United States.

CONCLUSION

We come, thus, to the conclusion that in 1959, American education is not geared to meet the needs of all children in a democracy. We see, however, in a spotty distribution throughout the United States, small groups of educators who are concerned about the problem and who are attempting to broaden the horizon of experience for many children who logically *should* fall within our interest and within our scope. We, as educators, have a real responsibility thrust upon us. We should be challenged by the inadequacies of our present efforts to revitalize American education and to more adequately meet the needs of a large segment of our child population. The result of the induction figures concomitant with the second world war are frightening. That large segments of our adult population should be rejected from service in the armed forces of their country because of physical, mental, and/or emotional disturbance causes one to be concerned about the effectiveness of medical and educational sciences during the past twenty-five years. The challenge has been presented and certain suggestions have been made whereby the situation may be rectified. If we can institute a program of early discovery and early therapy, if we can be honest in our diagnosis and honest in our prognois of the limitations of handicaps on the lives of children, if we can increase the financial reimbursement on the part of the state and federal governments to local school systems, if we can educate teachers and bring parents to a new understanding of their contribution to the adjustment of exceptional children, then we are, in large measure, coming to a relatively early solution to a current unmet need.

3

PERCEPTUAL AND LEARNING DISABILITY

Overview of the Problem

*L*EARNING DISABILITIES as a term, now widely used in professional education and in many related disciplines, is not synonymous with all of the problems of learning found in children and youth. Learning disability is a technical concept which, since 1963, has been subverted to mean anything which educators wished to sweep into this bin. The subversion of the term and the concept, essentially to meet the needs of educators, has been a tragedy — a tragedy compounded by many well-intentioned persons as well as by agency administrators who may never have had a thorough understanding of it.

In 1974 there was published the report of a study committee (Hobbs 1974) which, among many other committees which were requested to examine terminology, produced a significant definition of learning disability. Most of the previous definitions, including that of the United States Office of Education, have defined this problem by exclusion, i.e., indicating what it is not rather than what it actually is. The committee, headed by Joseph Wepman, reporting in Hobbs's publication, defines this problem by inclusion. It states that learning disability is essentially a problem of perception and perceptual disorder. If it is perception, that means without question that the problem is centered in the neurological system of the human organism. As such this does not mean that all children admitted to programs for learning disability must be submitted to a neurological examination, for neither neurology or psychology is yet sufficiently sophisticated to be able to ascertain the exact neurological problem. Furthermore, since the therapeutic program for these children is essentially psychoeducational, the exactness of the

Reprinted from *Educational Leadership* 32, no. 8 (May 1975): 499–502, by permission.

neurological diagnosis is not absolutely necessary except in situations calling for controlled research. We mention the neurological basis of learning disability here, only to support our concern for exactness in definition and educational conceptualization of what the problem really is. The Wepman Committee report defines these children in terms of the psychoeducational reality as those, of any age, who demonstrate an inadequate ability in functions such as "recognizing fine differences between auditory and visual discriminating features underlying the sounds used in speech and orthographic forms used in reading; retaining and recalling those discriminated sounds and forms in both short and long memory; ordering the sounds and forms sequentially; both in sensory and motor acts . . . ; distinguishing figure-ground relationships . . . ; recognizing spatial and temporal orientations; obtaining closure . . . ; integrating intersensory information . . . ; (and) relating what is perceived to specific motor information."

For the first time since the early 1940s a national committee also states another truism. These *perceptually handicapped children with learning disabilities will be found to be of any and all intellectual levels.* Learning disability is not a problem characteristic only of children above an intelligence quotient level of 80! Federal, state and local regulations and definitions pertaining to these children which state the contrary are definitely in error. They perpetuate an erroneous concept which unfortunately was assumed about 1963. Those definitions are wrong. Perceptual disabilities resulting in learning disabilities are to be found among mentally handicapped children where indeed the most significant research was done which established this clinical problem. Although definitive demographic data is not readily available, it is likely that this problem characterizes a very large percentage of mentally retarded children, larger probably than that which will ultimately be found as an acceptable incidence figure for the child population above an IQ level of 80. This latter quotient, frequently found in state education regulations and in local board of education definitions, is without any scientific base whatsoever, and to perpetuate it means that thousands of children with ability lower than that figure are being denied their educational birthright. It is essential that perceptual and learning disability in children and youth be understood and accepted for what it really is.

Sometimes learning disability as formerly defined is accepted as a term almost synonymous with remedial reading. Certainly it is not that. A child with perceptual and learning disability does not need remediation in reading or in any other learned skill. The child needs a new learning experience of a developmental nature — a developmental program which may need to begin much below his chronological or mental age levels. Such programs are widely described by Kephart, this writer, Frostig, Ayres, Barsch, Cratty, and other senior authors who have devoted their professional lives to this problem. No one will find remediation the key word in the writings of any of these authors. "New learning," "developmental learning," "psychomotor match," "psychoeducational match," "perceptual-motor training" are the terms these authors use. Those who pursue the concept of remediation are not concerned with the best interests of the child in question.

Where does this type of new learning take place for these children? Some children with understanding teachers may be assisted in the ordinary classroom, although this situation will have its drawbacks for the child. If the teacher is assisted by an aide or by a team of well-oriented volunteers or both, the child's growth and educational development may be more insured in the ordinary grade placement. Although he wrote concerning the mentally retarded child with perceptual handicaps, J. J. Gallagher's fine volume illustrating the potential of the tutorial approach to these children has great value. The resource room, if the teacher is appropriately prepared, is a valid solution for the majority of these children, but there will be others for whom a special clinical teaching station, relatively self-contained, is the most appropriate decision. Here too the teacher's preparation is the keystone to the problem.

We feel that a structured program is the most appropriate for these children, structure being utilized as a tool for teaching and growth. A permissive environment for these children pays less dividends for the children and their families. Although only passing comment can be made here due to limitations of space and appropriate editorial writing, there is a full literature available on every topic here mentioned which the thoughtful reader can pursue. We have made numerous definitive statements in this editorial. They are made from years of close personal relationships with these children, with classroom situations, and with extensive clinical data.

The "field" of perceptual and learning disability is relatively new, certainly very new as a wide-spread educational concern. There are dozens of pressing problems which must be solved. Some of them need solution before children will receive appropriate learning experiences in appropriate settings. The field lacks a sufficient corps of well-prepared educational specialists in the public schools. The fad of "mainstreaming" which has engulfed American education in the past few years is not a new concept, but it is one which is being employed in thoughtless ways at a high cost to thousands of exceptional children and their families. Speaking only of perceptual and learning disability, we guess that ordinary classroom teachers who know how to work with these children in anything by the global concept of "individualization," is a miniscule percentage of the total national teaching corps. If integration of these children is to be undertaken, general educators and administrators must know something more about it than they now do. Psychologists in great numbers who function in schools, must also learn how to present to the educators a psychological picture of these children which can be matched to educational methodology appropriate to the child's needs. The IQ and the MA are not helpful data to the teachers of these children, but what constitutes the mental age is helpful if it is properly conceptualized.

Reference in all facets of this problem is needed and demanded. It is impossible to estimate the number of dollars which have been wasted to date in the interests of learning disability because the concept was not properly understood and because research was almost totally lacking. Research is needed in both epidemiology and demography related to the problem. It is needed in terms of the structure-nonstructure issue. It is needed in terms of the role of perceptual-motor training. It is needed in terms of the control of children's behavior with medication. It is needed in the relationship of these problems in children and the ingestion of artificial food colorings, genetic implications, biochemical imbalances, environmental deprivation on the total ecological spectrum, and nutritional deprivation (both prenatal and postnatal). Research is needed in the areas of neurological, educational, and psychological diagnosis and the development of instrumentation to make diagnosis more exact. Studies are needed regarding a logical attack on this problem when it is found in or persists into preadolescence and adolescence. Little consideration has been given this problem in terms of the secondary school levels.

Training programs based on content are needed for all professional personnel who proport to work in this complex field of child growth and development. Not only is content-oriented training and professional preparation required, but so is an understanding and practice in the function of an interdisciplinary team attack on this problem. The traditional interdisciplinary team approach is not that of which we speak here, i.e., that moderated by medical personnel who function within the school. The interdisciplinary team which is needed with perceptual and learning disabled children is that in which professions function as equals among equals. It supports the education program and has minimal direct relation with the child. It has as its focus the ultimate return of the child to the educational and social community as fully a participating person as is possible with what we know and will know regarding his needs and approaches to learning and adjustment.

REFERENCE

Hobbs, N., *Issues in the Classification of Children.* San Francisco: Jossey-Bass, 1974, Chapter 11.

4

SPECIAL EDUCATION, THE COMMUNITY, AND CONSTITUTIONAL ISSUES

*S*PECIAL EDUCATION for exceptional children faces challenges to its very existence. Some of these are of its own making; others are products of historical attitudes and of the time in which we write. In juxtaposition, however, these factors have produced a situation which all educators must solve if the basic tenets on which the field is founded are to survive and if exceptional children are to be served. A unique and historically unprecedented situation is developing in the United States, the significance of which is immense, but in no manner is it appreciated yet by all professional educators, members of boards of educations, or the citizens of the community. So powerful is its potential thrust that the face of special and general education could be completely changed at almost a single stroke.

As we see it, the problem is at least of a two-fold nature. The first deals with the broad issue of psychological diagnosis, labeling and placement of children. The second issue concerns itself with the quality of special education for these children once psychologists and administrators have made decisions regarding them. Both of these matters are intimately related and both are subject to professional accountability.

In this paper we wish first to examine a matter of growing concern on the part of the consumers of education, and to note the legal challenges which are being made to psychological evaluation and judgment, and to the placement of children. The prediction of this type of community challenge

Reprinted from *Special Education: Instrument of Change in Education for the 70s,* edited by Walker and Howard. Charlottesville, Va.: University of Virginia, 1970–71, by permission.

was well stated by Dunn (1968),[1] one who spoke for many concerned educators. The predictions he made are indeed coming true. Secondly, we wish to couple this development with issue of consumer self-determination which has a significant impact on education generally and on special education in particular. The third and fourth issues to which we wish to address ourselves deal with the responsibility of both special and general education for dissatisfaction with school programs, the crisis around which the legal arguments are developing. Finally, we shall look at some solutions which may be important, if the needs of handicapped children are to be met. Let us turn first to the community concern with psychological judgments and special education placement.

THE COMMUNITY AND THE LAW

As special classes for the mentally retarded and for children with learning disabilities in the public schools continue to contain a disproportionate number of children from racial minorities, parents, educators, and psychologists are becoming increasingly concerned over the validity of currently used psychological tests as a tool for educational placement. In 1969 Mexican-American children made up 13 percent of the California school population though they accounted for almost 30 percent of special education students within the state.[2] Nationwide there are fifteen times as many blacks as whites in programs for the mentally retarded.[3] School districts have generally been unresponsive to the pleas for change in placement criteria, so parents have turned to the courts and a ground swell of litigation has followed.

The first of the arguments which are most frequently leveled against current placement procedures says that present *educational testing does not accurately measure the learning ability of the public school child.* It is argued that intelligence tests are standardized on groups consisting primarily of white, middle class children. In addition, the tests are heavily verbal, and therefore discriminate against those whose cultural background does not emphasize the development of verbal skills. The questions themselves are unfair, because they are more easily answered by white, middle class school children, e.g., "What color are rubies?" "Who wrote *Romeo and Juliet*?" "What are checks for?"[4]

In 1967 Judge Skelly Wright held illegal in *Hobson v. Hanson* 269F. Supp. 401 (1967) the method whereby examinations of achievement and ability were used to determine the placement of a student in a particular curriculum of the Washington, D.C., public school system. In the court's opinion:

The evidence shows that the method by which track assignments are made
depends essentially on standardized aptitude tests which, although given on
a system-wide basis, are completely inappropriate for use with a large segment of the student body. Because these tests are standardized primarily on and
are relevant to a white middle class group of students, they produce inaccurate and misleading test scores when given to lower class and Negro students.
As a result, rather than being classified according to ability to learn, these
students are in reality being classified according to their socio-economic or
racial status, or — more precisely — according to environmental and psychological factors which have nothing to do with innate ability. (p. 514)

Judge Wright's holding with respect to standardization was primarily based upon William Kunstler's cross-examination of Dr. Roger T. Lennon, Vice-President and Director of the Testing Department of Harcourt,
Brace, Jovanovich, Inc., publishers of the Stanford Achievement Test and
the Otis Quick-Scoring Mental Ability Test series, typical of other tests
which are used in many of the nation's public schools. A significant interchange between Mr. Kunstler and Dr. Lennon includes the following:

Q Now, as I understood your testimony earlier, your standardization group
includes a certain percentage of Negro children, and I thought you said five
to seven percent?
A Yes, I think you are right, Mr. Kunstler, I believe I did.
Q Would you indicate to the Court why the number of Negroes, the percentage of Negroes, is approximately half that, according to your figures, of
the Negroes in the total American population?
A I would say two things, Mr. Kunstler. First in citing the figure five to
seven percent, as you know, I was quoting from memory; but taking those
figures at face value, the only thing that I could say was that this deviation in
terms of representation from the national picture represents nothing more
than a certain lack of control on our part. We would wish it were otherwise,
but you will also recall that we have not sought or concerned ourselves immediately and specifically with the matter of race as a dimension of our
sampling matrix. So to other factors, and what has emerged is not the result
of specific, immediate attention to racial representation but the natural outgrowth of the operation of the other sampling bases.
Q Does that mean, Dr. Lennon, that Harcourt, Brace, for example, your
department, came to a policy decision that race was not a factor to be considered in the standardization of the achievement and aptitude test?
A Yes, sir. We have very definitely taken the position that in the standardization of our tests and the definition of samples, we will not use race *per se*
as a dimension to be controlled.
Q You don't use race at all as a dimension?
A That is correct, sir.[5]

Judge Wright then examined the emphasis of the tests upon verbal skills, and stated:

The scholastic aptitude tests used in the District school system are verbal, with the exception of one series (TOGA) which includes a nonverbal component. . . .

The chief handicap of the disadvantaged child where verbal tests are concerned is in his limited exposure to people having command of standard English. Communication within the lower class environment, although it may rise to a very complex and sophisticated level, typically assumes a language form alien to that tested by aptitude tests. Slang expressions predominate; diction is poor; and there may be ethnically based language forms. The language spoken by Negro children in the ghetto has been classified as a dialect.

Other circumstances interact with and reinforce the language handicap. Verbalization tends to occur less frequently and often less intensively. Because of crowded living conditions, the noise level in the home may be quite high with the result that the child's auditory perception — his ability to discriminate among word sounds — can be retarded. There tends to be less exposure to books or other serious reading material — either for lack of interest or for lack of money. (p. 481)

The unfair nature of the questions themselves was noted:

The disadvantaged child has little or no opportunity to range beyond the boundaries of his immediate neighborhood. He is unfamiliar, therefore, with concepts that will expand both his range of experiences and his vocabulary. He has less exposure to new things that he can reduce to verbal terms. For example, one defense witness, a principal of a low-income Negro elementary school, told of how most of the children had never been more than a few blocks from home; they had never been downtown, although some had been to a Sears department store; they did not know what an escalator was, had not seen a department store Santa Claus, had not been to a zoo. These experiences, common in the subject matter of tests and textbooks, were alien to the lives of these children. (p. 481)

On appeal, the District of Columbia Circuit Court of Appeals in *Smuck v. Hobson* 408F. 2d 175 (1969), affirmed the lower court's decree abolishing the track system.

Following the Hobson case, the Federal District Court of Southern California found in the Pasadena school district, racial discrimination of a designed nature as a consequence of grouping students according to their abilities as recognized by standard intelligence tests and teacher recommendations.

In its January 1970 ruling on *Sprangler v. Board of Education* 311 F. Supp. 501 (1970), the Court found:

> The racial effect of the grouping procedures generally in use in the District is to increase segregation. At every secondary school a higher percentage of black than white students is in slow classes in every subject matter, and a higher percentage of white than black students is in fast classes. ***The racial segregation that exists within integrated schools as a result of interclass grouping doubtless has numerous causes, not all of which are treated in the record. ***One is that grouping assignments are based in part on scores obtained on achievement and "intelligence" tests. As the District's assistant superintendent for elementary education acknowledged, such tests are racially discriminatory, based as they are primarily on verbal achievement. (p. 519)

Additional suits filed in the District Courts of California on behalf of Mexican-American students further reinforced the case against current testing techniques.[6] *Diana v. State Board of Education,* C-70 37 RFP, cited the Civil Rights Act of 1964 (42 U.S.C. 2000d, 2000d–1), contending deprivation of a citizen's right to an equal education and required special testing of minorities.

Covarrubias v. San Diego Unified School District, 70 394T, sought both damages for a conspiracy to deprive citizens of equal protection under the laws, and an injunction against special education classes until placement procedures were modified; while *Stewart v. Philips,* 70 1199F in Boston asks recognition of the influence of black culture on learning as well as the affects of poverty. Closely related to this argument is a decision of a three-judge federal panel (October 8, 1971) in the *Pennsylvania Association for Retarded Children v. the State of Pennsylvania,* which ruled that all children are capable of benefiting from an education and are entitled to one. This judgment stemming from a charge by the Association that Pennsylvania unconstitutionally discriminated against many retarded children by allowing school psychologists to decide if a child were educable. The implications of this ruling will be felt both in residential care facilities as well as in public school systems, wherever the mentally retarded individual may be.

A second argument leveled against current placement procedures, to which only passing reference will be made here, states that the *administration of tests is performed incompetently.* The plaintiffs in *Hobson, Stewart,* and *Covarrubias* argued that those public school officials administering the intelligence tests were not adequately trained to do so. "The skilled tester should be aware of the cultural backgrounds of the children so that anxiety created by the testing situation or inability to understand directions because of language problems can be detected."

The third argument against placement is that *Special Education programming itself is inadequate.* At the heart of the *Hobson* decision and underlying most arguments which attack the criteria for special education placement is the finding that "once a child is improperly placed in an educable mentally retarded class, there is little chance that the student will leave it. Insufficient attention is given to the development of basic educational skills and retesting occurs infrequently if ever. Contributing further to the lack of upward mobility is the student's self image which is formed by improper placement and creates the self-fulfilling prophecy of low achievement." Judge Skelly Wright states in *Hobson*:

> The real tragedy of misjudgments about the disadvantaged student's abilities is, as described earlier, the likelihood that the student will act out that judgment and confirm it by achieving only at the expected level. Indeed, it may be even worse than that, for there is strong evidence that performance in fact declines. . . . (P. 491).

Once locked into the special track "the social stigma surrounding the label 'mentally retarded' remains with the child his entire life. Obtaining a job may be difficult if not impossible" and the psychological damage caused by low self-esteem may be great. Improper placement, therefore, produces irrevocable imprisonment in a system which relegates "the victim to an economic, educational, and social position far below that which he is in fact able to achieve."

Considerable time has been spent in discussing the legal ferment which is growing in several areas of the United States and which portends to become contagious. We do not fear such contagion, for from our point of view judgments in the favor of the plaintiffs might require a favorable overhaul of all aspects of special education and probably general education as well. This could be positive.

It is appalling that special education and psychological practice in the schools often have been permitted to function on low levels of professional performance without something being done about it internally. If intelligence tests are so poor in many of their characteristics; if they are sometimes misused on one population when originally intended for use on another; if inadequate personnel are administering them and making judgments about children from the resultant data; and if educators in gossip or in misguided judgment make unethical statements about children from the data at hand — if all or any of these things are true and can be documented, why in the name of conscience have not psychologists done something to correct the issue of tests and testers; and why have not educators been brought to the high level of the professional ethic practiced by sister professions?

As pollutants from cars have become recognized as a detriment to clean air and life itself, state legislatures, the federal congress, and other political and environmental groups have moved to insist that automobile manufacturers correct the defect by a certain fixed date. Alfred Binet's first test was published in 1895, but after several revisions, the latest of which was but a few years ago, this commonly used test still retains defects and its continued use in its present form permits misdiagnosis, labeling for life, and deprivation of the birthrights of thousands of children, when those children often are not the ones for whom the test was intended nor on whom it was standardized. And yet psychologists, the American Psychological Association, the Council for Exceptional Children, and other powerful professional groups have literally done nothing to correct the situation. The Wechsler series of intelligence scales, the infant scales, the famous social maturity scale, and others are each and all subject to the same criticism. The profession has not done responsible monitoring. Often it may have served to protect the failures of its membership. This cannot be further tolerated. These insights are not newly acquired, but go back through many generations of children.[7]

PARENT PARTICIPATION AND SELF-DETERMINATION

The abovementioned three arguments against special education placement which have been heard in the courts are coupled with a fourth argument of major proportions. It is stated that *"parents are not given an adequate opportunity to participate in the placement decision."*

In a case currently proceeding to trial, a group of eleven Mexican-Americans primarily school children, have filed a complaint at Superior Court of California (*Arreola v. Board of Education* 160 577), seeking an injunction against further continuation of special education classes for the developmentally disabled until parents are given the benefit of a hearing before placement, and the intelligence tests being used recognize the cultural differences of Mexican-Americans. As a result of the changes in the California Education Code prompted by *Diana,* the plaintiffs attack upon the cultural bias of the intelligence tests appears insignificant. The real focus has now become the question of parental participation in the placement decision. The argument is grounded on the Due Process clause of the Fourteenth Amendment.

As in *Arreola,* an important part of *Stewart* is the argument advanced by the class of plaintiffs representing "all the parents of students placed in classes for the mentally retarded in the Boston public schools who have been denied the opportunity to participate in the placement decision." They ask that the school board establish consultation procedures by which parents might participate in the placement of their children.

It is difficult to isolate trends clearly one from the other for obviously they are interrelated. The legal issues involving parental participation which we have noted are intertwined with the self-determination which large segments of our society are accepting as a mode of life. The black citizens of our nation have made black beautiful to themselves, and they have said to the rest of the nation, "Recognize that beauty within the constructs of our Constitution. There is no alternative." Chicano citizens, the American Indian, the Chinese-American, the Japanese-American, and the other ethnic groups on which the greatness of America is based, have individually and collectively insisted that their place in the sun be insured. They are succeeding in their effort.

As success motivates the search for more success, it is right that these groups look at those elements in the community which remain as binding forces to their earlier segregation and inequality. The schools and poor special education are convenient and early targets of their attention. White America in its more thoughtful moments is agreeing with the minorities, and much of the white leadership is now being brought to bear on the matters which minorities have highlighted. The large bulk of the university and college student group, fortunately the leaders of the next decades, sees the injustices and hypocrisies of our present ways of living and is appropriately demanding redress for the affected.

Those things which can be interpreted in the light of segregation will fall into the focus of a tremendous and powerful social spotlight. Special education is one of these things, and parents in *Arreola* ask redress. General education also is not safe from community inspection, nor is it innocent in the eyes of the consumer. Tract systems, homogeneous groupings, ungraded classrooms, social promotions are all administrative tools which educators have used to serve their own ends. However, they have not served society as our citizens now wish to be served. The recourse to the courts which some parents are using to protect the interests of their children is now visible, and this method will be used more and more by citizens as another useful tool of self-determination to correct injustice. Significant constitutional issues are yet to be resolved, but the trend is clear and unmistakable. Educational leadership wisely exercised now can avoid the necessity of conforming later to judicial decree.

Special education would not be judged as discriminatory, as a technique of structuring social classes, or in any negative light if it had always produced a good product during past years. We have had time to develop a good product, but we have not risen to the opportunity nor to the social obligation to do so. Some years ago Mr. Richard Hungerford, then Director of the Bureau for the Education of Children with Retarded Mental Development in the City of New York Public Schools, with his colleagues, created a significant concept of education and curriculum development for retarded children. This concept was specifically based on the children's identified needs as retardates and on the opportunities in the community for their employment as adults. That he was professionally attacked for his seemingly unorthodox efforts by special and general educators in the New York City public schools is a matter of history. When one compares the fundamental truths of his effort against the quality of curriculums published by many public school systems in the United States, one finds little in the latter to defend as special in special education. We still operate most of special education for the retarded on the basis of a watered-down academically oriented curriculum, on handicrafts, and within the concept of second-class citizenship. Special education is a stepchild not generally wanted by the educational profession, and we have brought this situation essentially on ourselves. From a position of weakness, it is not easy to withstand the pressures of the community. It is never pleasant to operate from the defensive position, yet special educators may not long be able to operate in a position of healthy and socially responsible offensiveness. It is easy to understand why, in a climate of self-determination and self-respect, many parents question the appropriateness of labels and the means by which decisions regarding labels and placement in special education were made.

SPECIAL EDUCATION'S RESPONSIBILITY

We have alluded to several factors inherent in special education itself which contribute to the situation we face today and against which the consumer is beginning to protest. Among these are the failure to create appropriate curricula for children, the failure to correct our own deficiencies when ample time has been provided, and the failure to produce a product which the community recognizes is the result of good school programs. All these things serve to create more than a few doubts in the minds of thoughtful parents. Other criticisms can be extended toward special education which are not easily justified or countered. Not all of these are the responsiblity of special education alone; many may be the result of political selfishness and parental desperation.

Beginning in the early part of the decade of the forties, parents rose up by the thousands in the states and nationally to demand that services be extended to their children — mentally retarded and those with cerebral palsy, particularly. Parents in the Association for Children with Learning Disabilities have likewise done the same. These lay people rightfully assumed that educators and psychologists and physicians knew what should be done about these children, and that the only thing which was needed was a sufficient quantity of dollars to provide service supports. Parents often didn't sense that we had few adequate curricula for educable mentally handicapped children and fewer for trainable children. They frequently didn't know of the professional infighting among educators around educational concepts, the concept of occupational education for the retarded, for example. Parents had no reason to know that psychological tests were inadequate or that some individuals functioning as psychological diagnosticians were in reality ill-prepared for their work. Parents didn't realize that basic research on the way retardates learned was essentially lacking, that little information was at hand regarding vocational training, that teacher certification for this work operated on minimums rather than maximums, or that the minimums were received too often from poorly prepared college professors. On these unknowns parents obtained vast sums of money for services and essentially gave it to professionals to perform services. It is our considered opinion that these services have failed to produce a product of quality commensurate with the investment made for the very reasons we have stated that parents could not know, or which they took on faith as truths. While the education of children with mental retardation is better off than some fields, due to its long history, an examination of the presently popular field of learning disabilities will illustrate the point here being made.

The history of this field is indeed short. While the work of Montessori, Fernald, and some others antedate the early 1940s, essentially the first publications concerned with psychopathology of brain-injured mentally retarded children were published in 1941–42. The first application of these findings to intellectually normal, neurologically handicapped children took place about 1952. The first attempts at any organized research with these children in an educational frame of reference was begun in 1957 and published in 1961. The first published conceptualization of teacher competencies in this field appeared in 1966; the first report of a teacher education program, in 1969. We are dealing here with a contemporary phenomenon.

Simultaneously, parents of children with learning disabilities have become very well-informed regarding their children from the literature which does exist. They have begun effectively to put pressures on school personnel to create service programs, and they have been instrumental in having federal legislation passed in behalf of their children. This parental effort has taken place again on the assumption that dollars would produce results.

However, if one looks at this field, one is appalled at the fact that in all of the United States there is but a small handful of college professors in the area of learning disabilities who are equipped to prepare teachers for this work, and that there is no significant effort to increase the size of this corps. There is a large number of college professors who call themselves professors of education for children with learning disabilities. This has been a very popular bandwagon in the past decade, and one sees the phenomenon of the instant specialist on hundreds of occasions. We think the greatest emergency in all of special education exists in the large number of well-intentioned young people who represent themselves as professors in the field of learning disability without ever having had an organized orientation to the problem. Too few have had direct experience with these children for a long enough time to understand the problem. Few have had opportunities for even superficial exposure to research in psychology or learning related to this field, or indeed time themselves to mature in relations to this most complex challenge of human development.

In spite of the absence of qualified professors, federal agencies continue to provide teacher traineeships for the summers mostly, but for academic year programs occasionally. It is politically significant to provide large numbers of traineeships to teachers. These traineeships are used in institutions of higher education where teachers come under the tutelage of poor professors and thus perpetuate mediocrity. Would it not be better to declare a moritorium on learning disabilities for two or three years while a crash effort be made to thoroughly prepare a corps of fifty to a hundred well-qualified educational professor-specialists who are basically founded and comfortable in all aspects of this subtle, technical, difficult field of child growth and human development? In a country with the resources of this nation, it is appalling to state that in 1972 there are indeed only a few universities in the United States and Canada where teachers can learn in depth to deal with the complex problems of children with specific learning disabilities. Without adequate professors, there will be no adequate teachers. Without adequate teachers, there will be no adequate community programs. Parents will accept what is given them until they come to realize that it is in large measure a fraud. How can we then be surprised that parents take special education to court and show it for what it is? The United States Office of Education and Bureau for the Education of the Handicapped could rectify this situation within a five-year period if it were prone to do so. We cannot continue to espouse in learning disabilities a program of mediocrity as a national policy.

As a nation we still have no policy to insure educational quality. Education as a right reserved to the states and delegated to local communities is a high-sounding tenet, but no where have we seen the right as reserved to the states sufficiently monitored to ascertain that quality as a birthright of American citizens is insured. Furthermore, academic freedom in universities and colleges does not give college presidents and deans the right to employ poorly prepared faculty members whose appointment and subsequent tenure mean that they will be in positions of power for many years—power to deliver a poorly prepared product for employment in the education of children. Federally funded traineeships in special education under PL 88-164 required only two years of relevant experience before the award was granted. With this minimum, with often inadequate screening of candidates, young men and women moved swiftly through programs of graduate training to become professors of special education in hundreds of colleges and universities which hastily organized departments to profit from the federal bonanza. In our considered opinion not all by any means of the rewards of PL 88-164 are good. Students who could not get accepted in one university because of deficiencies in their records turned to others where standards were not so high and still entered the profession with the doctorate a year or so later. As much as we personally resent the implications of certification, we need in special education and in general education something akin to national boards in medicine and hospital boards of review to protect the educational patient. The responsibility of special educators is indeed great in the etiology of the problem we face.

GENERAL EDUCATION AND ITS RESPONSIBILITY

General educators also have a responsibility in this difficult situation. Ignore for a moment the problems of class size and teacher-pupil ratio, both factors of major significance in a good educational program. General educators, both teachers and administrators, have been all too comfortable to use special education classes as dumping grounds for the unwanted, as temporary or permanent placements for the management problems, as sources for supplemental income from outside the community. It is no secret that school principals have occasionally commented to psychologists just before a test-ing situation that it would be helpful if this child's intelligence quotient were found to be within the limitations of special class placement. It is also no se-cret that many special educators have hoped a given child's IQ would be found low enough to permit him to be removed from the unholy competition of the regular grade and to allow him the more relaxed atmosphere of the special class. These policies, among others, produce unteachable teaching situations, and create learning vacuums for children.

General educators as a group have never made an effort to learn about exceptional children, yet many become instant authorities in any con-versation. Dunn strongly says special educators "have been living at the mercy of general educators who have referred their problem children to us. . . . Let us stop being pressured into continuing and expanding a special education program that we know to be undesirable for many of the children."

Teachers' attitudes toward exceptional children reflect those of the culture. The historical stereotypes are present among educators as they are in other social groups. These stereotypes limit the capacity of educators to accept the child who on any measurement is on the periphery of the social group. Teacher attitudes towards exceptional children can be changed, but change can be brought about only through a planned educational attack.[8] This has never been done by general educators, and it has been resisted by them for many years. Until general educators know about exceptional chil-dren, no program of integration of such children into the regular grades will be effective. To continue special education as it now is would be a tragedy, but to move in response to community pressures to a program of integration into the regular grades would be a catastrophe for thousands of children.

We are at a point in our educational development where all the alter-natives must be carefully assessed. That which can be used with profit to children should be developed, and those plans which cannot be used in the favor of the consumer must be dropped even though they be sacred to some individuals or to groups. This means that quality special education must be developed as a bona fide educational service to children who can profit from it. It means that appropriate programs of integration of the exceptional into regular grades should be implemented which provide rich learning experi-ences for every child. It means that resource rooms, itinerant teachers, the creative use of volunteers and teacher support personnel be employed and used effectively. Just to face a barricade in the road and run blindly to an-other exit is not the solution. Careful assessment of what we have that is good must be undertaken immediately. That which can be proved to meet the needs of all children or groups of children must be culled out and im-proved; that which cannot, must be discarded immediately.

There is no single way to provide for all exceptional children, but if general education is to play any part in this program at all, then all general educators must have educational experiences during their training period which will permit them to understand and to serve the consumer of their services. That elementary school administrators and teachers can be appointed to their positions in 1971 without having had any training and little understanding related to approximately a fifth of the clientele they serve is a fact which would happen only in public education and in no other field of professional activity in the United States.

Elsewhere we have written of misfits in the public schools.[9] We have never defined exceptional children as misfits, but we do point the finger of professional irresponsibility at elementary and secondary administrators and at college professors of education who fail to realize the full dimension of the obligation to all children. These are the misfits, and these people allow special education to become a scapegoat or whipping boy as an alternate to their own guilt. These are strong words, but stronger words than these are going to be required in the days ahead to protect children, to force changes in teacher education, and to bring all education to a new level of professional responsibility and acceptance in the community. As this problem of special education placement becomes more frequently verbalized in the community, do not let general educators escape from their responsible role. General educators have often said the better way is total integration of the exceptional into the regular grades. If this be true, which is very doubtful, then elementary and secondary teacher education must provide the theoretical and curricular supports to its teachers which to date it has never undertaken.

SOLUTIONS ARE AT HAND

The problems which have been discussed are not the total list. They are basic to the legal actions which have been taken and are being prepared for still other court actions. It is a sufficient list of problems to remind us that all is not right with the world of psychological diagnostics and special education. We must put our house in order, or the privilege of doing so may indeed be taken from our hands. If general education cannot understand the proper role of the specialist or cannot itself find ways of dealing appropriately with its own inadequacies, then others to whom the right has been reserved may well find it appropriate to intercede for their children. There are some solutions which can be offered for immediate implementation, not all of which will be popularly received. We place them in no priority list, for each is a high priority in and of itself. Neither is the list we present complete. It is suggestive of the rigorous attack which must be made if special education is to achieve the expectancies the community holds for it.

First, *professional review panels* must be established to monitor the adequacy of psychological and educational diagnostic programs operated by schools and clinics throughout this nation. This is not a matter of centralization of control nor infringement of the rights of individual professionals. Psychological diagnosis is equally as technical and as significant as any aspect of medical diagnosis. Medical practitioners have not found their independence curtailed when through their own mediums they have been required to maintain high standards of service delivery using the technique of the professional board of review. The system is not fool-proof, but it goes far to insure for the public a high quality of medical service in an area where the public cannot itself be authoritative. Psychological diagnosis is likewise an area where the public must rely on the profession. If this be the case, the profession itself must insure that the public receives its just due.

Review boards should be established at all levels to review credentials of personnel, the capacity of the individual psychologist to provide services to children particularly those who represent extreme physical or mental deviations, the adequacy of instrumentation used, the quality of interpretation of data which are made, and the appropriateness of recommendations. Commercial firms should not be allowed to sell imperfect psychological tests any more than pharmaceutical houses can sell drugs harmful to human life.

We would proceed further and recommend review panels for all programs of special and general education. State departments of education should properly perform this function, but these agencies are historically weak and are inadequately staffed so it is rare that they are able to serve in this role. Certification handled by the state education office, a point where some control can be exerted, is customarily the interpretation of minimums, and is essentially a clerical matter.

Parents, as previously stated (*Arreola*), are demanding a vital role in education. Citizens in a parallel activity are demanding that there be citizen review committees of all local police action. The professional policeman doesn't like this suggestion. The citizen demand comes, however, from the fact that policemen have not apparently performed their duties at a level expected of them by the community. Brutality directed to any man, regardless of color or race, is not condoned in the tradition of this country. In the failure of some police systems to maintain a standard compatible to tradition, citizen review panels have demanded and have been developed in a number of cities.

If this is to happen in professional education, educators too will resist. Better we immediately provide a mechanism which is effective in insuring the level of education which the community expects. In so vital a function to the life of any nation, no one can avoid the utilization of any review body which may better insure quality of the product. Education is often as brutal to children as police are reputed to be brutal with some university students, arrested prisoners awaiting trial, or convicted felons. It is simply an interpretation of what adults do to children which has not yet been viewed in the same light. Our house must be put in order, and review panels properly conceptualized and widely using their powers could go far in producing quality.

Second is the matter of *accreditation*. As much as it was distasteful to many department chairmen and university presidents, the American Psychological Association and the American Speech and Hearing Association have provided instructional strength to programs of graduate and undergraduate training in their respective areas. Approval or the withholding of approval of training programs, assessment of the quality and number of staff, clinical facilities, and library resources has permitted strong programs to mature, and has caused weak programs appropriately to go out of business. If they have not followed the latter course, the employer is aware that he is hiring graduates from a program recognized to be weak. In education we do not do this. The greatest university program in special education in the United States is equivalent to the weakest in the eyes of the uninformed superintendent-employer of teachers, if he deals in certification concepts alone. He needs to be protected as much as do the children of his system.

We object to accreditation personally, but we are of the opinion that its benefits are greater than its limitations, and that regardless, it is another mechanism to insure quality quickly. Accreditation of special education programs by a professional organization, whose findings are respected by the funding agencies in terms of training grant awards, would go far toward increasing the stature of professional training.

Third, we would recommend the *removal of tenure* from teachers and administration at both the public school and university levels. Incompetent teachers and professors who have somehow achieved a tenure status should not be protected or permitted to continue their incompetence. Semester after semester serious undergraduate and graduate students complain about the same professors for the same reasons. Year after year a few teachers in secondary and elementary schools continue to be recognized by parents as ones who should be avoided by their children at all costs. There is almost no recourse on the part of university students to instructional mediocrity. At the public schools level, the tenure laws are so binding that removal is at best a long and expensive undertaking, and at worst it may result in reinstatement.

Good teachers, administrators, and professors have nothing to fear. Legal controls can be developed which protect the educator from the whims of a board of education or of an individual administrator. Children, however, have a right to be free from mediocrity. Children throughout their education have a right to be challenged by the best minds of this nation whether the child is normal, mentally retarded, gifted, physically handicapped, or in other ways exceptional. We in the United States place a high value on education, but we sacrifice quality by the continued protection of mediocrity obvious to peers, administrators, children, and youth alike. Tenure laws, while important at one point in educational history, have been misused. They have protected poor special education teachers as well as inept general educators at the expense of the programs and to the detriment of children. University students, being more mature, soon learn to deal with mediocrity in instruction in their own way, but even at the level of higher education, the expense of supporting poor instructors who are comfortable in the security of the tenure law adds immeasurable cost to the student and negates the very purpose of higher education. There is little question that, if tenure were removed, methods of merit rating coupled with educational and administrative accountability could be brought to a high level of professionalism.

Fourth, special educators must come to a realistic understanding of the meaning of the concept of the *whole child* (Cruickshank *et al.* 1969). The child development movement has returned many important dividends to professional education as well as to children and families. We recognize these contributions and acknowledge their significance. The concept of the whole child likewise was important in bringing to the attention of adults, who in some capacity dealt with children, the fact that the child needed to be viewed from what we now term an ecological point of view. The child's total mental health, his physical health, and his relationships with the environment together constitute a whole child.

Educators, however, have been taught to teach to the whole child without ever being told just how to do that. The phrase "the whole child" has become a meaningless shibboleth. Its definition is often clouded. Its meaning to the instruction of children has rarely been fully clarified to those who teach children.

We deal with our automobile as a whole automobile. We replenish its gas and oil supply, its air, its water. It is oiled and greased, washed, and painted. It is handled with propriety on the road, and cautiously parked to avoid damage. It is indeed a whole concept. But if the oil filter, the spark plugs, or any part of the machine fails to work, the whole ceases to function properly.

Similarly, in special education, the whole must work. General educators have stressed the whole child so much that special educators have felt forced to adopt the concept to avoid being criticized. In doing so they have ignored a major portion of their professional responsibility, namely, to make the parts work so the whole will function properly. There will be no whole child, for example, if the deaf child has no communication skills. Hence, special educators must teach communication. There will be no whole child if braille is not accomplished successfully. Hence, special education should teach braille to the blind child for all it is worth. There will be no whole child if perceptual-motor disorganization exists. Hence, special educators of children with specific learning disabilities should focus on these deficient parts with a crash program early in the life of the child, and continue it until the parts smoothly blend into a whole function.

It is our considered opinion that the total lack of, or a misconception of the concept of the whole child on the part of most educators has served to impede positive educational programming. In special education particularly, we must realize that there is no such thing as a whole child, except in the geographical parameters of his body, until we as educational specialists put the pieces of the mosaic together in such a way as to permit their total coordinate function. In special education the primary emphasis should be on defective parts. When these are corrected, replaced, or their effects minimized as much as possible, a whole child can be delivered to general education and to society. When this is done, special educators have done their job. Special education must be viewed as the technological support to general education. It is the arm of education which makes it possible for the child to experience the richness of the total education process. If special educators do in another classroom that which general educators can do as well in another setting, there is no reason for the existence of special education. If special education performs well its technological skills in making a strong attack on the psychoeducational deficiencies of children and on the needs of children, which when neglected make adjustment difficult or impossible, then it has fulfilled its mission.

The fifth solution which we wish to discuss is the *removal of medico-clinical categories* as a basis for viewing special education programming. The present typing system in education has its historical antecedents, but they are no longer relevant to modern programming. Part of special education's problem is that it has adopted the medical taxonomy and applied it to the educational scene. This has not worked, but we nevertheless continue to persevere in the concept.

For example, cerebral palsy, a medical concept, is not a functional term in education. There is no curriculum for cerebral palsy. There is no such thing as a teacher of cerebral palsy. What is the child like who has cerebral palsy in one of its forms? He may have, for example, a visual-motor problem. Research indicates that approximately 80 percent of the athetoid type do have this type of learning problem. But this problem is also often found in exogenous mentally retarded children, in some deaf children, in some children with epilepsy, in hyperactive and emotionally disturbed children — each a medical category. Instead of preparing teachers of cerebral palsy children, of the deaf, of hyperactive children or others, we should prepare many teachers to deal with visual-motor problems of children wherever they are found.

The audio-motor problems of the aphasic child — a medical classification — are the same types of problems found in many children with diagnosis of perceptual handicap, cerebral palsy, mental retardation, *ad inf.* One doesn't teach aphasic children; one teaches to the unique problems of these children which are similar in type to problems found in numerous clinical categories. Similar cross-category characteristics of children can be identified of many other types.

The visual-perceptual and auditory-perceptual characteristics of children underlie their capacity to achieve skills in spoken language, in handwriting, in reading and in number concepts. Emphasis in teacher education should be on learning of the psychopathology of childhood and learning how to translate these characteristics into a specific defect-oriented educational program. If teacher education in special education were directed toward the issue of what specifically must be done in cases where dissociation, for example, is a problem in a child, irrespective of his medical classification, dramatic changes would be observed in special education. If the rational implications of hyperactivity on a visual, auditory, or tactual basis were understood by special educators, a fundamental alteration in classroom environments would follow. Most teachers in their training programs never hear the terms dissociation or learn the educational significance of hyperactivity.

Special educators should teach to the specific psychoeducational pathology in the child, not to the generalized concepts of disability as in the historically defined medico-clinical categories. There probably is no such thing as a teacher of the deaf, of the blind, and certainly not of the crippled child. To persevere in these notions will continue inadequate educational programming. To reorganize our notions of special education along the lines of the individual learning disabilities of children will mean that teachers will focus on the defective parts which prevent the child from being whole.

To move to accept this idea will require a restructuring of all special education: teacher education, certification, state reimbursement to local schools, local special education pupil class assignment and organization, and indeed probably of our professional organizations. Not to restructure the total field is going to mean the continuation of the downward spiral of special education toward increased mediocrity. Quality special education will come when teachers fully understand the meaning of the specific learning disabilities found in children within whatsoever medical characteristics and, through teaching programs, are able to minimize their roles, to negate them entirely as hurdles to learning, or to exploit them and thus enhance the child's capacity to learn and adjust.

The final point we wish to make may not be so much a solution as it is a hope for a better educational climate for children and teachers. We must *bridge the gulf* which exists *between special and general educators* at all levels: in universities, in state departments, and in local schools.

We are, after all, all concerned with children. There is enough for all to do if the job is well done. General educators cannot serve all children. There are limits beyond which the skills of the best teacher cannot be extended. There is a technology in good special education which when properly applied can help children with problems. General educators have not always been honest with special education, and special education has rarely prepared its teachers to teach to the specific problems of the children it proposes to serve.

The demand of the community for professionally honest solutions to the problems of children is upon us. Educators of any category can ill afford to fight among themselves any longer. They cannot be allowed to continue to hide their inadequacies from the general public. Educational leadership must find ways of bridging the gaps and a unified corps of professionals must be developed. There must be a recognition that each qualified member of the profession has a significant role to play in the total educational fabric. An honesty must exist which is intolerant of mediocrity, of educational inefficiency, and of irresponsibility to children's needs.

REFERENCES

1. Dunn, L. M. "Special Education for the Mildly Retarded — Is Much of it Justifiable?" *Exceptional Children* 35 (September 1968): 5-24.

2. Palomares, U. H., L. C. Johnson. "Evaluation of Mexican-American Pupils for EMR Classes." *California Education* 42, no. 3 (April 1966).

3. Jensen, A. "How Much Can We Boost IQ and Scholastic Achievement?" *Harvard Education Review* 83, no. 39 (Winter 1969).

4. From Stanford-Binet Test and Wechsler intelligence scales.

5. *Testimony of Doctor Roger T. Lennon as Expert Witness on Psychological Testing* (New York: Harcourt, Brace and World, 1967).

6. Ross, S. L.; H. G. DeYoung; J. S. Cohen. "Confrontation: Special Education Placement and the Law." *Exceptional Children* 38 (September 1971): 5–12.

7. Chenault, J. J. Mental Retardation as a Function of Race, Sex and Social Economic Status. Unpublished doctoral dissertation, Michigan State University, 1970.

8. Haring, N. G.; G. G. Stern; W. M. Cruickshank. *Attitudes of Teachers Toward Exceptional Children*. Syracuse: Syracuse University Press, 1958.

9. Cruickshank, W. M.; J. L. Paul; J. B. Junkala. *Misfits in the Public Schools*. Syracuse: Syracuse University Press, 1969.

5

MODELS FROM SPECIAL EDUCATION FOR EDUCATIONAL RESEARCH IN CHILDREN WITH LEARNING DISABILITIES OF SOCIAL AND ECONOMIC GAIN

*I*T IS INDEED LOGICAL to look to the field of special education for exceptional children regarding guidelines for research with children whose disabilities are of a social, ethnic, or economic origin. Special education should be able to suggest answers. However, special education per se has not produced the volume or quality of research which might be expected of it. Until about 1950, special education was essentially theoretical. The educational programs which were in effect — and some of them had been in operation for many years — were based on opinion and mere modification of what was already being done with normal children. Very little research with any type of exceptional children was available prior to this date, and most research subsequently has been produced from fields ancillary to special education.

Following the Second World War, personnel with research interests and skills began to become concerned with educational, social, and psychological problems of various groups of handicapped children. Some research, mostly non-educational, which had been undertaken for the war effort had peacetime implications for the field of disability, and this was continued with different populations and with children. Beginning with the signing of PL 85-926, advanced graduate students began to be recruited for the field of mental retardation in sufficient numbers to cause special education faculty members in universities to turn their attention to doctoral research in increasing quantity. The federal government through the numerous agencies of the Public Health Service began to channel large sums of money into research related to education, although not specifically educational research. With the amendment of PL 85-926 by PL 88-164, a remarkable stimulation

Address, *circa* 1966–67.

to educational research efforts was experienced. However, this is a contemporary action and insufficient time has lapsed to bring major studies to fruition or to have longitudinal studies continued sufficiently to provide significant data. All this is said by way of pointing out that special education as a professional field may not provide the many guidelines which it should or which are desired when models are sought for the area of the cultural disadvantaged child. A serious effort can be made to cull from special educational research those things which may have significance for the sister field, and to this end this paper will be directed.

HOMOGENEITY OR HETEROGENEITY?

For many years in the education of mentally retarded children it was assumed that the population, except for the usual individual differences between children, was homogeneous in nature. With this assumption, educators grouped mentally retarded children for instruction according to intelligence level. The groups were smaller than in the ordinary classroom, but children were grouped within a broad chronological age span as a homogeneous population. A single teacher was assigned to a group of from fifteen to twenty children who were assumed to have the same characteristics of learning.

In the latter part of the 1930s Dr. Heinz Werner and Alfred A. Strauss, working at the Wayne County Training School in Michigan, discussed two different types of mentally retarded children[1] and suggested that the educational needs of these children were uniquely different. These men spoke of an *endogenous* mentally retarded child as being one in whose case history there was evidence of familial tendencies toward retardation and in whose case history there was no evidence of birth injury, neurological signs, accident, illness, or injury which might account for the disability. This is the hereditary or genetic type of mental retardation. They also brought to the attention of educators the term *exogenous* mental retardation. A child in this classification was one in whose case history there was no evidence of the familial factor which could be considered etiologic but in whose case history there was evidence of birth injury, neurological signs, accident, injury, or illness which might have contributed to the intellectual state of the child.

More important than the delineation of the two groups of children was the fact that these two scholars also were able to identify the learning characteristics of the children as being quite different one from the other.[2] A more detailed consideration of these differences will be undertaken in a later discussion in this paper. Suffice at this point to say that generally what is done educationally for exogenous children is inappropriate for endogenous children and *vice versa*. It is generally agreed, although rarely implemented, that the two groups of children cannot be adequately educated in the same classroom.

Later research to be mentioned in the following pages has demonstrated that the two groups of children, endogenous and exogenous, present problems which are typical not only of mentally retarded children, but of children at any and all intellectual levels. In other words, while in the literature the terms are generally restricted to the levels of mental retardation, there is such a thing as an exogenous child of normal intellectual ability or even of superior intellectual ability. What we are saying is that the psychological characteristics of exogeny, originally believed to be restricted to retardation, may indeed be characteristic of some children at any point in the intellectual spectrum.

It occurs to this writer that it is important to keep these facts in mind in considering the culturally disadvantaged child. It is obvious that there are both types of children within the total population of disadvantaged children. One hears both professional and lay persons refer to "culturally disadvantaged children". In this sense it is obvious that they are being considered as a single group. It appears that to perseverate in this notion of homogeneity is to fall ultimately into the same trap as was so typical of educators of retarded children for such a long time. In reality, it will undoubtedly be found that there are large numbers of endogenous culturally disadvantaged children and perhaps equally large numbers of exogenous culturally disadvantaged children. Communities will be assisted in their planning for this segment of the child population if they are aware that dual planning may be a requisite. The preparation of teachers, and of the teaching materials as well, will be different particularly for the exogenous group if indeed the two groups exist in readily identifiable form. It is the opinion of this writer that the incidence of exogeny among the culturally disadvantaged may be considerably larger than in either the populations of mentally retarded children or intellectually normal culturally advantaged children for reasons which will be discussed later. The exogenous culturally disadvantaged child represents another type of multihandicapped child.

The first major issue, however, in considering any population of human beings is to know of what it is comprised. Incidence and prevalence studies need to be undertaken to ascertain exactly what the educational problem may be from the point of view of psychopathology particularly as it related to exogeny. The endogenous issue, while requiring special consideration is more nearly comparable to that with which educators are already familiar. The exogenous problem inserts new concepts, new methods of teaching, and new approaches to children with which educators generally are unfamiliar. It is one thing for educators of culturally disadvantaged children to plan for certain types of educational experiences; it is another thing if instead of one plan of education there are two or more distinctly different learning problems inherent in this large group of children for whom different educational models must be constructed. Studies of an epidemiological nature are then indicated as an initial, but significant step.

NEGLECT AND MENTAL RETARDATION

Strauss and Werner also discussed a third group of mentally retarded children, i.e., neglected.[2] These are children who, because of lack of stimulation in very early childhood, grow to function as mentally retarded children throughout their life experience. This group of children is closely related to the problem of the culturally deprived and disadvantaged child. Skodak, Skeels, and Dye,[3] in their early studies of the effect of stimulation on the mental development of children provide support to the clinical identification of the neglected child in the mentally retarded population.

It may be recalled that these researchers identified two groups of infants who were wards of a fondling home. One group of children (Group I) was left in the home where the adult-child ratio was approximately one to 15; the other group (Group II) was taken to an institution for high grade mentally retarded girls and there each infant was made the responsibility of four to six retarded women. In the first situation, Group I children received very limited stimulation, for the adults were able to meet only the basic physical needs of the babies. In the case of the children in Group II, one can easily imagine the tremendous amount of stimulation which was provided to them by the women who played a foster-mother role. The two groups of children were equated by the researchers as much as infants at this age can be. At the end of the third year the children were re-evaluated and at this time all of the children were provided with individual foster home placements. At the chronological age of three, Group I children were characterized as functioning at a high grade retarded level; Group II children had a mean intelligence quotient in the upper normal range. The two groups were re-evaluated each five-year period for three periods. At every re-evaluation Group I and Group II retained their relative positions and the mean intelligence quotients for the groups did not vary significantly. The large amount of early stimulation for the Group II children apparently was significant in establishing the intelligence at a normal functional level. In contrast the lack of early stimulation for Group I children apparently resulted in an irreversible situation even when in foster homes they were brought into a much more stimulating environment. The intervention of stimulation at and after the chronological age of three was not sufficient to counteract the impact of earlier deprivation.[3]

Dr. René Spitz has depicted beautifully the dramatic and socially negative adjustment which infants and small children make when separated from their mothers. While he is illustrating trends toward emotional apathy in these children, it is not unrealistic to assume that, if the separation continues for a sufficient period, intellectual atrophy may also be experienced.

In good institutional programs for the mentally retarded, the neglected type of child apparently learns, perceives, and adjusts in a manner similar to the endogenous type of child. They are able to achieve to the maximum of their mental level, but as school-aged children rich institutional programs of education and stimulation do not increase the level of intellectual function perceptibly.

It is the considered opinion of this writer, that among the huge population of culturally disadvantaged children there are thousands whose ability to react with profit to any type of learning experience is absolutely limited by low intellectual level. This low intellectual level it is suggested is the result of stimuli deprivation in the first three years of life. In addition to the continuing burden of cultural deprivation which the child carries during school age, these children in reality are neglected type of mentally retarded.

While it is not to be assumed that this writer agrees with the philosophic or political theories which are involved, the issue which is herein being considered might well lend itself to some of the techniques which have been utilized within the Soviet Union for many years with infants of working mothers. The government of the Soviet Union is not content to assume that parents would provide the type of desired learning environment. The government is intent on providing the infant and young child with a prescribed type and amount of stimulation and learning. These children at a very early age are brought for long periods of time into nurseries. Here programs involving varied stimulation is provided to them. It is obvious from the statements of Bronfenbrenner[4] and others that the impact of this effort has had favorable results from the psychological and the political points of view involved.

In the United States no effort has ever been made to attack the problem of cultural deprivation, neglected mental retardation, and educational unreadiness in these children through the extensive use of infant and nursery school programs. The highly popular Head Start Program has significant characteristics in this direction, but, in the opinion of this writer, it comes four years too late. With the utilization of control groups, a careful study needs to be undertaken in which nursery education for culturally deprived children could be made available beginning no later than six months of age. Obviously in a large group of infants there would be included unintentionally some infants who were genetically retarded and others who were retarded by reason of adventitious factors (exogenous retardates). These too, however, from Kirk's observations would profit immeasurably from the educational regimen which could be provided. The concept of the well-baby clinic could be expanded for these children to include extensive periods each day for several years. These daily periods should be endowed with much adult-child contact, with much social and individual stimulation involving many sensory avenues, and with as full a range of experiences as it would be possible to provide. It is this writer's considered opinion that were this done, these children would come into school age with a reservoir of experience and human contact which would carry them into and through elementary education at a level of success not predicted in terms of their economic or cultural backgrounds. Oscar Lewis' *La Vida*[5] gives evidence that from the worst of socio-economic living conditions mentalities can develop which in small degrees rise above the source of their origin. His report indicates that infant stimulation produces emotional relationships which alone can carry the individual through adversity. If this type of relationship, in more gentile form, could be coupled with an educational point of view, a major impact on the effects of deprivation of whatsoever type might well be made.

Environmental deprivation is not only associated with economics, social factors, or ethnic causes. In blindness there is the basis of a major type of sensory deprivation. In this writer's experience, blind children have been referred for evaluations who, because of the lack of parental insight and knowledge, at the age of two years had never left the crib. Totally blind twins, for example, could neither walk, sit up, talk, or control their bodily functions. The only stimulation, except for physical care which they received, was from one another in their random movements within the crib. They were entered into a rich nursery school experience at two years. These twins began to receive a major stimulation thrust. The effort was apparently undertaken in sufficient time, although both as teen-agers are slow learning children. Walking, talking, socialization, eating, and orientation to space and mobility were established within six months. The issue we are stressing here is that children who are extremely deprived can under programs of early stimulation positively respond. We have seen blind infants who have been treated by their parents as if they were sighted who when they had reached school age were fully capable of competition on almost every basis of comparison with their normal peers. On the other hand, other blind infants, from heredity not characterized in any way by mental retardation, have reached school age functioning as low level retardates. When this situation is investigated, often what amounts to severe emotional and social deprivation has been found to have existed in the parent-child relationship. Emotional rejection is comparable to any degree of deprivation insofar as intellectual and social growth is concerned.

One can carry this example still further in the case of children with profound hearing losses. These children if exposed to an auditory environment coupled with tactual, olfactory, and visual stimuli develop into inquisitive, interested, and intellectually aggressive children. On the contrary, deaf children, who as infants and young children are not provided with rich programs of education or with close adult-child relationships often appear as children of school age to function as retarded individuals.

One cannot over-estimate the significance of early environmental stimulation on the development of the infantile nervous system. There is little question but that a multidimensional sensory program is required to bring children to a level wherein they can profit from learning experiences. There is little question but that this thrust must begin at a very early chronological age level. It cannot wait until the age of four nor will a summer program as an antecedent to the beginning of kindergarten be sufficient to counteract the impact of neglect of the previous four years. An infant-early childhood program must be conceptualized.

BRAIN INJURY AND CULTURAL DEPRIVATION

We spoke earlier of the exogenous-endogenous dichotomy in the area of mental retardation. We mentioned also that children with the characteristics of exogeny were to be found at any intellectual level, not just among the mentally retarded. At upper intellectual levels these children are referred to by an immense number of terms including brain-injured child, child with minimal cerebral dysfunction, child with language disorders, child with special or specific learning disorders, dyslexic child, and many others.

The opinion of this writer has been indicated and it has been suggested that culturally deprived children, because of a lack of early stimulation, may indeed have suffered a central nervous system insult in some degree. This possibility has also been suggested by Berne[6] and others as being a basic consideration to a fuller understanding of these children's behavior. In the experience of this writer numerous socially and economically deprived children have demonstrated the same psychopathology as brain-injured children, although a diagnosis of central nervous disorder could not be ascertained in the case of the former in every instance. The lack of a positive diagnosis of neurological insult, however, does not necessarily rule out the presence of such insult in view of the present level of diagnostic sophistication. Irrespective of the presence or absence of positive neurological diagnosis, positive psychopathological signs, comparable to that in brain-injured children, have been observed in culturally deprived children. It is unnecessary to go into this matter in detail, for these characteristics have been described in the writings of this author[7] and those of others[8] too frequently to bear detailed repetition here. Suffice to say that culturally deprived children oftentimes show marked degrees of sensory hyperactivity, i.e., the inability to refrain from reaction to unessential stimuli insofar as any or all sensory modalities are concerned. Often they are also motoricly disinhibited, i.e., being unable to refrain from reacting to stimuli which elicit motor responses. Closely related to the matters of visual and auditory hyperactivity are the interesting phenomena of figure-background pathology, dissociation, perservation, angulation problems, compression, tendencies toward immaturity, and grossly immature and distorted self-concepts and body images. These characterize the brain-injured child. They also characterize many culturally disadvantaged children for whatsoever reason.

We suggested earlier that within the field of mental retardation, there would need to be programs for the exogenous retardated youth and others for the endogeneous retardated pupils who are also culturally disadvantaged. We are now suggesting that the mass education of culturally disadvantaged children may for many children need to be substituted with a highly structured clinical type teaching which has been found to be beneficial with hyperactive emotionally disturbed and brain-injured children. The structured approach of Cruickshank[8] is not being suggested as a solution to the problem of lack of early environmental stimulation and its devastating effects on mentality, but it is being suggested to have clinically demonstrated value for intellectually normal hyperactive culturally disadvantaged children who may or may not also be brain-injured. More important, it may be appropriate to wrench professionals away from the stereotype of the culturally disadvantaged and to envision individuals within this large group as having quite distinct types of problems one of which may be the psychopathology typical of brain-injured children. If this group can indeed be identified, of which there is little question, then dramatic changes are indicated for educational methodology. Either the individual tutorial approach of Gallagher[9] or the small group approach of Cruickshank,[8] both of which are based on the same philosophical structure and learning theory, might be appropriate for culturally disadvantaged children identified as having the psychopathology mentioned in a previous paragraph. Educational programs for the culturally disadvantaged child may, in many instances, be better if the program is considered in terms of the psychopathological needs inherent in the child rather than in terms of social, economic, ethnic, or cultural factors. A different educational emphasis is required if the former can become the reality which it should.

EDUCATION IN A REALISTIC SOCIAL SETTING

The Maryland Educational Research Project under the direction of Mrs. Rozelle Miller is currently in the third year of a four-year study dealing with educational approaches to the hyperactive emotionally disturbed children.[10] While certain of the approaches are either similar to typical educational practice or to the structured approach of Cruickshank mentioned above, one approach would appear to be unique appropriateness to the culturally disadvantaged child. The Maryland Educational Research Project, being carried out in Anne Arundel County, has not been reported in the literature, although a final report will probably be prepared during the summer, 1967. However, information could be obtained regarding the aspect of the project which will be discussed herein.

The MERP is based on the social studies aspect of the educational program. Other elements are not overlooked, but they are inherent to and outgrowths of the social studies activities. The program is conceptualized in seven well-coordinated steps around the concept of "Simulated Environments." To quote directly from one release prepared by MERP: "There are two conditions under which the simulated environments are to be used in . . . classes and these depend, in part, upon the children's reading ability. Assuming little or no reading ability, there are specific games and techniques which [have been] developed, specifically to help these children to learn to read and to overcome emotional blocks they may have concerning reading. In cases where some of the children can read and some cannot, a combination of reading, other academic games, and/or role playing simulating social environments, geared to ability levels, [have been] used."

The second condition assumes a reading ability on the part of most of the children. In this situation the emphasis on the simulations and the remedial reading became a by-product of the simulated environment. "The purpose of these simulated environments is to place the children in situations which simulate life situations and to have children play various roles in these situations, moving from one simple problem or one simple role to a more complex problem or situation as the pupils are developmentally ready for the change. These problems [were] presented to the children on 'situation' cards and thus be controlled as to type. Each child [received] one situation card for each round of the activity, and on this card he [was] told the role he [was to play] and the problem to be solved."

The seven steps which are involved in the simulated teaching activity include: (1) creation of a situation, (2) the identification of a specific problem, (3) class planning, (4) small group planning on assumed aspects of the problem, (5) roll playing and discussion, (6) conclusion, and (7) evaluation.

Children originally in the fourth grade at the beginning of the experiment were identified as hyperactive emotionally disturbed children. Twenty-four class groups were selected for the experiment. These classes, of different sizes and different administrative arrangements, established for the duration of the experiment. The children are now completing the sixth grade. Simulations have been utilized throughout this three-year period as the major controlled instructional method. Measures of achievement, self-concept, and socialization have been made of the children. In every significant measure, positive growth equal to or in excess of established developmental norms have been obtained.

There have been certain "unmeasurables" which nevertheless appear to be significant as this writer has observed the children involved. There is little question but that nonverbal children have become verbal. Scared children have found security in their identification with the objective roles which they have played. Tolerance of the opinion of others has been developed. Feelings of responsibility for social problems of the simulations has been created. Self-concepts quite obviously have taken on new dimensions which are positive and social in nature. The children have learned the technique of problem-solving.

It would seem to this writer that the concept of the simulations would have significance to the socially disadvantaged children as an educational tool. It lends itself to both the reader and the nonreader. It can be as concrete or as abstract as is desired in terms of the children, their background, and the realities of the group behavior. Its implications for developing wholesome social attitudes and for providing solutions to the social situation inherent in the simulation bring an aspect of reality to the educational process which is all-too-often lacking for socially disadvantaged children.

LANGUAGE AND THE DEAF

It would be well to look to the field of the education of the deaf for certain research models regarding "concept-expansion" for other groups of disabled children, including the culturally deprived. While much of the discussion in this paper relates to sensory deprivation, the chief learning problems of the culturally deprived often center around this variable. More than one observation has been made of the extraordinarily limited spoken vocabulary in the homes of many culturally deprived individuals. In a superficial study completed by a student of this writer, it was observed that the average speaking vocabulary recorded among members of fifty culturally deprived families consisted of slightly more than 120 words. Language deficit results in concept deficit. The lack of concepts means restricted perception of the social order in which the family lives. Persons concerned with the learning problems of the culturally deprived would do well to familiarize themselves with the psycho-educational and psycho-social research literature of the deaf for numerous clues which would be germain to the former area. These studies are entirely too numerous to review in this paper. In more complete form than herein possible, they have been more adequately reviewed elsewhere. A suggested clue of the significance of these studies is observed in a summary statement of McNeill in which he states:

> To the degree that a child tests rather than formulates hypothesis with parental speech, the expansion situation presents itself as a model for educating deaf children — that is, a situation where new information is presented to a child in a form that differs minimally from what he already knows, and where the changes seem maximal that the presented information is relevant to what he wants to know. Perhaps the education of the deaf approximates this model already. But the beneficial effects of expansion-like instruction might be increased by first introducing a deaf child to *child* language as it appears in the studies of Brown, Ervin, and Braine. That is to say, it is possible that a deaf child's acquisition of linguistic competence would be faster if his first exposure to English took the form of nouns, verbs, and undifferentiated pivot clauses, presented in sentences that are generated by simple hierarchical rules free of transformations. Such speech would greatly simplify a deaf child's testing of hypotheses, a fact that may help compensate for his generally impoverished sensory output.

McNeill goes on to say

> To take one example, all children who have been studied in this country, and apparently also children who are growing up in Russia. . . . initially form negatives in the same way; a simple affirmative is prefixed by a negative element — no or not in the case of a child acquiring English, *nyet* in the case of Russian children. They produce such negatives as *no drop mitten, not*

Rusty hat, etc., which are quite different from the adult equivalents *I didn't drop the mitten, that's not Rusty's hat,* etc. Perhaps a deaf child would be benefitted by first encountering English negatives in the firm of *no drop mitten,* not in the full form *I didn't drop the mitten.* Obviously, a child would later have to develop the full negative form. The point here is that primitive negatives, such as *no drop mitten,* lead hearing children to full negatives in a very natural way. Perhaps deaf children can be induced to follow a simpler course. Moreover, the primitive negative is actually part of adult competence, though deeply buried under much other grammatical paraphernalia, and so must be acquired if full gramatical competence is to be achieved. The suggestion being made here is that the various aspects of adult competence, some of which are completely covert in native speakers, often appear as overt stages in normal language acquisition. By presenting deaf children with child speech, the task of acquisition may be significantly simplified in that they will overt examples of essential, but often covert, aspects of competence.

If the reader will re-read these last two paragraphs of McNeill and substitute the words *culturally disadvantaged* each time the author employs the word *deaf,* significant guidelines to a long series of studies involving speech and language acquisition by the culturally disadvantaged child may well present themselves. Earlier reference was made to the importance of initiating programs of sensory stimulation early in the life of the child. A final remark of McNeill's is significant in this respect with reference to the acquisition of language. He says:

The capacity to acquire language may be transitory; it may reach a peak around the age of two to four and decline thereafter. It may even disappear altogether as a special capacity with the beginning of adolescence [here the research of E. Lenneberg[12] is most significant to the education and learning problems of the deaf and the culturally deprived.] There does seem to be a cut-off at puberty in the ability to acquire a second language. A second language learned before this time is generally acquired with relative ease and the result is often a native fluency. A second language learned after this time is far more difficult to acquire and often does not result in native fluency. At least one difference between these periods is the greater relative importance of rote learning in post-adolescent acquisition. Perhaps this is what we should expect if a basic capacity to acquire language has by then disappeared. The implication is obvious: In view of the possibility of a critical period for language acquisition, which peaks at two to four years and declines steadily after that, any effort to take advantage of a deaf child's [socially and culturally disadvantaged child's] capacity for language acquisition must be an early effort — the earlier the better.[11]

The close relationship between language acquisition and measured intelligence has been a known factor for many years. This is true not only in the area of the deaf but also in the area of the blind and other groups of the physically disabled, e.g., the cerebral palsy. In socially and culturally disadvantaged children the lack of language-concept development undoubtedly has a significant impact on the development of intelligence per se irrespective of the innate potential of the organism. In a crash program of language development, however, it is apparent that two approaches must be taken to the problem: one, conceptualized in terms of the "peak" concept for children under the age of four; the other, based upon much more rigorous conditioning models and memory for children older than that age.

It is important for investigators of the learning problems of the culturally disadvantaged to explore fully the recent research for the deaf. In the past several years the *Volta Review* has increased its effectiveness by providing periodic summary statements of significant research pertinent to learning characteristics of the deaf. A specific example of this can be seen in the January 1966 issue which is entitled "Language Acquisition." A second is to be found in the November 1963 issue entitled "Research — 1963." Other similar reviews are to be found in other volumes of this periodical. (While reference to courses is being mentioned, the reader should not overlook the *Annual Review of Psychology* which contains summaries of leading research in the areas of learning, audition, visual perception, and related matters of direct import to the study of the culturally disadvantaged.) Finally the role of "Language and the Education of the Deaf" in relationship to the culturally deprived has been the object of an important recent summary statement by Herbert R. Kohl and the Center for Urban Education. In this latter publication Kohl assumes the same point of view as was requested of this writer and explores fully the research in the education of the deaf as it relates to learning with culturally disadvantaged children. The intimate relation between language acquisition and thinking, between language acquisition and cognition, and indeed to motor development is significant not only to the deaf, but also to the culturally disadvantaged.

THE SPECIAL EDUCATION TEACHER

One of the most significant books on the culturally deprived has been Reissman's, *The Culturally Deprived Child*. P. J. Groff[13] submitted 78 Reissman statements to nearly 300 teachers who then agreed or disagreed with statements. Remarkable variance was observed, or to put it differently little concensus was observed in the attitudes of these teachers toward the Reissman tenets and in turn toward the culturally deprived. (Groff's article lists at least 35 statements which are ideas waiting to be researched. Here is a nucleus of a broad series of learning investigations.) The attitudes of teachers toward children constitute one of the most significant influences upon the learning of the children. The attitudes of adults toward the culturally deprived child reflects the stereotypes with which the adults have been associated throughout their lives. This fact has been found to be true in a study related to the attitudes of teachers toward exceptional children. The significant fact, however, is that attitudes can be modified toward greater acceptance of the disabled child and toward greater reality. Superstitions, old wives' tales, misconceptions, untruths, and irrational concepts can be replaced by intelligent concepts and realistic understanding. The study to which reference is herein being made involved, mentally retarded children, gifted children, emotionally disturbed children, and all types of physically disabled children.[14] It utilized simple and inexpensive techniques of lecture, group discussion, and non-directive group counseling. Opinions toward the epileptic, for example, were as ingrained and as reality-distorted in the groups of teachers who were studied as are many opinions which are held by teachers regarding culturally disadvantaged children or toward religious or ethnic groups.

Whalen[15] has addressed himself to a broad group of techniques now being referred to as "behavior modification procedures." His paper has been called "the most complete and systematic coverage of this particular point of view to be found in the professional literature — especially in terms of its focus on relevance for classroom teachers." While his paper addresses itself to the teacher concern for ways in which one can effectively break into the cycle of self-defeating behavior exhibited by emotionally disturbed children, its appropriateness to the teacher of the culturally disadvantaged will be observed quickly by a thoughtful reader. Because it is easily obtainable and more easily read, it is appropriate here only to note the areas of research and theoretical concern included in the paper, namely, psycheducation therapy, life-space interviewing, structured approach, and behavior modifications. In this regard the important work of Bijou[16] related to the learning environment and its relationship to behavior modification with retarded children is also significant as is, of course, the entire literature of reinforcement theory. The application of these points of view, however, to the learning situation for culturally disadvantaged children has not been undertaken with sufficient thoroughness nor in any respect in a longitudinal context.

Closely related to teacher attitudes and to intervention approaches as discussed by Whelan is the matter of behavioral modification of retarded children discussed by Lindsley.[17] Lindsley is concerned with modification of behavior in retardated children through the manipulation of certain environmental variables. This has application to the education of the culturally deprived children. William Morse *et al.*[18] also consider this issue insofar as emotionally disturbed children are concerned in their discussion of classroom behavior viewed from several diverse frameworks. Roger Barker[19] and his associates likewise attempt to determine the effect of melieu on the behavior of children through the sampling of behavior specimens, and this research could easily relate to culturally deprived children as well.

MISCELLANEOUS STUDIES

The issues of hetrogeneity, stimuli deprivation, simulations, language acquisition as a tool in expansion of concepts, modification of teacher attitudes, and the modification of child behavior and attitudes through educational milieus appear to this writer to be fundamental in consideration of any group of disabled children including the culturally disadvantaged. Simultaneously, however, there is a myriad of other significant problems which can only be mentioned as being pertinent to the study of the culturally disadvantaged child. These will be referred to in almost outline form from this point on.

1. It would be well to investigate the role of incidental learning in culturally disadvantaged children in somewhat the same manner as has been done by Stevenson and Zigler[20] with retarded children. Zigler's studies (with his co-workers) of rigidity, negative reaction tendencies, and cosatiation effects in both normal and retarded subjects has meaning for the culturally deprived as well. Discrimination learning and rigidity has been investigated by Stevenson and Zigler in retardates and this has, of course, been the basis of extensive study by Kounin (also with retarded subjects).[21] Heinz Werner[22] has made some significant early studies of the impact of rigidity on the learning of mentally retarded children, and he and his associate, Strauss, have carried this into a significant study of the clinical symptom of perseveration as it relates to the learning of exogenous mentally retarded children in particular.[23] Rigidity, as a factor in learning, has not been investigated sufficiently with respect to the adjustment and achievement of children who are culturally deprived.

2. The field of cognition, perception, and motor development is one which has received a great deal of attention on the part of investigators particularly with respect to brain-injured children. While conflicting points of view are to be observed in the literature, these are to a degree healthy signs

of a new and active field. Of particular significance in the area of cognitive structure with brain-injured children is the work of Riley Gardner (the author is fully cognizant of the status of Jerome Bruner in this area, but in an attempt to focus only on the exceptional child Bruner's work has been excluded from this discussion).[24] While largely theoretical, Gardner has submitted some concepts to empiricle study. Recently he has prepared a yet unpublished paper concerned with the effects of emotional disturbance on cognitive behavior.[15] These sources provide a rich resevoir for the stimulation of research with culturally disadvantaged children.

Ralph Reitan has made significant thrusts into the problems of psychoneurology as it relates to learning and achievement, particularly in the area of reading. Significant sources for initial inquiry into the research of both Reitan and Gardner are to be found in a recent publication entitled *The Teacher of Brain-Injured Children: A Discussion of the Bases for Competency* (Syracuse University Press, 1966).

Rubin and his associates[25] have been especially effective in handling the matter of cognitive-perceptual-motor function and its relation to child maladjustment (emotionally disturbed children). The report of the research of these authors, together with those of Haring and Philips,[26] and Cruickshank *et al.,*[7] constitutes a significant reference for those concerned with cognitive structure and its relation to the education of culturally deprived children and youth.

Frostig, Rappaport, Strother, Gallagher, Kephart, Barsch, and Gaddes[27] have each contributed significantly to an understanding of the relationship between perception, cognition, and motor development to learning and adjustment of brain-injured children, in particular. Getman, in his studies of the physicology of readiness, has added still another dimension to the understanding of this problem.[28] The work of Arthur Benton[29] is a classic in relating cerebral dominance, laterality, and handedness to the learning of children. These concepts need to be explored in relation to the culturally disadvantaged child.

3. Little significant research has been done in the area of the learning seriously visually limited child. However, two or three studies are important from the point of view of this paper. Cowen and his associates[30] have quite thoroughly investigated the relationship between visual problems and adjustment in the adolescent as Sommers[31] did several years earlier. Sommers' interests were particularly related to parental attitudes with reference to adolescent adjustment. One of the significant lessons which can be learned from the Cowen studies is in the point of view which the authors assumed. They indicated that their interests were to determine the adjustment factors which were present in visually handicapped children, not what caused these

factors. They contended that it was not necessary to know cause in order to point directions for research regarding causation. These studies each contain certain values in their internal structure of design which are significant to research in the related field of the culturally disadvantaged. Given a certain set of attitudes, they said, one can predict the behavior of children. No causation is indicated, but attitudes which can be identified are declared useful predictors of behavior in blind children. It is the internal design element which is significant here insofar as the culturally disadvantaged child is concerned rather than the instruments employed or the conclusions reached.

4. The basic study of G. O. Johnson[32] (cf. also the literature of sociometry as prepared by Bronfrenbrenner, and the studies of Force with physically handicapped[34] and J. J. Johnson[35]) related to the social status of mentally retarded children in the special class and in the regular grades is important in conceptualizing research related to integration and segregation concepts. It is important in considering the problem of class and social placement of culturally deprived children in educational communities other than their own. Orville Johnson's study was important in indicating that factors of personality rather than intelligence were significant in the acceptance or rejection of mentally retarded children. Cruickshank, Summers, and Wiberley also found this to be true with physically handicapped children of normal mentality when these children were integrated into the regular grades of an elementary school system. One wonders to what extent the identification of children as being culturally disadvantaged is a factor in rejection by other children in an integrated situation or to what extent personality characteristics of certain culturally disadvantaged are the factors which cause them to be isolates in an integrated social situation. Does the contagion factor in the isolation of one or more emotionally maladjusted culturally disadvantaged children spread and characterize all culturally disadvantaged children in the opinions of members of social groups surrounding them?

5. The issue of programmed instruction has received some, but insufficient attention by research personnel in special education. Malpass and Blackman,[36] Capobianco and Blackman,[37] Ellson,[38] and Sturlow[39] have reported on several investigations. Ellson's work has been essentially in the field of reading, while the other investigations have centered around instructional programs with the mentally retarded. While conclusive data is still to be achieved, sufficient positive results have been achieved by children who have experienced programmed instruction to warrant its further refinement. Certainly this poses an area of research which might well prove fruitful with socially disadvantaged children.

6. Some years ago Cruickshank[40] undertook a comparative investigation of normal and mentally retarded children of the same mental ages re-

lated to the psychological characteristics involved in the arithmetic process
(see Volume 1). This study, although extremely limited in number of subjects
and scope, has played a significant part in the thinking of numerous persons
since its publication. Dunn,[41] some years later, applied the same reasoning to
the area of reading somewhat similar findings to those of Cruickshank. Although it is unnecessary to go into the details of the investigations here, the
two studies indicated that in several characteristics mentally retarded children exceeded the achievement levels of their matched normal partners while
in others there were deficiencies attributable apparently to the innate mental
deficiency. Although the two investigations of necessity were restricted to
very small populations, it was apparent from them that neither intelligence
nor mental age alone could be considered as the basis upon which curricular
adaptations for the mentally retarded children were made. The basis for
educational programs for the endogeneous mentally retarded children was
indicated to be a definitive understanding of the psychological characteristics of the child. The individualization of instruction in terms of the molecu-
lar aspects of mental age, it was suggested, will produce a much more realistic educational program for the retarded child than will the consideration of
mental age as a unity or than will the arbitrary down-grading of the curriculum in terms of preconceived notions of what the achievement levels for the
mentally retarded child should be. Insufficient comparative studies of the
learning characteristics of groups of children have been made. They are essential if educators are to obtain a realistic understanding of the manner in
which groups of disabled children learn and the variations in the group characteristics which are typical of individual children within the clinical groups.
This thinking needs to be applied to culturally disadvantaged children. Comparative studies are needed matching culturally disadvantaged children by
mental age with culturally advantaged children; matching mentally retarded
culturally disadvantaged children with mentally retarded culturally advantaged children. From these studies would come a more accurate understanding of the nature of an optimum curriculum for the former groups.

     7. One of the great needs in educational and psychology research as
it pertains to exceptional children is for well-conceived and well-executed
longitudinal studies. Such studies are lacking except for a few modest attempts. Longitudinal studies which cannot only develop patterns of growth
for disabled children but can also reflect the results of specific intervention
techniques are needed in all phases of disability and special education. Four
citations can be mentioned which may serve as partial models for what must
ultimately be undertaken with socially disadvantaged children. These are
studies reported by Goldstein, Jordan and Moss,[42] by Blatt and by Cassidy.[44] Heber and Stevens provide a good review of studies which have been

done on a longitudinal basis with mentally retarded children.[45]

8. One final problem should be noted and this pertains to work-study programs. Few studies pertaining to pre-employment programs or to any facet of the educational program as it related to employment have been completed with groups of disabled youth other than in the field of the mentally retarded. The pay-off of a special educational program is the ease with which disabled youth are able to be assimilated into the competitive work world. Two studies warrant examination by those seeking models for the culturally disadvantaged child, i.e., those of Carriker[46] and of Porter and Malazzo.[47] Cohen[48] likewise has a good study dealing with job placement failures and successes with mentally retarded youth which, although not longitudinal in nature, relates to this problem and is one which could provide important guidelines.

ADDENDA

In preparing this paper and in thinking about the problems of special education as they may relate to the culturally disadvantaged child, numerous problems came to mind which would warrant study. Although time has not permitted a complete assessment of the research of special education, many of the topics which are listed below would undoubtedly relate to investigations which have been undertaken with one or another of the clinical groups of exceptional children. These suggestions are incorporated into this paper as a basis for some discussion as appropriate:

1. Are there skills which a teacher of culturally disadvantaged children needs which are unique to this clinical group? If so, what are these skills or competencies?

2. Socialization skills have been indicated as important variables for the culturally disadvantaged child. However, the development of such skills has not always resulted in improved social behavior — improved in terms of adaptability to middle class standards. Is there a way that socialization skills can be developed which will enable culturally disadvantaged children to adapt to middle class culture if this indeed be an important goal?

3. Values of culturally deprived children differ from values of middle class children. One research study might investigate how values can be altered in children of school age, prior to school, or even during adult life. Kluckhohn has done some interesting work along this line. It might be interesting to investigate how values can be inculcated in a person who is in an environment which possesses different values.

4. Rewards to behavior are many. What rewards are significant for culturally deprived children? Do these rewards differ in terms of the significant rewards for middle class children? Studies of rewards might rely on Rotter's social learning theory or on other learning theory models.

5. In any area of low socio-economic status, some children "make it" and others don't. Whatever success is defined as, an investigation could look at those who make it and who don't. A comparison might then provide some variables which are critical for the developing child.

6. In school, certain reinforcements (rewards) are acceptable and desirable for culturally deprived children. Other rewards are not (referring to rewards which are rewards for middle-class children). An investigation might locate the behaviorial reinforcements which exists among culturally deprived children. If these factors were isolated, then systematic use of them might be made.

7. Married student housing adjacent to many universities is often characterized by low income, relatively low prestige, some apathy, temporary instability, many children, and some degree of female dominance (while husbands neglect families to pursue studies), and various other variables which approximate or correlate with variables found in lower class American cultures. However, the children in married student housing situations do not grow up with feelings of apathy, hopelessness, or powerlessness. What are significant differences in the two low-income groups, both having many children, in terms of the learning abilities of children?

8. Self-concept is an important variable. Culturally deprived children are often termed low in self-concept — or negative rather than positive. What are contrasting differences in the self-concept of culturally disadvantaged children and children from married student housing areas and what are the significant variables which determine self-concepts?

9. Significant "others" range from Hollywood stars to baseball heroes to neighborhood persons. Which significant "others" as models for behavior are chosen by culturally disadvantaged children? How are they different from models chosen by other of children? How do significant "others" affect behavior? Can these models be used as educational media?

10. While children may live under conditions of low economic and social status, when do they recognize that other families live under different conditions? It is when they start school? When they begin dating? When they begin job seeking? When do they (the children) lose hope or realize their level of aspiration can only be x, y, or z? When do Black children and when do White children realize that marriage may only be for members of their race? What are the factors which bring this realization about? Can these factors be altered?

11. What is the impact of the advertising system — especially TV? Presumably it produces a desire for various products — is this desire universal or do some groups reject desires for these products? Particularly the culturally deprived — deprived — do they desire the same products, to the same degree, as do non-culturally deprived?

12. Can teaching bring about an ability to cope with social norms? If the same values and desires predominate, then can teaching bring about the behavioral forms necessary to produce fulfillment of those values and desires? While stealing Aqua Velva may produce a "sweet-smelling person," it is not desirable to steal. Are there alternative approaches which "work" for the culturally deprived person and specifically child, which may or may not differ from the middle class method of buying Aqua Velva? Because the culturally deprived child can't buy Aqua Velva, are there other acceptable ways he can acquire it? Can these other ways be taught in special education programs?

13. How can motivation be rechanneled when present? Assuming that the motivation is present, and the means to the end are not available or acceptable to other parts of society, then can this drive to get certain ends to be used to get these ends or other ends by alternative means?

14. It was theorized that if jobs could be found for students in the 18 to 25 year range, then children under 18 would observe their older brothers and sisters and friends and emulate their behavior. They would have respectable goals to aim at. This would produce an interest in jobs — i.e., school, and an interest in learning. Can levels of aspiration be measured? Do levels of aspiration change in younger children when older children and youth have success in the labor market?

15. It was once thought that teachers should be selected from that group of people who "made it" out of the slum. However, this business of "making it" out of a slum leads to rejection of the slum, its people, and frequently seems to result in a conservative attitude. Why do people who succeed in terms of social mobility lose identification with their origins? What are the factors involved? Are there ways to lessen this rejection of humble beginnings?

16. Busing children around town has become commonplace. Much of the result has been adverse to the culturally deprived child. Are there ways or places in which visits by culturally deprived to neighborhoods, homes, schools, or whatever of middle class children can take place with positive results? Perhaps school is the wrong location. Conversely, can middle class children visit the homes, habitats and schools of lower class children and receive positive experiences in greater awareness and sensitivity of an unsolved problem, and also awareness of and some respect for a different culture? Perhaps jazz music fits in here?

17. Redl and anthropologists have done work on culture contact. How can contacts between different groups be arranged which result in positive feelings for both groups?

18. In terms of special education models, traditionally the handicapped child has been given a better chance with special teachers, special materials, and special programming. How about trying this with the culturally deprived under experimental conditions so that such a program's effect could be rigidly measured and manipulated to achieve maximum results?

19. One of the greatest conflicts is that between the middle-class teacher and the classroom filled with 30 or so culturally deprived children, when they are oriented to different behavior, goals, and thinking. Is there a way to change the teacher rather than the children to minimize such conflicts?

20. The goals for the culturally deprived child should be adequately defined. What type of life will he or she lead? What type of work will be available for him or her? Is the goal the same as for the blind, deaf, crippled, brain-injured or otherwise handicapped child? These are goals both for the child to emulate and the education system to aid toward.

21. Middle class children have certain behavioral skills which enable some degree of competency in the middle-class oriented school system. Can these be identified, then taught to culturally deprived children as skills?

22. Studies of the aspirations and feelings of culturally deprived families, persons, and groups are very much needed. Anthropological investigations perhaps of the sort Oscar Lewis has done, could be one approach.

23. The administrative superstructure of the educational system has a key role in adapting to or working with the problem posed by cultural deprivation. What are the attitudes of administrators? Are they willing to pay the costs of special programs? What about their knowledge of the situation?

24. Some claim that all the "don'ts" are present in classroom teachers attitudes. What are the implications of this attitude for busing in children from a different social level or of different culture? Can these attitudes be changed? This would call for a longitudinal study.

25. Learning patterns appear to be similar for mentally retarded children, normals, and gifted—the only difference being rate of development. How about for the culturally deprived? Are there different learning patterns?

26. What about overthrowing the schools and having teachers go out on the streets with neighborhood groupings, gangs, and families? This would use the method of that great teacher—Socrates. While perhaps far-fetched, the above idea could be compromised with at least getting teachers out into homes, neighborhoods, or local hangouts in the area from which

the culturally deprived come, and doing this under conditions that result in positive interchange. What is the effect of a teacher visit to the home of a student—for dinner or for a casual visit or whatever? Here the effect must be measured on both the teacher and the student.

27. Dr. John Johnson had a program going, apparently much like Dr. Peter Knoblick's program in which a university consultant went to the school and talked with teachers during lunch hours or at other times, about such problems as they were having and how some research studies might provide ideas. A reality group of sorts in which the teachers were told about a specific skills to use in handling their problems in a better way.

28. Culturally deprived children have problems relating to teachers, middle class persons, and others linguistically. The barrier of a different dialect or language produces separateness. How can speech therapy, or speech teachers instill different speech models to prevent this barrier? Studies are needed for this area. One suggestion might be to have housewives—with appropriate speech patterns spend time on a one to one basis or on a one to say three basis with culturally deprived children. Although it is hard to justify such a program, it may lead to important results.

29. Howard University has a program for Black college students in which there are evaluations of speech behavior. This type evaluation was done in terms of interviews for jobs and it was found that Black students were less effective in speech patterns and self expression during such interviews than were whites. What are the differences at various age levels of speech patterns and what importance does this have—on teachers, employers, peers, the community at large?

30. To improve speech patterns—to bring speech behavior more in line with that of the community at large—or the middle class—it would be useful to bring about adult domination of the speech situation and cut down on class sizes in culturally deprived areas.

31. It is time to investigate whether a new speciality is needed—the expert in cultural deprivation. Rather than follow traditional disciplines, we are turning more and more to a problem oriented approach—such as mental retardation (using several disciplines) or brain-injury (where a person might counsel parents, teach not only academically oriented subjects, but also special physical skills and even social skills, act as a junior psychologist, help as a vocational advisor, etc.). Experts in cultural deprivation might work with gangs, teach in schools, organize neighborhoods, serve as a speech model and behavior model, etc.

32. Many persons are attracted to the field of cultural deprivation. We need to know more about such people—we need personality testing to learn why they are interested, about their motivation, etc.

33. Special education as taught in universities sometimes has an opportunity to grapple with one problem area such as cultural deprivation. As the meeting proved, the interchange of information and ideas was very helpful to understanding other disciplines and other ideas. This type of meeting of students, faculty, and or teachers should be continued, and if possible, it would be interesting to set up a series of such meetings with a variety of students and include in the meetings some culturally deprived children as participants. It would be interesting to measure the differences in attitudes and behavior of the students.

34. Consultants to the schools could set up demonstrations in which they would actually teach a class while teachers watched and learned, and then later would discuss the techniques of teaching they used with the regular teachers.

35. The Neighborhood Youth Corp, among other programs, apparently provided some monies to get jobs for children. How about getting children jobs—this includes such children as drop-outs and the culturally deprived—in schools as teacher aides and assistants? Employment in the school would provide jobs in a stimulating environment.

36. Special education has always used the special class. How about monies for this from Neighborhood Youth Corp and from HEW to set up special classes for one or two or three children who appear to be culturally deprived—using special classes—resource rooms, or such?

37. Rokeach and others have postulated rigid personality syndromes. How do teachers fare with such personality research? Are teachers rigid? Do rigid teachers have different attitudes toward and different behavior toward the culturally deprived?

38. A demonstration class at a university would provide a laboratory of learning for culturally deprived children, for teachers who observed, for teacher trainers, for students at the university, etc. This would provide an experimental situation in that variables could be controlled and manipulated at will.

REFERENCES

1. Strauss, A. A. "Typology in Mental Deficiency." *American Journal of Mental Deficiency* 44 (1939): 85–90.

2. Strauss, A. A., and H. Werner. "The Mental Organization of the Brain-Injured Mentally Defective Child." *American Journal of Psychiatry* 97 (1941): 1194–202. Strauss, A. A., and H. Werner. "Disorders of Conceptual Think-

ing in the Brain-Injured Child." *Journal of Nervous and Mental Diseases* 96 (1942): 153–72.

3. Skeels, H. A., and H. B. Dye. "A Study of the Effects of Differential Stimulation on Mentally Retarded Children." *Proceedings and Addresses of the Sixty-Third Annual Session of the American Association on Mental Deficiency* 44 (1939): 114–36. Skeels, H. A. "Mental Development of Children in Foster Homes." *Journal of Genetic Psychology* 40 (1936): 91–106. Skeels, H. A., and M. Skodak. "Adult Status of Individuals Who Experienced Early Intervention." Paper presented at the 90th Annual Meeting, American Association on Mental Deficiency, Chicago, Ill., May 12, 1966.

4. Bronfrenbrenner, U. "Soviet Methods of Character Education: Some Implications for Research." *American Psychologist* 17 (1962): 550–64.

5. Lewis, O. *La Vida.* New York: Random House, 1966.

6. Berne, E. *Games People Play.* New York: Grove Press, 1964.

7. Cruickshank, W. M.; F. Bentzen; R. Ratzeberg; and M. Tannhauser. *A Teaching Method for Brain-Injured and Hyperactive Children.* Syracuse: Syracuse University Press, 1961.

8. Kephart, N. *The Slow Learner in the Classroom.* Columbus: Charles Merrill, 1961.

9. Gallagher, J. J. *The Tutoring of Brain-Injured Mentally Retarded Children: An Experimental Study.* Springfield, Ill.: Thomas, 1960.

10. This material is as yet unpublished.

11. McNeill, D. "The Capacity for Language Acquisition." *The Volta Review* 68 (1966): 17–33.

12. E. Lenneberg. "The Biological Basis of Language." Mimeographed, Harvard University, 1966.

13. Groff, P. J. "Culturally Deprived Children: Opinions of Teachers on the Views of Reissman." *Exceptional Children* 31 (1964): 61–66.

14. Haring, N. G.; G. G. Stern; and W. M. Cruickshank. *Attitudes of Educators Toward Exceptional Children.* Syracuse: Syracuse University Press, 1958.

15. Whelan, R. J. "The Relevance of Behavior Modification Procedures for Teachers of Emotionally Disturbed Children." Chapter 4 in P. Knoblock, ed., *Intervention Approaches in Educating Emotionally Disturbed Children.* Syracuse: Division of Special Education and Rehabilitation, Syracuse University, 1966, pp. 35–78.

16. Bijou, S. "Application of Experimental Analysis of Behavior Principles in Teaching Academic Tool Subjects to Retarded Children." In *The Learning Environment: Relationship to Behavior Modification and Implications for Special Education,* edited by N. Haring and R. Whelan. Lawrence, Kan.: University of Kansas Publications, 1966.

17. Lindsley, O. "Direct Measurement of Prothesis of Retarded Children." *Journal of Educational Psychology* 147 (1964): 66–81.

18. Morse, W. C.; R. Bloom; and J. Dunn. *A Study of School Classroom Behavior from Diverse Evaluative Frameworks: Developmental, Mental Health, Substantive Learning, Group Process.* University of Michigan, U.S.O.E. # SAE 8414, November, 1961.

19. Barker, R. G.; Tamara Dembo; and K. Lewin. "Studies in Topological and Vector Psychology, II: Frustration and Regression: An Experiment With Young Children." *University of Iowa Studies in Child Welfare* 18 (1941).

20. Several studies are pertinent here: Shallenberger, P. and E. Zigler. "Rigidity, Negative Reaction Tendencies, and Cosatiation Effects in Normal and Feebleminded Children." *Journal of Abnormal and Social Psychology* 63 (1961): 20–26. Stevenson, H., and E. Zigler. "Discrimination Learning and Rigidity in Normal and Feebleminded Individuals." *Journal of Personality* 25 (1957): 699–711. Zigler, E. "Social Deprivation and Rigidity in the Performance of Feebleminded Children." *Journal of Abnormal and Social Psychology* 62 (1961): 413–21. Zigler, E. "Rigidity in the Feebleminded." In *Research Readings on the Exceptional Child,* edited by E. Trapp and P. Himelstein. New York: Appleton-Century-Crofts, 1962. Zigler, E.; L. Hodgden; and H. Stevenson. "The Effect of Support on the Performance of Normal and Feebleminded Children." *Journal of Personality* 26 (1958): 106–22. R. Shepps, and E. Zigler. "Social Deprivation and Rigidity in the Performance of Organic and Familial Retardates." *American Journal of Mental Deficiency* 67 (1962): 262–68.

21. Kounin, J. "Experimental Studies in Rigidity I. The Measurement of Rigidity in Normal and Feebleminded Persons." *Character and Personality* 9 (1941): 273–82.

22. Werner, H. "Subnormal and Abnormal Forms of Rigidity." *Journal of Abnormal and Social Psychology* 41 (1946): 15–24. See also Werner, H. "The Concept of Rigidity: A Critical Evaluation." *Psychological Review* 53 (1948): 43–53.

23. Strauss, A. A., and H. Werner. "Experimental Analysis of the Clinical Symptom 'Perseveration' in Mentally Retarded Children." *American Journal of Mental Deficiency* 47 (1942): 185–88.

24. Gardner, R. "The Needs of Teachers for Specialized Information on the Development of Cognitive Structure." In W. M. Cruickshank (ed.), *The Teacher of Brain-Injured Children: A Discussion of the Bases for Competency,* edited by W. M. Cruickshank. Syracuse: Syracuse University Press, 1966.

25. Rubin, E. Z.; C. B. Simson; and M. C. Betwee. *Emotionally Handicapped Children and the Elementary School.* Detroit: Wayne State University Press, 1966.

26. Haring, N., and E. L. Phillips. *Educating Emotionally Disturbed Children.* New York: McGraw-Hill, 1962.

27. The following papers in W. M. Cruickshank, ed., The Teacher of *Brain-Injured Children: A Discussion of the Bases for Competency.* Syracuse: Syracuse University Press, 1966, provide a remarkable summary of the basic concepts concerned with perception, cognition, and motor development: J. J. Gallagher, "Children with Developmental Imbalances: A Psycho-educational Definition," pp. 21-44; S. R. Rappaport, "Personality Factors Teachers Need for Relationship Structure," pp. 45-56; M. Frostig, "The Needs of Teachers for Specialized Information on Reading," pp. 87-110; E. S. Freidus, "The Needs of Teachers for Specialized Information on Number Concepts," pp. 111-28; N. C. Kephart, "The Needs of Teachers for Specialized Information on Perception," pp. 169-80; R. H. Barsch, "Teacher Needs—Motor Training," pp. 181-96; C. R. Strother, "The Needs of Teachers for Specialized Information in the Area of Psychodiagnostics," pp. 197-207; W. H. Gaddes, "The Needs of Teachers for Specialized Information on Handedness, Finger Localization, and Cerebral Dominance," pp. 207-18.

28. Getman, G. N., and E. R. Kane, *The Physiology of Readiness,* Minneapolis: P.A.S.S., 1964).

29. Benton, A. *Right-Left Discrimination and Finger Localization Development and Pathology.* New York: Paul B. Hoeber, 1959.

30. Cowen, E. L.; R. P. Underberg; R. T. Verillo; and F. G. Benham. *Adjustment to Visual Disability in Adolescence.* New York: American Foundation for the Blind, 1961. See also R. P. Underberg, R. T. Verillo, F. G. Benham, E. L. Cowen. "Factors Relating to Adjustment to Visual Disability in Adolescence." *The New Outlook for the Blind* 55 (1961): 253-359.

31. Sommers, V. *The Influence of Parental Attitudes and Social Environment on the Personality Development of the Adolescent Blind.* New York: American Foundation for the Blind, Inc., 1944.

32. Johnson, G. O. "A Study of the Social Position of Mentally Handicapped Children in the Regular Grades." *American Journal of Mental Deficiency* 55 (1950): 60-89.

33. Bronfrenbrenner, U. "The Measurement of Sociometric Status, Structure, and Development." *Sociometry Monograph* 6. New York: Beacon House.

34. Force, D. G. "Social Status of Physically Handicapped Children." *Exceptional Children* 23 (1956): 104-107.

35. Johnson, J. J., and J. R. Ferreira. "School Attitudes of Children in Special Classes for the Mentally Retarded." *California Journal of Educational Research* 9 (1958): 33-37.

36. Malpass, L. F.; M. Hardy; A. S. Gilmore; and C. F. Williams. "Automated Instruction for Retarded Children." *American Journal of Mental Deficiency* 69 (1964): 405–12.

37. Blackman, L., and R. J. Capobianco. "An Evaluation of Programmed Instruction With the Mentally Retarded Utilizing Teaching Machines." *American Journal of Mental Deficiency* 70 (1965): 262–69.

38. Ellson, D. G., et al. "Programmed Tutoring: Teaching Aid and a Research Tool." *The Reading Research Quarterly* (Fall 1965): 77–127.

39. Stolurow, L. M. "Programmed Instruction for the Mentally Retarded." *Review of Educational Research* 33 (1963): 126–36.

40. Cruickshank, W. M. "Qualitative Analysis of Intelligence Test Responses." *Journal of Clinical Psychology* 3 (October 1947): 381. Idem. "Arithmetic Vocabulary of Mentally Retarded Boys." *Journal of Exceptional Children* (1946): 93. Idem. "Arithmetic Work Habits of Mentally Retarded Boys." *American Journal of Mental Deficiency* (1948): 318. Idem. "Arithmetic Ability of Mentally Retarded Children: I. Ability to Differentiate Extraneous Materials from Needed Arithmetical Facts." *Journal of Educational Research* (1948). Idem. "Arithmetic Ability of Mentally Retarded Children: II. Understanding Arithmetic Processes." *Journal of Educational Research* 42 (1948): 279–88.

41. Dunn, L. M. "A Comparative Study of Mentally Retarded and Mentally Normal Boys of the Same Mental Age on Same Aspects of the Reading Process." Doctoral Dissertation, University of Illinois, 1953.

42. Goldstein, H.; L. Jordan; and J. W. Moss. *Early School Development of Low I.Q. Children: A Study of Special Class Placement.* U. S. Office of Education Cooperative Research Program, Project SAE 8204, Interim Report. Urbana, Illinois: University of Illinois Institute for Research on Exceptional Children, 1962.

43. Blatt, B. "The Physical, Personality, and Academic Status of Children Who Are Mentally Retarded Attending Special Classes as Compared With Children Who Are Mentally Retarded Attending Regular Classes." *American Journal of Mental Deficiency* 60 (1958): 810–18.

44. Cassidy, Viola M., and Jeannette Stanton. *An Investigation of Factors Involved in the Educational Placement of Mentally Retarded Children: A Study of Differences Between Children in Special and Regular Classes in Ohio.* U. S. Office of Education Cooperative Research Program, Project No. 043. Columbus: Ohio State University, 1959.

45. Stevens, H. A., and R. Heber. *Mental Retardation: A Review of Research.* Chicago: University of Chicago Press, 1964.

46. Carriker, W. "A Comparison of Post-School Adjustments of Regular and Special Class Retarded Individuals Served in Lincoln and Omaha, Nebraska Public Schools." Doctoral dissertation, University of Nebraska, 1957.

47. Porter, R. B., and T. C. Milazzo. "A Comparison of Mentally Retarded Adults Who Attended A Special Class With Those Who Attended Regular School Class." *Exceptional Children* 24 (1958): 410–12.

48. Cohen, J. S. "An Analysis of Vocational Failures of Mental Retardates Placed in the Community After a Period of Institutionalization." *American Journal of Mental Deficiency* 65 (1960): 371–75.

PART II

DEFINITIONAL CONSIDERATIONS

6

LEARNING DISABILITIES

A Definitional Statement

INTRODUCTION AND BACKGROUND

*L*EARNING DISABILITIES as a term can be defined. The term is used in the plural in this paper, since (a) that is the customary manner in which it is popularly used, and because (b) it is a phenomenon which rarely is singular in its characteristics as these are observed in a given child.

There are a variety of types of definitions possible, and as David Kendall as well stated there may be (a) diagnostic and etiological definitions, (b) educational, pedagogical, paediatric or biochemical definitions, and (c) legislative definitions. In this paper, the author has chosen to pursue the first strand, i.e., diagnostic and etiological, from which other definitions can ultimately flow. In the paragraphs which follow, a logical, step-by-step procedure will be offered, ultimately resulting in a definition which will hopefully achieve some common understanding of a very complex issue.

It is appropriate to consider some background information which is basic to a definitional statement of learning disabilities. The term learning disabilities itself is one of the interesting accidents of our professional times. It was never used prior to 1963, at least with the connotation which it presently has. Several parent organizations had been brought together at that time in Chicago, Illinois, in an attempt on the part of their members to organize themselves in an effective manner to represent their children on a national basis. Dr. Samuel A. Kirk had been invited to address the group at an evening dinner meeting. During his prepared, but informal remarks, he ruled out several clinical problems, such as *primary* mental retardation, as not being issues germane to the problem which the parents were considering. He did approach the matter positively, however, and indicated that these were children who showed "problems of learning," "learning difficulties," "learning disabilities," or other problems related (in Kirk's remarks) essentially to school learning (Hallahan and Cruickshank 1973, chapter 1).

Prior to this time a great variety of terms had been used to delineate essentially the same population as those which Kirk was considering. Kephart spoke of the child who was "perceptually handicapped"; Myklebust and often Kirk and Bateman, the child with "language disorders"; Cruickshank, the "brain injured child"; Clements, Payne and others, "children with minimal cerebral dysfunction" or "minimal brain damage". Still others referred to this population under the terms hyperactive, organic, strephosymbolic (Orton), clumsy child syndrome, Strauss syndrome, or any one of more than forty terms which have been reported in the literature (Cruickshank and Paul 1971). Early on Frostig and M. S. Rabinovitch also utilized the term perceptually handicapped, although the latter dropped it in favor of learning disabilities shortly after the term began to be used.

Immediately following the 1963 dinner, to which reference has been made, the parents on a national level in the United States organized themselves under the banner of Association for Children with Learning Disabilities, an organization which soon spread widely throughout Canada and the United States and in modified forms to other countries as well (see also Stott 1972).

The term learning disabilities was adopted as a functional term without precedents to guide those who attempted to define it, and without research or common usage which would assist in its appropriate formulation as a functional term. Although a small group of professional personnel met in 1964 to consider the term and its use (Kirk, Lehtinen, Barsch, Kephart, Strothers, Frostig, Cruickshank, Myklebust, among a few others), it was seen then as a term which could not satisfy both the professions and the parents, and one which would lend itself to innumerable definitions depending upon the orientation of the author. On the positive side it was a term which emphasized the primary problems of the child, i.e., learning, and focused these problems directly on the school's responsibility to solve them. It is a term which in general has positive connotations, and places the child in the best possible light. It is, however, a term which lends itself to misinterpretation, misdefinition, and misunderstanding. In this paper, the problem will be approached from two points of view, namely, (a) historical accuracy, and (b) neuropsychological accuracy. Out of these two strands comes an accurate concept of learning disabilities per se.

LEARNING DISABILITIES AND ENVIRONMENTALLY DETERMINED LEARNING PROBLEMS

Much of the confusion regarding learning disabilities, when not accurately conceptualized, comes from a failure on the part of many persons to differentiate between learning disabilities in children and those educational problems in children and youth which are primarily related to environmental causatives.

Special Needs

The total school population of a province or local school authority is the base for planning. A second smaller population is identified as including *children with environmentally determined problems* and those with *special needs* (psychoeducational, medical, nutritional, or others). For the purposes of this paper, but within the generally accepted construct, *this population refers essentially to problems of learning in children and youth which are environmentally produced.* There are some exceptions to this statement which will be mentioned later. These are children who may have had a difficult mother-child separation at the time of initial school entrance. These are children whose parents may have been undergoing a divorce when the child was in Grade One or Grade Two, at the time reading and other essential skills were being taught. These are the hungry children of a community; the non-English- or non-French-speaking immigrant children; those who are ill for extended periods of times. These are children who may have experienced the occasional poor teacher in Grade One or Grade Two at a time when basic skills should have been acquired. For each of these there may have developed deficiencies in school achievement, learning problems, and often emotional disturbances related to school and to school activities. The size of this population is actually unknown, although varying estimates and figures are available. Marked variability in incidence and prevalence is reported because of differences in the nature of the populations being studied, i.e., rural, urban, suburban, centre city, multiracial, etc. In this group the deficits are not chronic, but respond to educational or treatment regimens.

All children with learning disabilities, a third population group, have special needs, but they present a very special type of school, home, and community learning problems. These are the specific and central elements of this paper.

LEARNING DISABILITIES AND NEUROLOGICAL DYSFUNCTION

The relationship between learning disabilities and environmentally determined learning problems must be kept in focus in order to understand fully the issues of learning disabilities as a clinical entity. We have stated that the term learning disabilities is one which is subject to much confusion and misinterpretation. The term is with us, and for the present and undetermined future it will have to be accepted.

The definition of learning disabilities is a three-step process. (1) Learning disabilities, whether in singular or in complex forms, are the end result of other factors. (2) As the problem is being defined here in terms of its historical and neuropsychological accuracy, learning disabilities are the result of perceptual processing deficits of an extremely diverse nature. The moment one mentions "perception," however, one must account for still another level basic to the learning disability. (3) Perception is neurological. Perception is an inherent function of the neurology of the organism. Perception is not something separate and apart from the organism, but is the direct reflection of the capacity of the neurological system to receive stimuli, to transform them into neuro-electrical energy, to transport this energy to appropriate portions of the central nervous system, to provide a mechanism or mechanisms whereby experience, judgment, symbolization, the organization of symbols in linguistic structures, intelligence and other forms of higher intellectual function can be related to the energizing forces, and ultimately to activate efferent nerves (output) so that appropriate motor responses in the form of movement, speech, listening, viewing, or feeling can be experienced. Perception is a process through which the steps we have just delineated are accomplished and by which the individual accommodates or adjusts to its environment. Socially acceptable responses are those which are perceived and processed within the standards recognized by society. Reading, writing, acquisition of number concepts, as well as overt forms of more gross behavior, constitute such responses.

The neurological processes of the human organism are well documented (Gaddes, 1966 and 1975; Critchley, 1953, Luria, 1966), and will not be discussed here in any detail. The neurological aspect of learning disabilities is mentioned here only to indicate the specific base of the handicaps and to *differentiate learning disabilities from the environmentally determined problems of learning*. When this differentiation and the respective characteristics are kept in mind, it is easy to obtain clarity with respect to learning disabilities as an education and social set of problems.

To paraphrase and slightly modify Wepman and his associates (in

Hobbs, 1975), *learning disabilities are the result of neurologically based perceptual processing deficits.*

It must be pointed out that, since the sciences of neurology and neuropsychology are of relatively recent development, it is not always possible in the current state of the arts to make a specific diagnosis or neurological dysfunction in a given individual. We reiterate, if perceptual processing deficits are observed in a child, neurological dysfunction in some degree must be present whether or not it can be accurately identified or described through neurological examination, electroencephalography, or pneumoencephalography, — common techniques available to the neurologist. The future may indeed provide for greater accuracy and definitive diagnosis in these cases through the future development and refinements of the radio microscope, the "brain scan" and Computerized Axial Tomography (CAT scan) techniques, and possibly even holography when the latter science is perfected. No one of the techniques commonly used at present or suggested for the future provides fully accurate information today, but each contributes something and may be developed on a much more sophisticated basis for later diagnostic use. Certainly the brain scan holds much promise in this regard. Another investigator whose work has yet to be corroborated, but is related, is Julio Quirós (Argentina) who states that vestibular dysfunction in infants may prove to be a significant diagnostic clue to the future presence or absence of learning disabilities (1976). While fuller discussion of these matters is more appropriate elsewhere, it is essential to this paper to state that learning disabilities, the result of perceptual processing deficits, are based on diagnosed or assumed malfunctions of the neurological system of the organism. This is historically the point of view of those whose research and clinical studies gave form to the problems of children now called learning disabilities (cf. Weiderholt, in Mann and Sabatino, 1975). It is since 1963, and the widespread use of the less-than-satisfactory term "learning disabilities," that other inaccurate connotations have been given to it. If clarity regarding the essential problem is to be achieved, and if children and youth with perceptual processing deficits are to be helped, it is essential that clarity of understanding regarding the fundamental nature of learning disabilities be achieved. The needs of children with accurately defined learning disabilities are not being met, because of the confusion related to definition which is observed in many countries, and because classrooms are characterized by heterogeneity of learning disorders rather than a maximum of homogeneity. Educators are thus faced with insurmountable tasks, all essentially based on the absence of an accurate definition of the clinical problem for educational purposes.

In the sections which follow there will appear (a) a discussion and examples of perceptual processing deficits, (b) issues inherently related to learning disabilities, and some tangential to it, and finally (c) other elements which lead ultimately to a definitional statement.

EXAMPLES OF PERCEPTUAL PROCESSING DEFICITS

Perceptual processing deficits are of an unusual variety as they are observed in children and youth. Terminology commonly used is not always accurate either, so that the problem becomes confused for the parent or teacher. *The aspects of processing deficits which are included here are those which relate essentially to school learning and home adjustment. They are also defined here in terms of their psychoeducational realities,* since it is in this phase of adjustment that the greatest amount of attention is required. *It must be emphasized that,* although many examples are taken from the area of visual processing, *all sensory modalities are or may be involved*: auditory, haptic, olfactory, or gustatory as well as visual. Perceptual processing deficits may result in a variety of learning disabilities in children which, if unattended, in turn, will result in serious academic retardation. The Wepman Committee, the CELDIC Report, and the Australian Select Committee (1976) have emphasized numerous of these deficits as have others which will be mentioned. Since the issue of perceptual processing deficits is the result of neurological dysfunction and is subsequently the cause of the learning disabilities, considerable attention will be given to the manifestations of these problems. It is the clear delineation of the processing deficits which is the responsibility of the psychoeducational diagnosticians. Children and youth with perceptual processing deficits demonstrate inadequate abilities in a number of both overlapping and discrete functions. Some of these problem areas are delineated in the paragraphs which follow. The reader must keep in mind that all of the examples provided below may affect interactional learning which thus requires that those who work with learning disabilities children maintain a constant concern for social adaptation and development, effective emotional development, as well as the specific implications of the psychomotor match between perceptual deficits and educational management planning.

1. *Discrimination.* Children with learning disabilities frequently show an inadequate ability in the recognition of "fine differences between auditory and visual" and tactual "discriminating features underlying the sounds used in speech and the orthographic forms used in reading" (Wepman *et al.,* 1975, p. 309). Golick speaks of this same characteristic under the heading of inadequate "visual efficiency" (1970, p. 8). She emphasizes an important dimension which others have often overlooked, namely, that "With

some, the problems seem to be poor perception of the three-dimensional world; yet two-dimensional vision—for written material, pictures—is intact." Studies with cerebral palsy children have also indicated visual efficiency differences between two- and three-dimensional material (Cruickshank, Bice et al. 1965).

The Wepman Committee stressed discriminatory malfunction in terms of auditory and visual modalities. To these we have added tactual (haptic) discrimination in some children. Although the visual and auditory modalities are undoubtedly the most significant in terms of learning, some research of a minimal nature exists to indicate that the processing deficits here under consideration are probably to be observed in all of the sensory modalities. This fact, although not firmly authenticated, should be kept in mind as subsequent characteristics of perceptual processing deficits are briefly discussed.

2. *Memory*. Children with learning disabilities often show an inadequate ability in "retaining and recalling those discriminated sounds and forms in both short- and long-term memory" (Wepman *et al., ibid.*). The Australian Select Committee on Specific Learning Disabilities in its report to the House of Representatives, stresses, as a characteristic of "perceptual difficulties," "poor short-term rote memory" (1976, p. 129). Although failure to remember is an often-heard complaint of teachers and parents, it may not be a discrete processing deficit, but may be the result of other factors which will be mentioned later (see Inattentiveness and Failure to Refrain from Response to Stimuli). However, the inability to recall constitutes a tremendous hazard to successful achievement, is a characteristic noted by most authors, and indeed was stressed in what is perhaps the first published description of these children under the heading of a "Composite of a Child" (Cruickshank *et al.,* 1961, p. 55).

3. *Sequencing*. Many children with learning disabilities show an inadequate ability and a "poor grasp of sequence" (Golick, p. 9). The Wepman Committee likewise calls attention to this disability area in stating that learning disabled children often are characterized by difficulties in "ordering the sounds and forms (referred to in par. 1 above) sequentially, both in sensory and motor acts" (*ibid.,* Wepman 1975).

Sequencing and memory functions are undoubtedly closely interrelated. Sequencing requires an efficient memory by which to order things, events, or commands in a proper relationship. Irrespective of its independent or dependent status, the lack of ability to sequence is a fundamental characteristic of many children with learning disabilities, and is a significant hurdle to their school achievement and general adjustment. (See also Gaddes, 1977.)

4. *Figure-background relationship.* Children with learning disabilities frequently have an inadequate ability to distinguish visual, auditory, and/or tactile figure-background relationships (Wepman *et al., ibid.*; Frostig, Lefever and Whittelsey, 1961). This factor may also be related to attentiveness to be discussed below, but in isolation it is in itself a serious processing impediment for learning. Undoubtedly the most extensive studies of this problem have been carried out with the cooperation of cerebral palsy children, as mentioned above, of the athetoid and spastic subtypes (Cruickshank, Bice *et al., 1965*). However, studies of the figure-background pathology were completed by Werner and Strauss as early as 1941, and numerous other investigators have studied this phenomenon in relation to populations of children and youth with varying neurophysiological diagnoses. In practically every study which has examined the psychological characteristics of children with learning disabilities, the element of figure-ground pathology has been observed. Irrespective of its etiology, it is a serious impediment to appropriate development of reading skills, and its presence seriously impairs achievement in all forms of school-oriented learning situations.

5. *Time and space orientation.* The Wepman Committee (*ibid.,* p. 306) stresses that children with learning disabilities often have an inadequate ability in "recognizing spatial and temporal orientations." Problems of directionality, recognition of body parts, inadequate spatial and temporal orientation have been commented upon many times by clinical investigators (Hallahan and Kauffman, 1975) who work with the learning disabilities population. The interrelationship of these factors with others which are included in this section is obvious, but, as with some of the others, these problems stand out in such a manner as to isolate them. It is undoubtedly the failure to function well in these areas which in many children with learning disabilities contributes to the development of inadequate body-image concepts and poor self-concepts, other characteristics of a secondary order which are frequently commented upon by writers in this field (Kronick, 1973; Golick, 1970; Cruickshank, 1977; and others).

6. *Closure.* Children with learning disabilities have an inadequate "ability to obtain closure" on either an ideational or more concrete form. For example, a child asked to draw a square or a circle may produce something in the form of a letter "U". A child who starts to relate an event of the previous day may find that he cannot continue to the close of the story or idea (Wepman *et al., ibid.*; Gyr, 1975).

7. *Sensory integration.* Children with learning disabilities have an inadequate capacity in "integrating intersensory information" (Birch and Leford, 1964). Golick (1970) states that "Some children seem to be able to handle tasks that are purely visual or tasks that are purely auditory, but seem

to have difficulty in combining the information that comes to them through separate sense organs. For example, they may be able to see and recognize the letter *a*, and hear and repeat the vowel sound, *a,* but seem to be unable to learn to associate the two." Frostig (1975) writes of this aspect of processing deficits as "one of the most significant hurdles to learning and adjustment which faces the child with learning disabilities." How often does the following situation occur in the classroom? "*Listen,* boys and girls," calls the teacher, "listen to me. *Look* at the blackboard. *See* what I have written there. *Copy* what you see on paper." "Listen" (auditory), "look" (visual), "copy" (motor) involve three neurological systems. For children who have difficulty in associating activities which involve two or more systems, a failure experience is certain to take place. Intersensory integration is another aspect of processing which demands research at all levels of child growth and development. (See also Koupernik, MacKeith and Francis-Williams, 1975; Ayres, 1975).

8. *Perceptual-motor function.* Children with learning disabilities have an inadequate ability in "relating what is perceived to specific motor functions" (Wepman *et al, ibid.*; Kephart, 1975). In part this function is related to the poor grasp of sequence to which reference was earlier made (Golick, 1970), to an inadequate judgment of the amount of energy required to initiate and accomplish a given motor task, and to the inability to refrain from reacting to motor-eliciting stimuli until a task analysis of the required operation is completed by the child.

9. *Dissociation.* Children with learning disabilities very often have an inadequate ability to associate. To state it negatively, these children are characterized by dissociation. Dissociation is the inability to see parts in relationship to the whole. These children have difficulty in conceptualizing new concepts which are built upon previously learned or recognized elements. Dissociation contributes to the problems in sequencing and to figure-ground pathology. On a functional basis these children have difficulty with pegboard designs, block designs, parquetry blocks, lacing shoes, as well as with more abstract wholes which must be developed from related parts (Strauss and Werner, 1942; Cruickshank, 1977). The individual parts appear to have greater significance for the child than does the ultimate whole concept, probably because the parts contain many more stimuli. The Australian report refers to dissociation as a deficiency in "part-whole synthesis and analysis" (p. 129). This phenomenon, as with figure-background disturbance, and probably some of the other characteristics mentioned earlier, is closely related to the attention problems which these children often demonstrate.

10. *Attention.* Children with learning disabilities are often characterized by attention disturbances (Cruickshank, 1977; Werner and Strauss,

1942; and many others). Hagan and Keil (1975) and Lewis (1975) have made excellent analyses of the problems of attention and attention disturbances in children with learning disabilities. At least one point of view holds that the attention disturbances of the learning disabilities child are the result of being unable to refrain from reacting to extraneous environmental stimuli which may include those of a visual, auditory, tactual or other modalities. The extraneous stimuli may be internal as well as external to the organism (Rappaport, 1969). Kinesthetic stimuli resulting from clothing which bind (tactual stimuli) may be the source of real, but unconscious disturbances for the child. Extraneous stimuli may be of two major types: sensory or motor. Whereas the neurologically intact normal child or youth can negatively adapt to the unessential, the unusual, or the extraneous, the child with perceptual processing deficits at times appears almost driven to respond to them. Kurt Goldstein in a classic paper speaks of this characteristic in terms of "driveness" (1941). Homberger (1926) refers to the phenomenon as "being stimulus bound," i.e., tied to stimuli. Strauss and Werner (1941) and Cruickshank have referred to this behavior as forced responsiveness to stimuli (1966, 1977).

If the child is driven to respond to stimuli of whatsoever nature, the attention span will be significantly shortened (Kronick, p. 143). A short attention span is directly related to the amount of time the child has to learn. It is not unusual to see children in a clinical situation where the attention span is of two or three minutes in duration, and children with attention spans as short as fifteen to thirty seconds have been observed on many occasions. But even longer attention spans, yet short by normal standards, will produce learning and adjustment problems for the child in school or home learning situations.

Although little if any quantitative data is available, clinicians often also report that these children make deviant or unusual responses to reinforcement. While the etiology of this observed behavior may not be clear, it is possible that this also is directly related to short attention span or to attention disturbances of other natures. Likewise, these children may process stimuli at a different rate than normal children. If left alone these children are observed to have an erratic rate of processing, slower rates, or sometimes appear to be so overwhelmed by the task of processing that they function behaviorally on almost totally a trial-and-error basis.

Previously it was stated that the lack of attention or forced responsiveness to stimuli probably is related to dissociation and to figure-ground disturbance, among other characteristics, e.g., closure. The backgrounds of most visual situations and of many auditory and tactual representations contain much more stimuli than does the figure itself. Cruickshank, Bice *et al.*

(1965) have shown that it takes a relatively large increase in the value of a figure (through size, color, and commonness of concept) before a child with visual perceptual processing deficits can perceive it adequately on a routine basis. Grube has demonstrated that this capacity is developmental in normal children (at least during the chronological years of four through seven). The neurologically handicapped subjects in the Cruickshank and Bice study were between the ages of six and sixteen years.

The normal auditory climate of a classroom, home, or playground contains a great amount of stimuli. The visual environment of a printed page in a child's reading or arithmetic book contains hundreds, if not thousands of background stimuli in comparison to the few stimuli contained in the specific word or set of numerals which the child is attempting to respond to at the moment. Learning disabilities children are often characterized as having poor table manners. This may in part be due to the excessive number of background stimuli (many of which are motoric in nature) surrounding the child at meal time in comparison to the specific piece of food which is being put by him or her onto a fork or spoon. The psychologist often sees this characteristic of overreaction to stimuli defeating the child when the latter is asked to perform on marble boards, Rorschach cards, or other types of psychological testing material.

These comments are written by way of stating that the factor of stimuli attraction (a) reduces the child's attention span, and (b) may well be a significant deterrent to appropriate processing in other related areas, i.e., increasing chances of dissociation, hindering closure, producing figure-background confusions, and, among others interfering with the capacity to make fine discriminations (par. 1 above) which are so much a part of good initial reading and speaking.

(There is an interesting vicious circle which is often observed in the case of attention disturbances which is not a part of processing deficits per se, but which certainly serves to increase concept of failure in the learning disabilities child. Attraction to stimuli reduces the attention span. The reduced attention span produces the chances of failure experiences. Continued failure experiences may further reduce the length of the attention span, and may tend to drive the child to trial-and-error responses to environmental stimuli. In some children with severe manifestations of learning disabilities this cyclical behavior produces extraordinary adjustment problems for the child, his parents, teachers, and others who must cope with the behavior on a day-to-day basis.)

11. *Rate of processing.* Rate of processing has been mentioned above. However, it warrants special stress. Marjorie Golick writes: "There are some children whose difficulties in learning language are related to their

inability to process the stream of speech quickly enough to identify (and therefore remember) the component stimuli. This is evident at the beginning stages of speech development in their mispronunciation and misidentification of those parts of words (consonants articulated in clusters and unstressed syllables) which demand rapid temporal judgments. Later on it is apparent in their inability to repeat accurately polysyllabic words where several consonants follow in rapid succession; in their spelling errors (where sounds and syllables are omitted); in their difficulty in learning exceptions to linguistic rules (irregular parts and plurals which must be individually noticed and remembered); and in their difficulty in using and understanding those sentence structures which depend on precise tracking of unstressed elements whose forms or placements are unpredictable."

12. *Perseveration.* Some children with learning disabilities demonstrate varying degrees of perseveration which interferes with learning and adjustment processes. Perseveration is a characteristic which is not reserved to learning disabilities children and youth alone. Furthermore there appears to be more than one way in which perseveration is manifested. In the psychotic or the neurotic patient one frequently observes conceptual perseveration. This type of adjustment may or may not be a matter of perceptual processing deficit, but is the result of other dynamics not pertinent to this paper.

Perseveration in the child with learning disabilities has been described (Werner and Strauss, 1942; Kronick, 1973; Cruickshank, 1977) as (a) the prolonged after-effect of a stimulus, or (b) as the inertia of the organism preventing easy movement from one stimulus situation to the other. Whether perseveration is a genuine processing deficit or a learned emotional response serving to protect the individual is not clear and need not be argued here. It is, however, a very significant deterrent to learning and to appropriate adjustment in the child with learning disabilities when it does occur. It is probably one of the more difficult characteristics to deal with on either a psychological or an educational level.

13. *Language and communication.* Language and communication are learned behaviors based on essential neurological functions involving adequate reception of auditory stimuli, their transmission and translation into appropriate expressive behavior. These functions are basic examples of perceptual processing, and when undamaged systems convey stimuli appropriately, good normal speech, language as well as non-vocal speech is the result. When the system does not function adequately, as in the case of children with learning disabilities, then the commonly observed characteristics of faulty understanding of language and its use, poor speech per se, and their often-reported absence of "inner conversation" or subliminal language is reported.

On a related vein David Kendall states: "A characteristic of great importance is that *of language disturbance.* [Many] writers approached the problem of learning disabilities from the point of view of speech and language disturbances. It is quite possible, however, that some, perhaps even the majority of speech and language disturbances are the result of perceptual processing deficits. However, there does appear to be some evidence to support the construct of central language processing disorders, i.e., difficulties in the semantic and morphological aspects of language which can be separated from the modalities by means of which linguistic information is primarily received. For this reason it may be necessary to expand the concept of perceptual processing disorders to include those specifically linguistic aspects."

14. *Other characteristics.* Numerous authors have listed other characteristics of processing deficits, some of which are overlapping with those which have been mentioned above. Chief among these, however, are:

    a. deficits in size discrimination (Australian report);
    b. deficits in judgment of time (Australian report; Hallahan, 1975);
    c. deficits in judgment of distance (Australian report);
    d. deficits in abstract reasoning (Goldstein, Strauss, Cruickshank, Australian report, others);
    e. inadequate concept formation (Strauss, Werner, Australian report, Crichton *et al.,* Golick and others); and
    f. poor sense of rhythm (Golick).

LEARNING DISABILITIES: MULTIFACETED

Before the discussion of learning disabilities per se is concluded, it is important to note a number of subsets which fully or partially overlap within this population. The size of the learning disability population is unknown. There are many estimates, often guesses, which have been repeated so often that unfortunately they have become accepted as fact. The actual situation, however, is that there is not one adequate epidemiological or demographic study of learning disabilities in the world literature as of the time this paper is presented. There have been studies, very limited in size of populations of children with learning disabilities, but there have been no studies of total school populations to determine, with even rough screening devices, the number of children who accurately could be termed those with learning disabilities. This is a reflection of the newness of the field, the sudden use of the categorical term, the lack of adequate research, and the pressure to provide services in the absence of adequately prepared general educators and administrators, to say nothing of the almost total absence of qualified clinical teachers able to meet the needs of children with specific learning disabilities. It is this lack of accurate epidemiological data which makes the application of statistical definitions of learning disabilities unsatisfactory, although this problem will be discussed later in this paper. With this in mind it is possible to consider some of the elements central and closely related to learning disabilities.

Intelligence

Many definitions of learning disabilities include a cut-off point insofar as intelligence quotient is concerned. This is an historical slip which was permitted to occur in 1963, when the initial use of the term learning disabilities took place following Kirk's speech. Although it was stated earlier by Kirk that these were not children with *primary mental retardation,* his audience chose to hear that these were *not mentally retarded children.* Therein developed a situation which is without fact, and which has served to deprive thousands of children of their educational birthright. Parents wanted to put their child's best foot forward, and this is understandable. There were enough problems to be faced without the added one of mental retardation. And some of them had heard that these were children without primary mental retardation. To drop the word primary was a very easy thing for some parents to do, just as it was with some educators who did not understand the essential issues of learning disabilities. Thus early on the ACLD (USA) defined this problem in terms of intellectual normality. This led to numerous educational authorities defining the problem as being one reserved to children with intelligence quotients above 80, 85, or 90! Obviously any educational authority can define the problem as the citizens of that authority wish, but in terms of accuracy and child need, to equate learning disabilities with intellectual normalcy in all cases is to perpetuate inaccurate statements and to ignore much of what little research there is.

The basis for this statement lies in the early work of Werner, Strauss (as reported in Strauss and Lehtinen 1947), and their associates, studies which appeared for the first time in the literature between 1935 and 1945. All of these research studies, vigorously critiqued by Sarason (1946), were completed on endogenous and exogenous, educable mentally retarded boys between the ages of 12 and 16 years. Although their statistical sophistication accurately may be criticized, as Sarason has done, the studies of Werner and

Strauss demonstrate without a doubt the clinical presence of learning dis-abilities in mentally retarded youth (exogenous population). As a matter of record much which was known about children later to be called learning dis-abled in 1963, came from research done originally on mentally retarded youth. It is thus inaccurate to speak of learning disabilities, as we shall pres-ently define the problem, as being restricted to children and youth of average or above-average intellectual ability. It is accurate to state that the issues of *"perceptual processing deficits are respectors of no single intellectual level, but are to be found throughout the intellectual spectrum"* (a phrase used by Dr. John McLeod, University of Saskatchewan and Mrs. Barbara McElgrin, Montreal). Indeed, to perpetuate the inaccuracy regarding the relationship of intelligence to learning disabilities is not only to fail to serve many chil-dren in need, but to perpetuate an insidious form of racial discrimination as well. In some communities classes for the mentally retarded are essentially composed of minority group learners; those for the learning disabled, white learners. Estimates based on some institutional surveys indicate that the ex-ogenous group would constitute about 45 percent of the total group of men-tally retarded persons, probably less among the educable mentally retarded level. The exact percentage of exogenous *versus* endogenous retardation in the general population or within a given school system is not known, and is one of the factors which awaits a comprehensive epidemiological and demo-graphic study.

The terms *endogenous* and *exogenous* may require definition. In this paper and in general usage in the study of mental retardation, endoge-nous children are those in whose history there is no evidence of brain injury, neurological signs, accident, illness, or injury which could account for the intellectual retardation, but in whose history there is evidence of genetic, fa-milial, or hereditary factors which could account for it. Exogenous children, on the other hand, are those in whose history there is no evidence of genetic or familial entities, but where there is evidence of some adventitious factors (e.g., neurological signs, brain injury, accident, illness or injury) which oc-curred at some point during the fetal through the postnatal developmental period and which might or does account for the abnormal perceptual responses, the lowered functional intelligence, or both. It is the latter group to which reference is made here, and it is those who are indicated to have learning disabilities comparable to their intellectually more normal peers.

It must also be added that many learning disabilities children of whatsoever level of intelligence function may "test low" on initial psycholog-ical testing, but who with appropriate instructional regimens may later func-tion more nearly or fully normal. There are, of course, many learning disabilities children and youth who are fully functional at traditional levels of normal intellect, and some who are functioning well above "normal" insofar as measured intelligence is concerned. Irrespective of these latter comments, there is the person who can be differentially diagnosed as an exogenous mentally retarded learning disabilities child or youth. The careful differentiation required here to insure the appropriate therapeutic or educational regimens requires diagnosticians of excellent preparation and highly developed skills.

Cerebral Palsy

Illustrative of one of the more complex aspects of child growth and development is the relationship of cerebral palsy, mental retardation and learning disabilities. Although a relatively small population, it is a significant one on whom longstanding research data are available on this topic. The initial studies of Dolphin and Cruickshank (1951) illustrate the similarities between the perceptual pathology in cerebral palsy and in the exogenous mentally retarded populations of Werner and Strauss. As a matter of fact, the emphasis on intellectual normalcy which was seized upon by the parent groups may have come in part from the Dolphin-Cruickshank studies which were the first to be done on groups of intellectually normal children who had a definite diagnosis of neurological impairment. Following these, a comprehensive study of intellectually normal cerebral palsy children (Cruickshank, Bice, Wallen, and Lynch, 1965) was completed which corroborated in a much more definitive manner many perceptual similarities between exogenous mentally retarded youth and the cerebral palsy population. Four hundred children between the ages of 6 and 16 years were included in the latter study. However, the study was restricted to athetoid and spastic type cerebral palsy subjects only. The similarities between the mentally retarded and cerebral palsy subjects insofar as perceptual processing was concerned formed the first link between these neurophysiological disability groups and the population later to become known as learning disability, a fact corroborated by Wedell (1961) and Critchley (1953). In terms of certain aspects of perceptual processing, more than 80 percent of the two subtypes of cerebral palsy which were studied are so characterized.

A second characteristic of major significance pertaining to the cerebral palsy subset should be noted, namely, the high incidence of mental retardation in cerebral palsy. This fact has been known for many years through the research of Asher and Schonel (1950), Heilman (1952), Miller and Rosenfeld (1952), Bice and Cruickshank (1955), and others. The incidence of retarded mental development in cerebral palsy is variously reported by these authors, each working independently, to be overall in the vicinity of 70–80 percent. A high incidence of cerebral palsy-mental retardation-learning disability overlap is easily demonstrated, producing indeed a most complex psychoeducational diagnosic and teaching problem.

Aphasia and Dyslexia

Two subsets of aphasia and dyslexia are suggested to fall completely within the learning disability population. There are many popular concepts regarding these two clinical problems, but if they are accurately defined, they are seen to be very specific types of neurophysiological dysfunction involving severe forms of perceptual-motor input and output functions. McGinnis (1963) in her classic work on aphasia describes this population in almost exact terms comparable to the description of exogenous mentally retarded subjects of Werner and Strauss, the cerebral palsy subjects of Cruickshank and Bice, and the populations of children later to be called learning disabled as described by M. S. Rabinovitch, Gaddes, Kephart, Golick, Knonick, and many others. Similarly, R. Rabinovitch and others describe the dyslexic population, when accurately defined, from the same orientation, although each clinical subtype involves different central nervous system tracts.

Hyperactive and/or Emotionally Impaired

There is reason to believe that many hyperactive and/or emotionally disturbed children are actually learning disabled children who, on a motoric basis, are unable to refrain from reacting to stimuli which produce a motor response. Admittedly this forms a theoretical position. However, when some hyperactive and "brain injured" children were submitted to a similar educational model specifically designed for learning disabilities, and the teachers not informed regarding the diagnostic categories of their pupils, those with a diagnosis of hyperactivity performed equally well as those with a more definitive neurological diagnosis. This fact has been observed on frequent occasions in clinical teaching situations. Although there is no epidemiological data available, it is hypothesized that a significant number of hyperactive and/or emotionally disturbed children are learning disabled children, the latter with a severe emotional overlay which is probably the result of continued failure experiences. This, as with most aspects of learning disability, provides an important area of needed future research.

Other

Other clinical subtypes exist, some members of which undoubtedly demonstrate characteristics similar to the learning disabilities population. Some children with organic types of deafness have been shown to have many of the same characteristics of learning disabilities (McKay, 1952). Some blind children are observed clinically to have poor tactual perceptual processing, and thus have great difficulties in learning Braille, for example. Some children with epilepsy and others who have experienced encephalitis, meningitis, or other forms of central nervous system diseases, are often left with problems of perceptual processing among other handicaps. Autism, accurately defined, may well be considered here also.

The number of subsets which could be mentioned might be much larger. The point here, however, is not to make a complete inventory, but to suggest that there is a variety of clinical categories in each of which there is an identifiable percentage of children whose learning disabilities are due to the same basic neurophysiological dysfunction as are those of the larger group whose name identifies the problem per se. There is, of course, the learning disabilities child who does not have other complicating problems such as have been described thus far.

The skills of the neuropsychologist, the clinical or school psychologist, and the educational diagnosticians are crucial here, not only to identify the levels of intellectual functioning in these multiply handicapped children and youth, but to provide a differential diagnosis which will indicate the nature of the perceptual problem and the type of educational planning which is required (see also Crichton, Kendall, Cutterson and Dunn, 1972). Unfortunately not all of these professional groups are being prepared at the present time to be able to address adequately these complex problems of growth and development.

To this point in this paper learning disabilities have been identified as being:
1. a large subset of the population of children with special needs which is an identifiable population within any total school community;
2. characterized by numerous overlapping subsets, e.g., exogenous mental retardation, aphasia, dyslexia, among others, each of which has been demonstrated to have many common neuropsychological characteristics;
3. often present without the multiple characteristics noted in (d) below;
4. characterized as a condition to be found at all intellectual levels and frequently in relationship with numerous physical and emotional manifestations; and

5. the end result of perceptual processing problems which are an inherent manifestation of the neurological and physiological systems of the human organism.

OTHER DEFINITIONAL FACTORS

Etiology

As learning disabilities are being defined in this paper they may be the result of a wide variety of etiological factors, each of which may have a deleterious impact on the developing central nervous system. These may occur at prenatal, perinatal, or postnatal periods of development.

Typical of factors which may cause central nervous system impairment in the foetus (and subsequent processing deficits) are such things as rubella, maternal toxaemia, phenylketonuria (PKU), so-called "hard drugs," narcotics, such as heroin and methadone, and a wide variety of prenatal accidents and injuries. Injuries during the birth process constitute one possible perinatal etiological factor, but this may also be related to the failure of the bones and ligaments of the pelvic arch to give sufficiently to permit easy passage of the foetus, breach birth, abnormal position of the umbilical cord, and the failure to establish breathing immediately. Examples of postnatal etiological factors could be almost endless involving a wide variety of childhood illnesses, accidents, and injuries. It would appear, however, in terms of the present knowledge that most processing deficits are coincident with prenatal and perinatal etiological factors. Thus definitionally it is possible to state that *the central nervous system impairment with its subsequent processing deficits and learning disabilities may be related to almost any etiological factor.*

Age

Although most learning disabilities occur, it is thought, during the prenatal and early postnatal years, they *may occur at any age* in the developmental span of childhood and youth. In addition to chronological age, the age of the brain and the recency of trauma will be factors of significance in the ability of the individual to respond to treatment and educational regimens.

Genetic and Familial Factors

In recent years a number of studies has appeared in the literature which of necessity focused attention on the possibility of learning disabilities in some cases being related to genetic factors. Under no circumstances do these studies indicate this to be the sole source of perceptual processing deficits, but the matter must now be considered as another possible etiological factor. While admittedly more research is required, clinical observations alone would give one cause to wonder about the familial, if not the genetic, factors. The presence of nearly identical learning disabilities in a mother (age 43 years), for example, and in her daughter (age 25 years), her son (age 19 years), her second daughter (age 16 years), and her second son (age 10 years) is a convincing bit of evidence. Learning disabilities have been found in numerous sets of fraternal twins. Sons with learning disabilities quite frequently are reported to have nearly identical problems as those experienced by their fathers a school generation earlier. The familial incidence of learning disabilities is certainly recognized clinically. Whether or not the issue is genetic in the sense of a chromosomal abnormality remains one for further research. The relationship at this time appears sufficient so that both familial and genetic factors may tentatively be included as etiological factors, and as such should be evaluated carefully in all complete assessments of children and youth suspected of having learning disabilities.

Biochemical Imbalances

Although there is inadequate information available as yet, some evidence is accruing which relates biochemical imbalances to learning disabilities. Not enough is known about either normality or deviance in biochemical balance or imbalance to generalize. However, it can be postulated that this may be found as an etiological factor of significance. Abnormal retention or excretion of proteins, zinc, magnesium, among other items, must be viewed as having a potential impact on the developing central nervous system, perception and learning.

DEFINITION

Out of the structure which has been provided here, definitions which are applicable to any discipline can be drawn. Disciplines differ in the vocabulary which is used. Members of each discipline related to learning disabilities can utilize effectively the concepts contained herein for their appropriate disciplinary adaptation. The example which follows, while applicable in the final analysis to any discipline, focuses on the psychoeducational reality of learning disabilities. The elements which have been described in the preceding paragraphs and sections can be brought together to form a meaningful and historically accurate definition of learning disabilities. Two assumptions must be kept in mind, namely, (a) there is an inherent dysfunction in the learning process which is manifested in deficiencies in one or more academic skill subjects, language or communication problems and/or social adaptation problems; and (b) there is a significant discrepancy between measured potential and measured performance of both an academic and social nature.

Based therefore on these psychoeducational realities, it can be stated that (1) *learning disabilities are problems in the acquisition of developmental skills, academic achievement, social adjustment, and secondarily emotional growth and development, which are the result of perceptual and linguistic processing deficits.* Further defined, *learning disabilities* (2) *may be of any etiological origin,* (3) *may be observed in children and youth of any age and* (4) *of any level of intellectual function,* (5) *are the result of perceptual processing deficits which, in turn,* (6) *are or may be the result of a (diagnosed or inferred) neurophysiological dysfunction occurring at prenatal, perinatal, or (in the case of linguistic dysfunction) at the postnatal periods of development.*

QUANTITATIVE APPLICATION OF THE DEFINITION

The development of a definition of learning disabilities is a logical process. Unfortunately when a definition is reached, professional personnel are faced with a blind alley of unknowns. The lack of epidemiological data of a definitive nature, to which reference was made much earlier, leaves many perplexing problems. The clinical entity is known and relatively well understood. Knowledge regarding the size of the population is not available. This means a number of questions cannot be accurately addressed, *vis-à-vis*: (1) How many children should an area board of education and a director of education expect to find in a given school authority? (2) How many will need self-contained classrooms and how many could normally be expected to be included in the ordinary grades of the public school system? (3) What kind of in-service training is required for teachers of ordinary classrooms so they will be able to meet the needs of the learning disabilities children who are integrated? (4) How many teachers should be prepared by colleges and universities in a given province? (5) How much grant money should be requested by ministers of education from provincial legislatures to support local programs? These questions among others can now be answered only with guesses and estimates in spite of the fact, as has been stated, that some estimates have been used so widely and for such a long period of time that the figures often have become accepted as fact. Such cannot be permitted for the future. There is an immediate need for carefully conducted epidemiological study in a large school system which contains urban and suburban elements and which contains a sufficiently multiracial population to be able also to reach firm conclusions regarding the demography of the problem of learning disabilities. Such a study should include the total school population in order that the problem as it affects the secondary schools can be ascertained, an issue which is even more subject to the guess estimate approach than it is in the elementary school level. When this matter is concluded then the efficacy of the approaches to be discussed below can be determined.

Often quantitative applications and regulations of an administrative nature are confused with definition. In this paper there has been a serious attempt to keep these two matters separate. A definition has been presented. How that definition is applied may vary from one school to another. The problem of learning disabilities has become very confused over the years, confused essentially by those who have failed to recognize the historical antecedents to the problem. As a result, attempts at quantitative applications have likewise sometimes become cumbersome. It is difficult to establish education guidelines for anything when officials do not hold in mind a clear-cut idea of what is being administered, and when also there is lacking both a definitive idea of the size of the problem and qualified personnel to teach the child if and when they are accurately defined and diagnosed. This is a field of education which has grown with less than the best of logic and thought. It is obvious that *once a definition is agreed upon or accepted in principle, rules, regulations or guidelines for its implementation are required.*

LEARNING DISABILITIES OR THE LEARNING DISABLED?

It must be apparent to the reader that the term learning disabilities is one which is inefficient, and lends itself to much misunderstanding and misinterpretation. It is a poor set of words which has been used to describe a very technical problem of human growth and development. For the individual coming onto the term without a background of experience with it, the concept of learning disabilities provides a convenient niche into which a hetero-geneous series of childhood problems can be placed. For the teacher with little or no specialized training in the area of perceptual processing, the term learning disabilities can easily become synonymous with concepts of remedi-ation, lack of motivation, or behavior problems. For the parent who is con-fronted with the problem for the first time, the term learning disabilities can easily be translated to mean a problem for the schools to solve, since one of the chief aspects of the business of the schools is to deal with problems of learning and achievement.

Although we are not urging the adoption of another term, clarity and specificity of the problem would be much more quickly achieved if the pupils involved were termed children with perceptual processing deficits (PPD children). That is hardly an acceptable label, and it would only serve to create another category, the very thing which the few leaders who were ac-tive with this problem prior to 1963 tried hard to avoid. Their efforts were in vain, and a term — learning disabilities — was created which not only added to the classification nomenclature, but provided a term which produced ex-tremes in misunderstanding and confusion when it was accepted and utilized by novices in the field. Rather than to create yet another term, it is perhaps wiser to thoroughly understand the parameters of the present term learning disabilities, and to conceive it in the technical sense in which it has been described in this paper.

One further consideration regarding the term learning disabilities needs attention. The clients being served, and indeed the names of the very organizations purporting to represent them, place an emphasis on *children* with learning disabilities.

It is with children, of course, where it all started, but over time these children have grown up. The seven-year-old children in 1963 about whom parents were concerned are at the date of this writing adults of twenty-one years, often married, and sometimes with their own children, but regardless they are all coping with the responsibilities of adulthood. Just how many children with learning disabilities approach Grade Seven or Grade Ten still with functional characteristics or perceptual processing deficits is not known. The fact of the matter is, however, that many of them do. When their needs as youth with learning disabilities are not served by the secondary schools, the community often receives the brunt of their frustrations and maladjustment. The close relationship between the unsolved problems of youth with learning disabilities and delinquency has been demonstrated (Murray, 1975).

It is essential that these youth be served by the schools, a problem which has not been conceptualized by school personnel at this time to any significant extent. The question raised: can a problem which emphasizes children be accepted by secondary schools as typical of the youth they purport to serve? Should the issue become one of the problems of the *learning disabled*? Should formal associations functioning in behalf of these pupils be called "associations for the learning disabled?" The New York Association for the Learning Disabled, attempting to be an organization which speaks for those with learning disabilities of any age, may be the forerunner of change in emphasis.

If the term learning disabilities has been too broad an umbrella and has permitted too many educational problems not related to central nervous system malfunction to be included, the term learning disabled potentially may be even much more inclusive. Thus, if the future sees a change in the scope of interest of the associations, there is an even greater need than now for unanimity of thought and understanding about what is a learning disability. Unfortunately, parents and professions for too long have had to struggle with pseudo-definitions which were essentially definitions by exclusion. It is time that, even with some acknowledged deficiencies, a definition by inclusion be accepted and utilized by both lay and professional people working together to the end that confusion will be minimized, more exact educational programs and well-prepared educators will be provided, and the needs of the handicapped children and youth in Canadian schools will be better served.

REFERENCES

Asher, P., and Schonel, E. E., "A survey of 400 cases of cerebral palsy," *Archives of Disease in Childhood,* 1950, 25, 360–379.

(Australia) *Learning Difficulties in Children and Adults.* Report of the House of Representative Select Committee on Specific Learning Difficulties. Canberra: Australian Government Publishing Service, 1976.

Ayres, A. J., "Sensorimotor Foundations of Academic Ability; in William M. Cruickshank and D. P. Hallahan, *Perceptual and Learning Disabilities in Children,* Vol. 2 (Syracuse: Syracuse University Press, 1975).

Bice, H., and Cruickshank, W. M., "Evaluation of intelligence." In W. M. Cruickshank and G. M. Raus (Eds.), *Cerebral Palsy: Its Individual and Community Problems* (Syracuse: Syracuse University Press, 1955).

Birch, H. G., and Leford, A., "Two strategies for studying perception in 'Brain-Damaged' children," in H. G. Birch (Ed.), *Brain Damage in Children.* (Baltimore: Williams and Wilkins, 1964, 46–60.)

Crichton, J., Kendall, D., Cutterson, J., and Dunn, H., *Learning Disabilities; A Practical Office Manual.* (Victoria, B.C.: Canadian Paediatric Society, Norris Printing Co., 1972).

Critchley, M., *The Parietal Lobes.* (London: Edward Arnold, Ltd., 1953).

Cruickshank, W. M., *The Brain Injured Child in Home, School and Community,* 1966 revised as *Learning Disabilities in Home, School and Community,* (Syracuse: Syracuse University Press, 1977).

Cruickshank, W. M., and Bice, H. V., "Personality characteristics," in Cruickshank, W. M., and Raus, G. M., *Cerebral Palsy: Its Individual and Community Problems.* (Syracuse: Syracuse University Press, 1955).

Cruickshank, W. M., Bice, H. V., Wallen, H. E., and Lynch, K. S., *Perception and Cerebral Palsy.* (Syracuse: Syracuse University Press, revised edition, 1965).

Cruickshank, W. M., and Paul, J. L., "Psychological Characteristics of Brain-Injured Children," in Cruickshank, W. M. (Ed.), *Psychology of Exceptional Children and Youth.* (Englewood Cliffs, N.J., Prentice-Hall, Inc., 1971).

Cruickshank, W., Bentzen, F., Ratzberg, F., and Tannhauser, M., *A Teaching Method for Brain-Injured and Hyperactive Children.* (Syracuse: Syracuse University Press, 1961).

Dolphin, J. E., and Cruickshank, W. M., "The Figure-Background Relationship in Children with Cerebral Palsy," *Journal of Clinical Psychology,* 1951, 7, 228–231.

Dolphin, J. E., and Cruickshank, W. M., "Pathology of Concept Formation in Children with Cerebral Palsy," *American Journal of Mental Deficiency,* 1951, 41, 336–392.

Frostig, M., Lefever, D. W., and Whittelsey, R. B., "A Developmental Test of Visual Perception for Evaluating Normal and Neurologically Handicapped Children," *Perceptual Motor Skills,* 1961, 12, 383–394.

Gaddes, W. H., "The Needs of Teachers for Specialized Information on Handedness, Finger Localization, and Cerebral Dominance," in W. M. Cruickshank (Ed.), *The Teacher of Brain-Injured Children.* (Syracuse: Syracuse University Press, 1966).

Gaddes, W. H., "Neurological Implications for Learning," in W. M. Cruickshank and D. P. Hallahan (Eds.), *Perceptual and Learning Disabilities in Children,* Vol. I. (Syracuse: Syracuse University Press, 1975).

Gaddes, W. H., and Spellacy, F. J., *Serial Order Perceptual and Motor Performances in Children and their Relation to Academic Achievement.* (Victoria, B.C.: Department of Psychology, University of Victoria, Research Monograph 31, August, 1977).

Goldstein, K., and Scheerer, M. "Abstract and Concrete Behavior: An Experimental Study with Special Tests, "*Psychological Monographs,* 1941, 53, 1–151.

Golick, M., A Parent's Guide to Learning Problems. (Montreal: Quebec Association for Children with Learning Disabilities, 1970).

Golick, M., *She Thought I Was Dumb But I Told Her I Had a Learning Disability.* (Toronto: The Bryand Press, Ltd., 1970).

Grube, M. M., a doctoral dissertation in preparation at the University of Michigan, Rackham School of Graduate Study, *circa* 1978).

Gyr, J. W., "The Relationship Between Motor and Visual-Sensory Processes in Perception," in Cruickshank, W. M. and Hallahan, D. P. (Eds.), *Perceptual and Learning Disabilities in Children,* Vol. II. (Syracuse, N.Y., Syracuse University Press, 1975).

Hagan, J., and Kail, R. V., "The Role of Attention in Perceptual and Cognitive Development" in Cruickshank, W. M., and Hallahan, D. P., (Eds.), *Perceptual and Learning Disabilities in Children,* Vol. II. p. 165. (Syracuse, N.Y., Syracuse University Press, 1975).

Hallahan, D. P., and Cruickshank, W. M. *Psychoeducational Foundations of Learning Disabilities.* (Englewood Cliffs, N.J.: Prentice-Hall, Inc., 1973).

Hallahan, D. P., and Kauffman, J. M., "Research on the Education of Distractible and Hyperactive Children," in Cruickshank, W. M., and Hallahan, D. P. (Eds.). *Perceptual and Learning Disabilities in Children.* (Syracuse: Syracuse University Press, 1975).

Hallahan, D. P., "Distractibility in the Learning Disabled Child," in Cruickshank, W. M., and Hallahan, D. P. (Eds.) *Perceptual and Learning Disabilities in Children.* (Syracuse: Syracuse University Press, 1975.

Heilman, A., "Intelligence in Cerebral Palsy," *The Crippled Child,* 1952, 30, 11–13.

Kephart, N. C., *The Slower Learner in the Classroom.* (Columbus, Ohio, Charles Merrill Publishers, 1960).

Kephart, N. C., "The Perceptual Motor Match," in Cruickshank, W. M. and Hallahan, D. P. (Eds.). *Perceptual and Learning Disabilities in Children.* (Syracuse: Syracuse University Press, 1975, Vol I).

Koupernik, C., MacKeith, R., and Francis-Williams, J., "Neurological Correlates of Motor and Perceptual Development," in Cruickshank, W. M., and Hallahan, D. P. (Eds.). *Perceptual and Learning Disabilities in Children,* Vol. II. (Syracuse: Syracuse University Press, 1975).

Kronick, D., *A Word or Two About Learning Disabilities.* (San Rafael, California: Academic Therapy Publications, 1973).

Lewis, M., "The Development of Attention and Perception in the Infant and Young Child" in Cruickshank, W. M., and Hallahan, D. P., (Eds.). *Perceptual and Learning Disabilities in Children.* (Syracuse: Syracuse University Press, 1975).

Luria, A., *The Higher Cortical Functions in Man.* (New York, Basic Books, Inc., 1966).

McGinnis, M., *Aphasic Children.* (Washington, D.C. Alexander Graham Bell Association for the Deaf, Inc., 1963).

McKay, E., *An Exploratory Study of the Psychological Effect of a Severe Hearing Loss.* (Unpublished doctoral dissertation, Syracuse University, 1952).

Miller, E. A., and Rosenfeld, G., "Psychological Evaluation of Children with Cerebral Palsy and its Implications for Treatment," *Journal of Pediatrics,* 1952, 41, 613–621.

Murray, C., *The Link Between Learning Disabilities and Juvenile Delinquency: Current Theory and Knowledge.* (Washington, U.S. Department of Justice Law Enforcement Assistance Administration, National Institute for Juvenile Justice and Delinquency Prevention, 1976).

Quiros, J., "Diagnosis of Vestibular Disorders in the Learning Disabled," *Journal of Learning Disabilities,* Vol. 9, Jan., 1976.

Rappaport, S., *Education for Children with Brain Dysfunction.* (Syracuse: Syracuse University Press, 1969).

Sarason, S., *Psychological Problems in Mental Deficiency.* (New York, Harper and Row, 1953).

Shaw, M. E., *A Study of Some Aspects of Perception and Conceptual Thinking in Idiopathic Epileptic Children.* (Unpublished doctoral dissertation, Syracuse University, 1955).

Stott, D. H., *The Parent as a Teacher.* (Toronto: New Press, 1972).

Strauss, A., and Lehtinen, L., *The Psychopathology and Education of the Brain Injured Child.* (New York: Grune and Stratton, 1947).

Wepman, J. M., "Auditory Perception and Imperception," in Cruickshank, W. M. and Hallahan, D. P. (Eds.), *Perceptual and Learning Disabilities in Children,* Vol. II (Syracuse: Syracuse University Press, 1975).

Wepman, J. M. *et al.,* "Learning disabilities," in Hobbs, N., (Ed.), *Issues in the Classification of Children,* Vol. I. (San Francisco: Jossey-Bass Publishers, 1975).

Weiderholt, J. L., "Historical perspectives on the education of the learning disabled," in L. Mann and D. Sabatino (Eds.), *The Second Review of Special Education.* (Philadelphia, JSE Press, 1974, 103–152).

SELECTED ADDITIONAL REFERENCES

Prepared from a Selected Bibliography Provided by Dr. Robert Knights, Carleton University, Ottawa, Ontario.

Campbell, S. B., Douglas, V. I. and Morgenstern, G. (1971) Cognitive styles in hyperactive children and the effect of methylphenidate. *Journal of Child Psychology and Psychiatry,* 12:55–67.

CELDIC *One Million Children* (Toronto, Ontario: Crainford), 1970.

Cohen, N. J., Douglas, V. I. and Morgenstern, G. (1971) The effect of methylphenidate in attention behavior and autonomic activity in hyperactive children. *Psychopharmacologia,* 22:282–294.

Crockett, D., Klonoff, H. and Bjerring, J. (1969) Factor analysis of neuropsychological tests. *Perceptual and Motor Skills,* 29:791–802.

Czunder, G. and Rourke, B. P. (1972) Age differences in visual reaction time of "brain-damaged" and normal children under regular and irregular preparatory interval conditions. *Journal of Experimental Child Psychology,* 13:516–526.

Doehring, D. G. *Patterns of Impairment in Specific Reading Disabilities.* (Bloomington, Indiana: Indiana University Press, 1968.)

Doehring, D. G. and Rabinovitch, M. S. (1969) Auditory abilities of children with learning problems. *Journal of Learning Disabilities,* 2:467–474.

Douglas, V. I. (1972) Stop, look and listen: The problem of sustained attention and impulse control in hyperactive and normal children. *Canadian Journal of Behavioral Science,* 4:259–282.

Douglas, V. I. (1974, In press) Sustained attention and impulse control: Implications for the handicapped child. In J. A. Swets and L. L. Elliott (eds.), *Psychology and the Handicapped Child.* United States Government Publications Office.

Freibergs, V. and Douglas, V. I. (1969) Concept learning in hyperactive and normal children. *Journal of Abnormal Psychology,* 74:388–395.

Freibergs, V., Douglas, V. I., and Weiss, G. (1968) The effect of chlorpromazine on concept learning in hyperactive children under two conditions of reinforcement. *Psychopharmacologia,* 13:299–310.

Gaddes, W. II. (1966) The performance of normal and brain-damaged subjects on a new Dynamic Visual Retention Test. *The Canadian Psychologist,* 7a:313–323.

Gaddes, W. H. (1967) A new test of Dynamic Visual Retention. *Perceptual and Motor Skills,* 25:393–396.

Gaddes, W. H. (1968) A neuropsychological approach to learning disorders. *Journal of Learning Disabilities,* 1:523–534.

Gaddes, W. H. (1969) Can educational psychology be neurologized? *Canadian Journal of Behavioral Science,* 1:38–49.

Hardy, M. I., McLeod, J., Minto, H., Perkins, S. and Quance, W. R. *Standards for Educators of Exceptional Children in Canada.* (Toronto, Ontario: Crainford) 1971.

Hinton, G. G. and Knights, R. M. Neurological and psychological test characteristics of 100 children with seizures. In B. W. Richards (ed.), *First Congress of the International Association of the Scientific Study of Mental Deficiency.* (Surrey, England: Michael Jackson Company) 1971.

Klonoff, H. (1971) Factor analysis of a neuropsychological battery for children aged 9 to 15. *Perceptual and Motor Skills,* 32:603–616.

Klonoff, H. (1971) Head injuries in children: Predisposing factors, accident conditions, accident proneness and sequelae. *American Journal of Public Health,* 61:2405–2417.

Klonoff, H., Robinson, G. C. and Thompson, G. (1969) Acute and chronic brain syndromes in children. *Developmental Medicine and Child Neurology,* 11: 198–213.

Knights, R. M. (1966) Normative data on tests for evaluating brain damage in children 5 to 14 years. University of Western Ontario, *Research Bulletin* No. 20, mimeo.

Knights, R. M. (1973) A problem of criteria in diagnosis: A profile similarity approach. *Annals of the New York Academy of Sciences,* 205:124–131.

Knights, R. M. (1974) Psychometric assessment of drug-induced behavior change. In Proceedings of Abbott Laboratories symposium on *The Clinical Use of Stimulant Drugs in Children.* Chicago, Illinois, North Chicago.

Knights, R. M. and Hinton, G. G. (1969) Minimal brain dysfunction: clinical and psychological test characteristics. *Academic Therapy Quarterly,* 4:265–173.

Knights, R. M. and Hinton, G. G. (1969) The effects of methylphenidate (Ritalin) on the motor skills and behavior of children with learning problems. *Journal of Nervous and Mental Disease,* 1948, 643–653.

Knights, R. M. and Moule, A. O. (1967) Normative and reliability data on finger and foot tapping in children. *Perceptual and Motor Skills,* 25:717–720.

Knights, R. M. and Moule, A. O. (1968) Normative data on the Motor Steadiness Battery for children. *Perceptual and Motor Skills,* 26:643–650.

Knights, R. M. and Richardson, D. H. (1974) Automated assessment and training of retarded and disadvantaged children. Department of Psychology, Carleton University, *Research Bulletin* No. 10, mimeo.

Knights, R. M. and Tymchuk, A. J. (1968) An evaluation of the Halstead-Reitan Category Tests for Children. *Cortex,* 4:403–414.

Knights, R. M. and Viets, C. A. (1973) The effects of pemoline on hyperactive boys. Paper presented at the American Psychological Association, Montreal.

Knights, R. M. and Watson, P. (1968) The use of computerized test profiles in neuropsychological assessment. *Journal of Learning Disabilities,* 1:696–710.

Kronick, D. (Ed.) *Learning Disabilities: Its Implications to a Responsible Society.* (Chicago, Illinois: Developmental Learning Materials) 1969.

Kronick, D. (1970) Directory of learning disabilities help across Canada. *Chatelaine Magazine* (Toronto), 43, (10):100–104.

Meichenbaum, D. H. and Goodman, J. (1969) Reflection – impulsivity and verbal control of motor behavior. *Child Development,* 40:785–797.

Meichenbaum, D. H. and Goodman, J. (1971) Training impulsive children to talk to themselves: A means of developing self-control. *Journal of Abnormal Psychology,* 77:115–126.

Minde, K., Webb, G. and Sykes, D. (1968) Studies on the hyperactive child. VI: Prenatal and perinatal factors associated with hyperactivity. *Developmental Medicine and Child Neurology,* 10:355–363.

Minde, K., Weiss, G., and Mendelson, N. (1972) A five-year follow-up study of 91 hyperactive school children. *Journal of the American Academy of Child Psychiatry,* 11:595–610.

Rourke, B. P. and Czunder, G. (1972) Age differences in auditory reaction time of "brain damaged" and normal children under regular and irregular preparatory interval conditions. *Journal of Experimental Child Psychology,* 14:372–378.

Rourke, B. P., Dietrich, B. M. and Young, G. C. (1973) Significance of WISC verbal-performance discrepancies for younger children with learning disabilities. *Perceptual and Motor Skills,* 36:275–282.

Rourke, B. P., Young, G. C. and Flewelling, R. W. (1971) The relationships between WISC verbal-performance discrepancies and selected verbal, auditory-perceptual, and problem solving abilities in children with learning disabilities. *Journal of Clinical Psychology,* 27:474–479.

Spreen, O. and Gaddes, W. H. (1969) Developmental norms for 15 neuropsychological tests age 6 to 15. *Cortex,* 5:171–191.

Stott, D. H. *Studies of Troublesome Children* (London: Tavistock Publications) 1966.

Stott, D. H. *Flying Start Learning-to-Learn Kit* (Toronto, Gage) 1972.

Sykes, D. H., Douglas, V. I., Weiss, G. and Minde, K. (1971) Attention in hyperactive children and the effect of methylphenidate (Ritalin). *Journal of Child Psychology and Child Psychiatry,* 12:129–139.

Tymchuk, A. J., Knights, R. M. and Hinton, G. G. (1970a) Neuropsychological test results of children with brain lesions, abnormal EEGs and, normal EEGs. *Canadian Journal of Behavioral Science,* 2:322–329.

Tymchuk, A. J., Knights, R. M. and Hinton, G. G. (1970b) The behavioral significance of differing EEG abnormalities in children with learning and/or behavior problems. *Journal of Learning Disabilities,* 3:548–552.

Weinstein, R. and Rabinovitch, M. S. (1971) Sentence structure and retention in good and poor readers. *Journal of Educational Psychology,* 62:25–30.

Weiss, C., Werry, J., Minde, E., Douglas, V. I., and Sykes, D. (1968) Studies on the hyperactive child — V: The effects of dextroamphetamine and chlorpromazine on behavior and intellectual functioning. *Journal of Child Psychology and Psychiatry,* 9:145–156.

Wiener, J., Barnsley, R. H. and Rabinovitch, M. S. (1970) Serial order ability in good and poor readers. *Canadian Journal of Behavioral Science,* 2:116–123.

Witelson, S. F. and Rabinovitch, M. S. (1972) Hemispheric speech lateralization in children with auditory-linguistic deficits. *Cortex,* 8:412–426.

LEARNING DISABILITIES

Perceptual or Other?

*W*ITHIN THE TURBULENCE which surrounds the field of *learning disabilities* fifteen years after the term was first begun to be used popularly, are to be found many confusions relating to it. We have spoken about these many times before, and this paper may not add anything new which is of significance. Yet, in focusing on the title of this paper, perhaps a new look at old information may assist in a clarification of the problem as it really is.

In 1963, when the term learning disabilities was adopted by parents of these children in the United States, three things were apparent. First, those who wished to utilize the term were doing so to protect their children from terms which they felt were damaging to the child's best interests, i.e., minimal cerebral dysfunction, brain-injured, slow learner, neurologically handicapped, and many others. The decision was made to utilize the term learning disabilities in spite of the fact that the other terms, while not perfect, may indeed have been considerably more accurate and meaningful to the professions which would have to organize their energies to habilitate the child.

Second, other than the few persons who were actively working in the field and who were oriented to the problem as it actually was and is, those who adopted the term learning disabilities tended not to be fully aware of the complex neurophysiological aspects of the problem. Unless the child was severely involved motorically as in cerebral palsy, it was not generally recognized that neurophysiological dysfunction, which was not manifested in the observable motor performance of the child, could even be present in a

Reprinted from *Tijdschrift voor Orthopedagogiek* (The Netherlands) 9 (September 1978): 421-31, by permission.

111

form which would have subtle negative influences on the child's learning and adjustment. Today the matter continues to be so conceived by many professional people, and by what I suspect is a majority of the parents who belong to formal parent organizations. Most professional people have come to this field with a minimum of training and preparation. Often professional persons in this field of child development followed parents rather than leading them. This has not served to provide the strong leadership within the professions which would counteract innocent errors. The end result is a problem of multiple dimensions without concomitant well-conceptualized multiple solutions.

Third, those who accepted the term learning disabilities were unaware of, or failed to recognize, the genealogy of the problem. Had they done so, the present confusion would have been avoided or at least significantly lessened. The history of learning disabilities goes back much beyond 1963, and the numerous strands which Weiderholt (1974) and others have noted illustrate very clearly the orientation which illustrious early investigators and practitioners held toward the problem as we now should know it. Let us consider but a few examples. The first of which we will write is one of which I am proud to have been a part.

Alfred A. Strauss was a neurologist and a psychiatrist, and an exceedingly distinguished one in his native Germany prior to 1933 (Cruickshank and Hallahan 1973). Among his teachers and those who influenced him was Kurt Goldstein, whose neurophysiological orientation to the problems of the war injured is well known. Strauss likewise was influenced by August Homberger, a neurologist; by Kaufmann, a neuropsychiatrist; by Hans W. Gruhle, Director of the Neuropsychiatric Clinic at Heidelberg. Strauss' orientation was neurological, and this he imparted to those around him.

Heinz Werner was also a contribution of Hitler's Germany to the United States, and is viewed by many as the senior partner in the Werner-Strauss duo during the period when they worked together in the United States during and after World War II. He was one of the world's great developmental, genetic, and comparative psychologists of his day. Today he would be seen as a developmental neuropsychologist, and he then wrote as one. His interests were in brain mechanisms and their impact on learning. These two men influenced numerous younger persons in the United States: Samuel A. Kirk, perhaps chiefly known for his test of psycholinguistic abilities, an instrument which focuses essentially on auditory and visual input stimuli and output responses — neurophysiological; Cruickshank (1961, 1966); Kephart (1960); Lehtinen (with Strauss) (1947); and others who translated the work of Werner and Strauss into psychoeducational management programs. The common thread, however, which is woven through the work of the latter three and of the single work of Kirk quoted here is the neurophysiological basis of perception, and the educational dependency of programming on a sound understanding of the physical etiology of the program. From these who may be accused of having a vested interest in a point of view, we can turn to others who antedated them and who are related to the current, but unnecessary, dilemmas.

Weiderholt has presented an excellent and succinct chapter placing the field of learning disabilities into a perspective as he sees it. Weiderholt, from among others who could be named, recognizes thirteen individuals who between 1802 and 1933 made contributions essential to the field now known as learning disabilities. Each has a neurological orientation to his profession. Strauss and Werner were two of these. Twelve of these men were physicians who were deeply concerned with the neurological system of the human oganism. Gall (1802) sought to isolate the areas of the brain in which the localization of aphasia could be identified. Bouillaud (1825) also was concerned with localization of brain functions. Broca (1861), stressing hemispheric functional differences, related speech to the third frontal convolutions of the brain. Scientists speak now of *Broca's area* of the brain. This emphasizes the relation which this man sensed between motor function and neurological processes in humans. Jackson (1864), Bastien (1869), Wernicke (1881), Marie (1906), Head (1926), Orton (1925), Hinchelwood (1917), Luria (1966), and Goldstein (1927), to whom reference has earlier been made, each were concerned chiefly with the manner in which the brain functioned. Quirós of Argentina, Valk of the Netherlands, and Critchley of England, among many others, are the modern-day proponents of the emphasis which began in 1802 with Gall.

As one moves from the field of medicine to psychology in the United States the names of Kirk, Myklebust, McGinnis, Halstead, Cruickshank, Frostig, Eisenson, Wepman, and others, predecessors of the field of learning disabilities per se (1963), were all essentially concerned with the neuropsychological aspects of deviance in learning. Wepman emphasized the auditory mechanisms; Eisenson was concerned with aphasia as was McGinnis; Halstead, Frostig, and Cruickshank with various aspects of neuropsychology — the latter two applying their reasoning to the educational implications of disorders of perception and learning.

The interesting, yet discouraging aspect to the situation, is that since 1963, the neurophysiological aspects of the tremendous problem of learning disabilities has been essentially rejected by most parents and many educators in the United States and indeed in many other parts of the world. I suspect that this is the case because in the United States so few psychologists and

educators ever move into the basic sciences as an integral part of their preparatory training. Few in the field of learning disabilities in the United States
have studied in the area of neurophysiology, childhood psychopathology,
anatomy, or neuropsychology. What one does not know, one tends to reject
even though the unknown may be central to the problem under study as
these areas of knowledge we have mentioned are to the field of learning disabilities. Regardless of the cause, parents, educators, and many psychologists, among others, almost completely reject the concept of neurophysiological dysfunction, actual or assumed, as being synonymous with learning
disabilities. Until this situation is reversed, understood, and accepted; until
it is integrated into the management systems for the children involved, many
children and youth who could otherwise be helped will be denied their birthright. If the genealogy of learning disabilities is understood and recognized,
the relationship of this problem to the human neurological system becomes
apparent immediately. It is a very simple truism. The neurological base to
learning disabilities can only be rejected by those who do not know or are
unwilling to recognize either historical or neuropsychological facts. The
faulty neurological system gives rise to the perceptual processing deficits out
of which learning disabilities develop.

The title of this paper is in the form of a question, namely, is learning disabilities all perceptual? The answer is both "yes" and "no" depending
upon how extensive the definition of learning disabilities is. There is a large
subset or group of children and youth whose problems currently are included
with the term learning disabilities who are not characterized by perceptual
deficits.

In 1963 the term learning disabilities was first recommended by parents for usage. A small number of professional leaders came together in Chicago, Illinois, the following year to consider using the term. They were all
close friends, and each was fully aware of the work of the others. Almost
any term could have been used, and those few people would have been able
to function satisfactorily with one another with any term, because they understood each other's frame of reference regarding the problem under consideration. Thus in 1964 the leadership agreed to use the term learning disabilities, and this group *was oriented to the neuropsychological basis of the
problem.* No sooner had the term been released to the general professional
disciplines and to parents than a myriad of other concepts was attached to it.
To the educator, the term learning disabilities soon meant anything which affected the learning progress of the child. To the parent, the term was a positive one which put the problem in the hands of school people who were sup-
posed to be experts in learning. To the remedial reading specialists, the term
was magnificent for it expanded their professional territory immensely.

Learning disabilities were essentially reading problems they said; hence were synonymous with remedial reading.

Childhood problems of all sorts were brought under the heading of learning disabilities. This was accomplished essentially by people who did not know the history of the field, the neurophysiological technicalities of the original exploratory research which predated the generally unfortunate term, or who often used the term to advance their own personal professional goals without pausing to obtain the basic academic preparation so essential to the problem.

Thus when we say that learning disabilities is not all perceptual, we are saying that since 1964 a vast number of childhood problems has been brought via these avenues under the canopy of learning disabilities, and these are not those related to perceptual processing. We speak of these as *problems of learning* which, for example, may be caused by environmental deprivation, poor beginnings in school-related experiences due to problems of mother-child separation, parental divorce, poor teaching, hunger, and many other similar factors central to this issue. These problems of learning are environmental in nature, are of an exogenous order external to the organism, are not central to dysfunction of the nervous system. Poor teaching per se does not result in perceptual processing deficits. Neither do emotional problems which stem from child abuse or parental conflicts. Each of these may cause serious learning problems, but these are not of the same order as those of learning disabilities if the latter are correctly conceived historically and neurologically. However, it is these psychoeducational issues which have been appended to learning disabilities which have caused and still do cause the extreme confusion that exists, which make definition difficult, which has divided the field into feuding camps, and which makes appropriate service delivery to children and youth nearly impossible. When we state that these learning disabilities are not always perceptual, it is this vast group of childhood problems of learning to which we refer. We say "no" only to this part of the problem, to a part of the problem which while requiring the attention of educators and others, has diluted the field of learning disabilities accurately defined almost beyond repair.

The invention of the term learning disabilities in 1963 resulted in several things. It provided an acceptable term, albeit a poor one, to parents anxious to represent their children as best they could. It created an inclusive umbrella for numerous problems about which school officials were confused. These could be assigned to the new category learning disabilities, although they were often disrelated to the original issue. Finally, these two factors together served to minimize the original central problems, i.e., hyperkinesis, brain-injury, minimal cerebral dysfunction, organicity, and others which gave rise to the new term. These former terms had negative connotations to parents. They were not understood by the majority of persons flocking to the banner of learning disabilities. Yet each in its own way is essentially accurate as a descriptor. It is astounding to me that the long neurophysiological and neuropsychological history which antedated 1963 could be so easily ignored, and in some instances so aggressively attacked. The motivation for these actions of sensible men and women cannot easily be understood. At best they must be credited to innocence; at worst, to ignorance. The original focus of what we know as learning disabilities was neurological, and this is unequivocal. Those who deny this, ignore history and fact. Fortunately the thoughtful scientist, whether neurophysiolgist, neuropsychologist, or educator, recognizes this, and more and more they voice these understandings. To do otherwise is to deny logic.

We can accept the concept of environmentally produced problems of learning as a large subset of miscellaneous problems of childhood and adolescence. We can even give them a place within the concept of learning disabilities, provided that they are seen as quite different from the original central issue of learning disabilities. The latter are the result of perceptual processing deficits which in turn are neurophysiologically based. With respect to the latter, the answer is "yes;" learning disabilities are characterized by a form of perceptual dysfunction.

We will now consider and focus solely on the original group of children whose problems gave rise to the label, "learning disabilities." The one to whom we can say "yes," the problems are inherently related to perceptual processing deficits. A number of terms must be defined, for they are loosely used, and a number of concepts must be clarified. We have stated that learning disabilities are the result of perceptual processing deficits which are in turn based on an actual or inferred neurophysiological dysfunction. These may occur in children and youth of any age and be the result of any etiological factor. They are characteristic also of no single intellectual level, but to the contrary are to be found at every intellectual level. Although this latter statement is denied by many and officially by numerous organizations and governmental definitions. The fact remains that there is such a child. To deny this is to deny history and fact. Let us examine these statements more fully.

There is little argument, if a neurological base for perceptual processing deficits is fully disclosed by such instruments as the electroencephalograph, the pneumoencephalograph, the radiomicroscope, or the more recently developed techniques of computerized axial tomography, i.e., the brain scan or CAT scan. Older techniques utilizing X-Ray in conjunction with selective agents; fluoroscopy, and operative interventions, of course, verify what only may have been suspected in neurological examinations. In such specific verification few if any questions remain as to the etiology of the related perceptual pathology which may be noted in a given child. It is in situations where specific neurological injury or dysfunction cannot be isolated specifically, but where soft signs from the neurological examination or specific indicators of neurological dysfunction illustrated through neuropsychological tests or other diagnostic indicators are suggested, that some problems exist. In these instances *inferred* neurological dysfunction must continue as the basis of further management of the individual.

One can work backwards in reaching conclusions even though they may be tentative conclusions. If neuropsychological examinations indicate the presence of perceptual problems, one can assume with relative certitude that neurophysiological dysfunctions are present. Perception, in spite of popular notions to the contrary, is neurophysiological. This is unequivocal. It is, of course, possible to endow the term, perception, with artistic, poetic, and emotional connotations, but emotions are also physical so the issue is of little importance. Avoiding this issue, however, and adhering to the matter of learning disabilities, perceptual processing deficits as we have spoken of them over the years and as others have written before and since our efforts, are without question seen as derivatives of the neurophysiological system. When one factor is injured or disturbed, irrespective of the extent, the other may reflect that situation. Thus perceptual dysfunction in the absence of positive and observed neurological damage is the basis for inferring such damage whether or not laboratory evidence is present. We can say this because perception is a manifestation of a total neurological system. Perceptual deficit is itself evidence of neurological dysfunction. We are indeed saying nothing new in these statements. The relationship has been recognized for decades in the views of both neurologists and experimental psychologists.

It is important that we recognize the work of Julio Quirós of Argentina who speaks for others in raising an issue which, while closely related to the neurological system, may not be absolutely specific to it. Quirós feels that the vestibular system per se relates closely to the total perceptual development of the child particularly insofar as visual and auditory perception are concerned. He presents data to relate vestibular dysfunction in infancy to the presence of perceptual deficits and learning disabilities in elementary school-aged children. While the vestibular system is an integral part of the neurological system, it is of significance that Quirós and Schrager have isolated it for special study and for what appears may be a specific relationship to some learning disabilities (Quirós and Schrager 1978). These authors state that "some of the most outstanding psycho-neurological findings on vestibular-proprioceptive and visuo-motor integration can be summarized as follows:

1. Vestibular organs play a fundamental role in the regulation of eyes and head position.

2. Vestibular-cortical, vestibular-oculomotor, vestibular-cerebellar, vestibular-spinal, vestibular-reticular, and vestibular visual inter-relationships can clearly be distinguished.

3. Vestibular-oculomotor interrelationships are mainly stimulated by gravitational forces, and they could be useful for correct visual perception, with the participation of thalamic-cortical control.

4. Vestibular-spiral interrelationships are divided into two groups, which are affected by different inputs coming from muscles, joints, and skin.

5. Vestibular-visual interrelationships . . . seem to function as visuo-spatial coordinators of vestibular and visual inputs coming from vertical and horizontal axes."

That each of these emphases which Quirós and Schrager make is closely related to learning disabilities is obvious to anyone who has worked with these children for any length of time. The emphasis which these Argentinian scientists make is indeed significant and should be carefully considered. However, we have strayed somewhat from our original theme.

Three additional terms confront us in seeking to understand learning disabilities, i.e., perception, processing, and deficit. Each of these is loaded with definitional difficulties, for each may be defined in a number of ways depending upon one's point of view or theoretical structure. Floyd Alport (1955), a former colleague of this writer, speaks of perception as having something "to do with our awareness of the objects or conditions about us." Obviously perception also can be defined in terms of light waves or of impulses received in the external, middle and inner ear, or from other orientations. From the point of view of learning disabilities I am comfortable with a definition of perception as an awareness of things around us, and in so stating the issue I recognize that I am addressing the problem from a phenomenological point of view. Perception is here being addressed as a stimulus-reaction to things considered from the point of view of the behaver. A phenomenological experience of an object or situation is the way in which that thing appears to the individual, and is completely dependent upon his own neurological system. It would be helpful often in dealing with children who have learning disabilities if diagnosticians would seek to understand the perceptual act from the point of view of the child who is perceiving. Usually the child's world, from this orientation, is quite meaningful to him. Problems occur when the child's perceptions are matched against those of society, and when they do not correspond as judged by adults. Perception is an awareness of things. It is neurological. Processing requires that the individual endow these awarenesses with meaning. Meaning comes from experience and contact with the environment, i.e., learning. Learning is neurophysiologically based. If the percept or perception is inaccurate in relation to social norms, meaning will be distorted or inccurate. Deficits in achievement with respect to standards of society follow. In an interrelated chain of events, any part will be affected by the totality of the neurological system to which it is related. One aspect cannot exist without the other, and when specific damage characterizes the neurological system, specific perceptual disabilities will result. If the inherent problems of the neurological system are diffuse, affecting more than one or several areas of the brain or affecting the association fibers, then, not only will perceptual dysfunctions be observed, but also both processing actions and corresponding motor output responses may be unsatisfactory.

Although this must appear to many as *déjà vu,* or perhaps more accurately as *déjà entendu,* it follows easily from this point of view that learning is conditioning, and that the neurologic system is controlling. Except for purposes of completeness, one does not need to be reminded that efferent and afferent nerves together with complicated actions at the synapses constitute the unique elements in *processing.* Obviously processing involves more than this simplistic statement. Basal ganglia, the pyramidal and extrapyramidal tract systems, hemispheres, lobes, cortex, and internal brain structures are each and all involved. To these is added experiential learning which the neurological system has made possible. But these ultimately can be reduced to the basic neuron structure which in psychology is referred to as the S-R bond. This bond we view as processing in turn leading to learning. When all goes well, when the structure is intact, processing and positive conditioning are effected smoothly, and appropriate learning takes place. A normal child grows into a normal adult.

When, however, as the result of a myriad of etiological factors, disturbances, damage, injury, or by any other name something interferes with the normal growth or function of the neuron or the synapse, *processing deficits* result. The concept of processing deficit has been handled in a very cavalier manner by many writers and, at least in the English language literature, is conceptualized oftentimes in a very spurious manner. In English, the word deficit is defined to mean something in lesser amount, a deficiency in quantity. The word has been used in professional literature pertaining to learning disabilities to indicate less than normal relationships between a situation perceived by the individual and the response which that individual gives to what is perceived. In this sense deficit may still retain the concept of quantity deficiency, but in psychological terms quality deficiency is also involved. Thus problems of closure, which are often included within the concept of processing deficits in the learning disabilities child, may not be specific to perceptual processing as a total or complete neuropsychological act, but may simply be related to perception per se; the child does not perceive visually, auditorially, or tactically in a normal manner. It is only when processing and the motor concomitant to the initial perceptual phenomenon is required, that the deficit becomes observable. In the same manner such characteristics of learning disabilities children as dissociation and figure-ground differentiation are frequently mentioned as perceptual processing deficits. More accurately, they are the visual, auditory, or tactile motor evidence that a discrepancy exists somewhere in the perceptual processing activity, i.e., in the S-R bonds. Such characteristics as sequencing difficulties, memory problems, attention disturbances, distractibility, also often included within the processing-deficit concept, are undoubtedly more accurately motor manifestations of dysfunctions of the nervous system. If the motor phase of the cycle is included within the concept of perceptual processing deficits, then all of these learning disabilities characteristics may be included as a part of the phrase. Popularly this is being done. We make the differentiation here only to stress accuracy. It is important that we know whereof we speak, if not for the reason of more accurate approach to the child and its problems, then surely for the preparation of those who will function in the future in the professions. Characteristics, e.g., intersensory disorganization, dominance, or directionality problems, are more descriptive of the nature of the neurological problem than they are accurately viewed as perceptual processing deficits. However, in the literature these latter are often mentioned in the same lists as those characteristics which are truly processing deficits (Wepman 1975).

In the field of learning disabilities there are many "schools of thought," and differences of opinion: structure versus permissiveness, neurological dysfunction versus what must be viewed apparently as an "act of God" by those who reject the fact that learning is neurologically based. Self-contained classrooms versus mainstreaming and least restrictive placement has become the most recent educational argumentative fad in the United States. Learning disabilities as a function of remediation as opposed to developmental training and education is also a topic on which many would be happy to pit themselves one against another.

In my own case, age is perhaps providing the comfortable security of gradually withdrawing from these endless and non-rewarding debates. It is, I believe, of the utmost importance that children with learning disabilities be served and served appropriately. This is the least they can expect from those who call themselves experts. In the face of those who deny the neurophysiological orientation of perceptual processing deficits, or deny the validity of perceptual processing as fundamental to learning disabilities, I have had to pause to consider from whence I professionally have come and concomitantly from whence the field generally has come.

When one does this and considers the historical facts basic to learning disabilities; when one understands the focus of the study of thoughtful men for more than 150 years, i.e., the brain and its functions; when one considers the initial psychological studies of the 1930s and 1940s albeit with their clinical base, there is little to conclude but that the fundamental basis for all learning and for the potential for mislearning is neurological. When one further considers the conceptual misunderstanding, the emotional investments, and the inaccurate thinking with which the term learning disabilities was endowed in 1963, one is horrified. When one is faced by educators, psychologists, other professional persons, and by parents who either deny the existence of the neurological component of the child's problem or who stretch the accuracy of definitions to include childhood problems which were never originally conceptualized as learning disabilities per se, then one fears for the future of the field as a whole and for the nature of services which children now are receiving from well-intended, but professionally ignorant people. If one views this problem as it is, as logic, research, and history indicate it to be, then an appropriate management regimen can be conceptualized, appropriate professional preparation planned and executed for the disciplines, appropriate gains can be made by the children for whom these considerations are made, and research to continue to improve the child's lot can be undertaken with profit and direction. When this can be done, then one can say, "yes," learning disabilities as an integral part of the neurological system giving rise to the S-R bond is perceptual. When the environmentally produced problems of learning are included to contaminate true learning disabilities definition, then the answer to the question posed in the title of this paper is "no."

REFERENCES

Alport, F. *Theories of Perception and the Concept of Structure.* New York: Wiley, 1955.

Cruickshank, W. *A Teaching Method for Brain-Injured and Hyperactive Children.* Syracuse: Syracuse University Press, 1961.

Cruickshank, W. *The Brain-Injured Child in Home, School and Community.* Syracuse: Syracuse University Press, 1966.

Cruickshank, W., and Hallahan, D. "Alfred A. Strauss: Pioneer in Learning Disabilities." *Exceptional Children* 39 (January 1973): 321–27.

Kephart, N. *The Slow Learner in the Classroom.* Columbus: Merrill, 1960; 2nd ed., 1971.

Quirós, J., and Schrager, O. *Neuropsychological Fundamentals in Learning Disabilities.* San Rafael, Calif.: Academic Therapy Press, 1978.

Strauss, A., and L. Lehtinen. *The Psychopathology and Education of the Brain-Injured Child.* New York: Grune and Stratton, 1947.

Wepman, J., et al. "Learning Disabilities." In *Issues in the Classification of Children,* edited by N. Hobbs. Vol. 1. San Francisco: Jossey-Bass, 1975.

Wiederholt, L. "Historical Perspectives on the Education of the Learning Disabled." In *The Second Review of Special Education,* edited by L. Mann and D. Sabatino. Philadelphia: JSC Press, 1974.

PART III

INTEGRATION

8

INTEGRATION

A Conceptual Model

𝒯HE PROBLEM OF EDUCATIONAL PLACEMENT of children, whether because of physical or mental disability or because of race, color, social deprivation, or other generic characteristics, is a matter of serious concern to thoughtful people in the community. It is a problem on the racial scene, at least in the United States, which has touched every level of the court system of most states and, as well, of the federal system. Over and over again the courts have stressed the importance of equal educational opportunity for all children. Insofar as the racial situation is concerned, these same courts have spoken to the end that "equal" means integration of the races for educational experiences. The stress on integration, essential as one factor in alleviating the spiraling problem of the ghetto areas of our large cities and the economically deprived rural portions of the nation, has raised once again in the minds of many general educators the applicability of the same train of thought to the field of special education and to the educational planning for physically and mentally disabled children.

To follow the same line of reasoning with physically and mentally handicapped children as is applied to culturally deprived children, without understanding the implications of such reasoning, *will result in the fact that many children will be deprived of their birthright,* namely, an educational program geared to meet their needs and to bring them to the optimum of their potential physically, intellectually, and socially. The concept of integration, or special classes, has in the minds of many educators never been thought through with clarity or with a philosophic point of departure. For

Reprinted from *Individualism Och Samhoriget,* edited by T. Norbin and B. Sjovall (Lund, Sweden: Bokforlaget, 1977), by permission.

the past 150 years, in the United States and elsewhere for a much longer time, *a priori* decisions have been made on this matter by school administrators and community citizens on the basis of preconceptions, historical suppositions, emotional attitudes, and downright biases. Often these decisions have been made with little or no justification whatsoever from the point of view of research, reason, or logic.

School administrators are the greatest sinners in this respect. With little or no understanding of the nature or needs of handicapped children, they sometimes make decisions based not upon logic, but upon personal opinion and faulty reasoning. With little or no understanding of the nature or needs of handicapped children, they at times make decisions based upon emotion. With little or no understanding, they often make decisions based upon historical stereotypes. If one could find a way of ascertaining the honesty of the replies, I suspect that a majority of the administrative decisions made with respect to handicapped children and their placement in the schools is made more in terms of the personal convenience and emotional attitudes of the administrators of the school system than it is in terms of the needs of the children. The latter are made to appear paramount, but in reality there is little in evidence to support the fact that the needs of children are dictating the educational decisions.

If this appears to be a criticism of educational administrators, it is correctly evaluated. It is critical as the result of observing inept educational leaders, over many years, make faulty decisions regarding the life needs of disabled children—decisions which appear to the community to be adequate, which provide security to the individual who makes them, but which do not ring true in terms of the needs of the child or his family.

For many decades, educators in their wisdom have been telling the community that they are providing an educational program geared to meet the needs of all children. In their wisdom they have told parents that if indeed they are to be good parents, they too must provide a home climate to meet the changing needs of their children. Does meeting the needs of children mean that we provide an educational program where mentally retarded children have twice as long as their normal friends to accomplish a given task simply because their intelligence level is lower? This is the administrative rationale which is often encountered. Does meeting the needs of children mean that we group children with their mental equals because they will then be happier? This is repeated so often by some educators as to wear thin by mere repetition. Does meeting the needs of the retarded mean that by putting a saw or hammer into the child's hands he will ultimately find his way into the ranks of skilled labor? This is an assumption on the parts of many educators. Does meeting the needs of children mean that educators should permit a child with cerebral palsy to produce in a given school year forty-three hot pads? This is an observed situation and is duplicated in lesser or greater extent on many occasions. Does meeting the needs of handicapped children mean that a thousand dollars per year per classroom in a given school system is used to purchase leathercraft materials, raffia, metal craft materials, beads, and bits of glass with which bottles are covered with a mosaic? Is this education to meet children's needs? Is this education, or is it an evidence of inept educational leadership which would permit such a situation of unprepared teachers, or of a disinterested community citizenry which would permit children to be deprived of a fundamentally appropriate education?

At least two articles have appeared which are germane to the problem here under consideration. Johnson (1962) under the heading of a paradox raises a question regarding the value of special class placement and seriously challenges the value of the technique per se as appropriate for mentally handicapped children and youth. He uses one very old article by Perch as the basis of one of his conclusions that the special class does not result in an accrument of values to mentally handicapped children over placement in regular grades. This is what Perch says. What Perch does not say — and this is history relatively speaking, for Perch's study was published in 1932 — is that his special classes did not have a curriculum developed in terms of the needs of the mentally retarded. He did not say that he failed to have specially prepared teachers of the mentally retarded teaching mentally retarded children in the classes he studied. Without appropriate curriculum, without teachers knowledgeable in the area of the education of the mentally retarded, it is perhaps understandable that children placed in these classes would fail to respond in degrees different from other children left in the regular grades. There are many other variables, however, which were likewise uncontrolled, and which make his findings of less significance than Johnson suggests.

Likewise, Dunn raises this question again. He asks if much of special education for the mildly retarded is justifiable. Much, if not most of present special education for the mildly retarded is probably not justifiable from my point of view. However, it is not inept administrators which Dunn is judging. It is not poorly prepared teachers which he is criticizing. It is not the lack of well-conceptualized curricula which he speaks against. He is talking about the basic premise of the educational philosophy per se. Special education *is justified* under certain circumstances and under certain well-defined limitations. The way special educators and general educators have used the privilege of special education is not justified and, indeed, often warrants to them most serious criticism. We cannot further defend mediocrity. We cannot condone the sorry situation which exceptional children presently face in many communities. If educators themselves cannot put their house in order and provide for children that which they truly need, parents, tax-payers, legislators, or other groups of persons will, and ought to, take the responsibility away and exercise it themselves. What we have done too often in the name of special education is not worthy of the name, and this state of affairs exists in so many communities that, in my considered opinion, a crisis exists.

We mentioned a moment ago that the courts have said equal educational opportunity must be provided for all children and youth. Equal educational opportunity does not necessarily mean the same type educational opportunity, nor that all educational experiences for all children of a given age must be carried on in the same classroom nor with the same teaching materials if considerations of race particularly are recognized. Indeed, equal opportunity conceived as the same opportunity means "unequal" for many children. Equal educational opportunity does mean that all children will have the opportunity to experience an educational program which, in equal strength, will bring them to the maximum of their potential, whatever that may be.

If special education — which is necessary — is to play the role which it must and for which it has historically been intended, a crash program of a widely diversified nature is going to be required *immediately*. *Immediately* is emphasized, because we are speaking of something which should have happened years ago and cannot be permitted to continue ill-defined any longer.

We mentioned that a crash program of a widely diversified nature is required. This diversification will be discussed briefly because it is essential to the remaining portion of my remarks. A crash program must be instigated and carried through to *develop curricula for exceptional children* which are conceived of in terms of the adult needs of the disabled child, as well as in terms of his childhood developmental needs. The education of mentally handicapped children can no longer be tolerated if it is conceptualized as a mere modification of the program for normal children. We will deal with this more fully in a moment. Curriculum which is honestly conceptualized in terms of the different needs of the disabled is an absolute requisite from which there can be no departure or compromise. In this regard, we, as educators and as physicians, must get over the indefensible notion that all disabled children need special education. We now write of specialized curricula for those who really need them. But let us also consider this matter in more detail momentarily.

We need a crash program in the *preparation of teachers* who truly understand the educational process and who will be instruments of effective translation of the honest curriculum to the child who needs it. The preparation of teachers of exceptional children is subject to much valid criticism.

There is no need to go into the inadequacies of the programs, which are more than obvious. What, indeed, is necessary is a thorough reorganization of content and a new conceptualization of what our teachers need. Teachers of special education must have a fundamental understanding of biological intelligence. We are not here recommending a mere course in intelligence or individual differences. We are stating that, in depth, teachers who deal with manifestations of intelligence must understand fully the nature of intelligence as we know it from research and theory. Teachers frequently fail to possess even the most elemental understanding of this primary facet of all education. Second, teachers must have a thorough understanding of the concept of perception and of its diverse implications and relations to all learning. The relation of perception via all sensory modalities to learning, achievement, and adjustment of children is fundamental whether they be disabled or not. Third, teachers must have a thorough grasp of the concepts of cognitive structure, an issue which is rarely a part of teacher education programs. The work of Riley Gardner is fundamental to all special education personnel; the related work of Jerome Bruner is fundamental to all education, general as well as special. Where do the ideas of these men enter into the sequence of development for teachers, and when do they become guiding principles to all teachers and to all teaching? It is my considered opinion that the great majority of teachers, in their preparatory years, not only have never read or discussed these significant writings and ideas, but that most have never heard the term "cognitive structure" or "cognition." This is sad, for here is another strand in the essential fabric of teacher preparation. Fourth, teachers must understand the concepts of individual differences until these concepts can be applied as a matter of course in any and all situations. They must realize and thoroughly understand that the concept is something more than the replication of the so-called "normal curve," and that in every contact with children it has meaning. Fifth, all teachers of special education, if indeed not all teachers of all children, must understand the implications of emotional overlay on intelligence, on perception, on cognition, and on the variables of individual differences. This is an important strand.

On these elements of the warp and woof of teacher preparation can be added a liberal arts concept, and also the relatively few technical courses which teachers who will work with extremely disabled children may need. The assumptions of differential class placement, integration, or separation, are premised on the fact that there is present a teacher who truly knows what he is doing, what he is thinking, what he believes, and who knows how to translate what he believes into an honest and realistic educational program.

This is education at its best; anything less is not justified in these times, to use Dunn's words.

We need a crash program to sensitize all teachers to the nature and needs of exceptional children and to help them understand that they, as general educators, can and must solve the learning problems of the majority of exceptional children. They must understand that a blind child of any mental ability can function on an integrated basis with physically normal children of comparable mental ability. Blindness *per se* does not automatically dictate placement. The first line of special education is the general educator, but this means an understanding educator who deals in terms of children and their potential, not in terms of emotional or historical conceptions of disability. We need a crash program to prepare administrators as educators and to leave the mechanics of operating a school building to technicians.

We need a crash program to prepare many of the present school principals and other types of administrators to become the building educational technicians, and to bring new educational leaders in as the building educators. The attitudes and the programs of a group of teachers most often reflect the point of view of the building administrator. It is rare that a building administrator in the present educational scene knows special education (or, indeed, general education), is fundamentally interested in exceptional children, or, if he is, knows what to do about their education. It is depressing indeed to one who travels widely into school systems throughout this continent and elsewhere to find that often the most elemental concepts of education and of special education are not understood by many educational administrators, principals, superintendents, deans, and college presidents.

Among other items which might be mentioned is the fact that we need a crash program to free education from the medical stereotypes and clinical models which now throttle good special educational practice. We have so bowed to the medical model in education and have been so fearful of advocating that which we know is better, that the so-called special education programs for disabled children are, indeed, often nothing more than a hollow shell. What is the logic of the concept of a special class for the deaf? For the mentally retarded? For crippled? For the blind? In any group of blind, deaf, crippled or other clinical category, there is little evidence of appropriate instructional programs on the basis of the disability *per se*. The basis of instruction is, in terms of perception, intelligence, cognition, individual difference, and the other fundamentals which could be mentioned; not on the basis of motor disability, decibel loss, visual acuity, or morbidity data. But special education today is founded on these latter factors and, for this reason, it is generally poor. It is founded on the attempts of medical personnel to organize special education in terms of what is appropriate in a treatment setting or hospital; in terms of medical taxonomies, not educational taxonomies. For this reason, special education is poor.

Special education can be good. It can be something of which we are proud. It can prepare children to take their rightful places in society and function to the height of their capacities. It can demonstrate that, under the circumstances we have described, it need not be a paradox as Johnson states, nor would ever the question of its justification need to again be raised by Dunn or others. If we cannot be heroic and come to grips with the issues which face us to which we have given brief recognition here, then we should and, I think, will not long be permitted to continue in our too frequent presently inadequate and unjustifiable programs. The special education role is justifiable in terms of what we know about child growth and development; the special education program, as it is almost universally demonstrated, is not justifiable in its present format or quality.

With all of this background in mind, what is the issue of special class placement? To me it is never a matter merely of integration or segregation. We are not dealing with two ends of the spectrum. The problem facing educators — which administrators fail to recognize or do not wish to be troubled to face — is the more fundamental concept of *selective placement*. Selective placement is founded on a careful evaluation of the issues of child growth and development which I have mentioned previously, not on the basis of medical category, diagnosis or treatment. Grouping children is not a matter of fitting them into a class or room for the convenience of medication, convalescence, physician rounds, or because we wish to have an evidence that the emotional need of the community is being met. Special classes are not cages in a zoo through which a community's emotional catharsis is achieved. They are educational centers in which learning in terms of the honestly diagnosed needs of a child will be carried on. In this concept there are no pat answers regarding integration or segregation. There is a planned continuum of educational opportunity for children which will be applied to them in terms of their often ever-changing needs. Fluidity based on need is the concept for children. What are these different opportunities? There is little new in what we will say. There is something new in the dynamic way in which they are used. Remember, the basis of placement is in terms of the psycho-educational need of the child, not in terms of medical typology or category. Furthermore, be reminded that educational programs as we will mention them now are not ordered here in terms of good, better, best; nor poor, poorer, poorest. Every concept we mention is needed in every school system, and each must be judged best for the children it serves every hour of the day, every day of the week, month, and year. The quality of education must not suffer at the hands of politicians, vested interests, economic recession, or change in the person of the school administrator. Quality of education and educational opportunity is an inherent right of every exceptional child. We have stated that the first line of the special educational program is the regular classroom teacher and this brings us to the concept of integration as one point along the linear arrangement of several educational programs.

If it were justified to place all exceptional children in special classes, it would be impossible within this generation of teachers or the next one to prepare sufficient specialized personnel to staff the programs which would result. Fortunately this is neither a necessity nor is it justified. The needs of the majority of exceptional children can and should be met in the regular classes in their community and neighborhood schools. There is no special method of teaching spelling to a child who once had poliomyelitis. There is rarely a different arithmetic methodology required for the child with epilepsy which is medically under control. There is no special social studies methodology which is specific to the vast majority of other children with other types of physical ailments. The very great majority of mildly disabled children, and a much larger number of seriously disabled children than is now considered, can and should be the responsibility of the regular classroom teacher and the general elementary school principal.

When the regular classroom is considered as an element in the total special education program, certain considerations have to be understood. A few should be mentioned. Teachers who accept all children must be in these classrooms. The number of such children in a given classroom should never be so many as to itself create a management problem. Itinerary personnel as may be required must see that teaching materials are available for the classroom teacher. Special educational consultants must serve the regular classroom teacher *as well as the* special education teachers, in the same manner as music, art, and other types of specialists normally related to general education should also serve special eduation centers. There is little reason to outline here the tremendous successes which have been achieved in many communities in integrating blind children into the regular grades, in assimilating hard of hearing children into other classrooms. Crippled children in many communities are experiencing a much more greatly enriched program in their neighborhood schools than ever they would receive in a special class. This is not universal, however.

The primary reason for the failure of programs of integration is not the factor of the disability. It is not the lack of teaching materials. It is not the inaccessability of school buildings. The primary reason for failure is the unhealthy attitudes of general educators toward children with disabilities. A principal said to me, "I don't know what was ever in the mind of the superintendent when he put that crutch case in my school. He's a charming little boy, but we don't have what he really needs. He should be in the special school." "That child there with the hearing aid," said another principal of an elementary school, "should really be at the school for the deaf. We really don't have the training to handle him adequately." The facts that the child had adequate language development, was able to maintain a communicative relationship with his teacher and others, understood the use of his prosthesis, and was achieving quite satisfactorily in his school work were all lost on this administrator who really didn't want to be reminded that he must think in terms of the individual needs of children. It is so much easier to think about groups of children. This is why education so often fails.

It is a figment of the imagination of general educators that normal children isolate physically handicapped children. It is likewise a figment of other imaginations that normal children learn compassion and understanding by having a handicapped child in their midst. Studies show that the visible physical handicap *per se* is not a factor in the acceptance or rejection of handicapped children by normal children in regular grades. These children are rejected or accepted on the basis of the same personality factors as typify the rejection or acceptance of any child. The fact of the disability is not a matter of child attitude. The significance of the disability — so handicapped children tell us — *is impressed upon them by the adults who surround them.* We as educators are the factors which make integration succeed or fail, who determine the degree to which we imprint the disability as a matter of consciousness on the mind of the child who happens to own the disability. We define children in terms of disabilities. We accentuate their minority status by typology, by attitudes, expressions, emotions, and by other forces which draw children to us in a healthy way or repell them from us and make them isolates.

Integration is more than a mere administrative decision. It is an operational procedure determined by the needs of a child, not the needs of the adults. It is a concept of education which can provide for the total needs of the child and which should be assumed as the model for many exceptional children. We hasten to add, however, that integration into the regular grades is not the solution for *all* disabled children. There are many for whom this type of placement would not serve their best interests. Integration is for those who can profit from it. That this number now includes many who are presently in special classes is obvious. A thorough examination of our class rosters in terms of the learning needs of children — not their medical diagnosis should cause a considerable amount of pupil re-placement.

Let us move quickly to the other end of the placement spectrum and then think of intermediate positions. The opposite of the integrative concept is the special class. Here is where our big guns should be trained, and these should come under community magnification in a very intense degree. Who is in these classes? Why are they there? What motivated their creation?

Are the children in the classes the rejects from general education? Are they there because it is assumed that children grouped together as mental equals are happier? Is special education the result of attempts to relieve the regular classroom teacher of the slow child? Does all special class placement take place on the recommendation of physicians who seldom appraise the child in the learning situation from the point of view of his learning needs, but who recommend placement on the basis of medical characteristics, proximity of the child to physical therapy treatment, convenience to the physician's own programs of clinic visitations, or other such adult need? In the special class, is there a curriculum which is indeed different in terms of the needs of the children who are there? Can an identifiable curriculum for the retarded be demonstrated which is conceptualized in terms of the adult vocational needs of the retarded? Is the curriculum for the retarded an honest curriculum, or is it a watered-down academic program, a busy-work program, a program which merely extends the time for the acquisition of certain skills from that needed by normal children? Can educators justify the special class program in terms of the needs of the child, in terms of the later acquisition of readiness, in terms of the slower rate of achievement, in terms of the maximum achievement levels, in terms of the vocational outlooks for the future adult? If there are differences in these traits which are sufficient in degree to make integration difficult for the child, then special education is warranted. Special class placement — to be honest, realistic, and justified — must be predicated firmly on these positive factors. Anything else is less than honest. Anything else is inexcusable and must not be tolerated. There is a place for special classes. There is no place under the sun for inadequate special classes. There is the reality of the mentally retarded and his school-life-span needs for a different curriculum. There is, however, no justification for the continuance of many classes which are opportunities neither for the child nor for the teacher. There is the reality of the multihandicapped child. The almost total lack of thought as to the nature of the educational and training program for these children makes many of the so-called classes for these children almost a travesty. There is the reality of the neurologically handicapped child with severe and specific learning and perceptual disorders. If some of the programs we've seen for these children were not so tragically poor, they might have been considered humorous.

We as special educators may not be able to do much about what goes on in the general classroom, but we have it within our power to do something about the special class. The fact that even one special class in a community can be criticized is a commentary on the total special education endeavor. The fact of the matter is that the problem is far more fundamental than this, and the situation should be completely reversed.

On the placement spectrum at midpoints between integration on the one hand and special classes on the other, are several other techniques — each of which, if employed, must be of quality nature. Each should be conceptualized with a dual goal in mind; namely, to meet the needs of children and to retain the child insofar as possible with his peers. These administrative techniques need only be mentioned: the resource room, the itinerant teacher, the unassigned teacher, the use of teacher aides, the use of volunteers, the crises teacher, the helping teacher and probably others as well.

Our issue is not a matter of integration versus special education classes. It is not a matter of resource rooms versus special classes. It is not a matter of the residential school, to mention another program, versus the special class or the community school. The education of all of the children is all of these — all of these techniques, each receiving equal administrative support and an appropriate financial substructure commensurate to its needs. It is not a competitive situation. Educators have enough to do inside each classroom to make it quality to keep them busy; we need not fight among ourselves over our seemingly vested interests of special education or integration.

We said that the placement of children for their education is not a mere matter of an administrative decision. It is the manifestation of our philosophy of education and of our philosophy of child worth. Do we place a retarded child in a special class for twelve years, and there he finds an educationally empty cupboard or one stocked with relative inconsequentia? Or is he placed in a special class which has an honest curriculum geared to his needs and to his adult requirements? Do we require him to attend his community school and class and there he finds a teacher inhospitable to the outward manifestations of his separate needs, or a principal who defines him in terms of cultural and historic stereotypes? Or is he placed in a regular class where adults see him as a child and like all children one who needs to learn and has needs in meeting needs; where adults see their responsibility to be to stretch the horizons of his experience for him as for all children with equal energy and with equal motivation?

Let us not further argue the merits of one type of classroom over another. Let us make all classrooms places of challenge and learning. Let us not develop a hierarchy of values for educational settings, placing one over the other. Let us realize that if each is needed, each must be quality throughout. The hallmark of education which is firmly imprinted on the sterling is its quality. In the face of this all else is unimportant.

9

THE FALSE HOPE OF INTEGRATION

A SITUATION IS DEVELOPING in general and special education which is impregnated at the most with the reality of failure; at the least, with dangers to the children who are purported to be served. Suddenly, for a variety of reasons, the educational watchword is integration. A movement is developing against the utilization of the special class. Just as special classes were the solution to all of an administrator's educational problems a decade past, now, with equally as little or no thought, the same school officials are advocating that most exceptional children be assimilated into the regular grades. This situation needs to be examined with care, and from such an examination a logical policy of pupil placement needs to be developed. While some administrators are approaching this issue with wise decisions, many others are riding the new wave without direction.

Unfortunately, the issues must be discussed essentially from theoretical and philosophical points of view. There is no definitive research on either side of this argument, and indeed none may be possible due to the infinite number of uncontrollable variables. Logic can be applied from which certain conclusions appear sanguine to the unemotional thinker.

PRESSURE ON THE SPECIAL CLASS

Whether or not over the years special education has been permitted to demonstrate its worth, is subject to debate. Had it been given this possibility, it is

Reprinted from *The Slow Learning Child* (Australia) 21, no. 2 (1974): 67–82, by permission.

doubtful it could have risen to the challenge of universal quality education for exceptional children because of the nature of teacher education, and social and political attitudes. The issue is not one of opposing alternatives however much one might wish for simplistic answers.

RESPONSIBILITY OF GENERAL EDUCATORS

On the other hand general education and general educators must stand in judgment, for in the long history of special education, from as early as 1830, special education has been used by generalists as a place for the educationally unwanted children of the schools. To justify their decisions, general educators without data rationalized that children were happier when placed with those of the same mental age. Hence, special classes were created which were heterogeneous on half a dozen other bases and thus essentially were unteachable. Maturation and experience, for example, often were ignored in grouping children.

Educators at all levels and of all types have created and have taken comfort in rigid categories with specifically defined limits. Children were assigned into these categorical slots, some of which were borrowed directly from medicine and psychology irrespective of their educational suitability. There are many reported instances in almost every school system where these category boundaries were bent and twisted in order to place a child in special education, not because his needs would be met there, but for the convenience of general education. Dunn has pointed to this situation very well, and he sees the responsibility for poor special education resting in two places.[1]

First, he justly criticizes general educators, as we do, for placing in special classes any and all children who could not be educated in regular classes. The appellation "dumping ground" is an outworn description of special education classes, yet a more accurately descriptive term can hardly be found for the special education classes in many of our largest and smallest school systems. Programs for the mentally retarded, socially maladjusted and educationally disturbed children have received the greatest number of unholy placements, but classes for acoustically, visually, and physically handicapped children have also felt the brunt of general educational ineptitude and mismanagement. The developing field of education for children with specific learning disabilities is currently at the mercy of poor educational decisions. Even now, in the latter program's infancy, heterogeneity exceeding the bounds of educational logic is to be seen in a preponderance of these programs.

In emphasizing this situation, Dunn and others justly point an accusing finger at the decision-makers in general education. These are administrators who force misplacement of children for their own convenience or for the convenience of regular class teachers. Special education is viewed by them as an administrative device to relieve the regular educational system of problems for which solution escapes the general educator. Too often, the easier way out of an educational problem has been its transfer rather than its solution.

FAILURE OF SPECIAL EDUCATION LEADERSHIP

On the other hand, Dunn appropriately points an accusing finger at special educators who willingly or unwillingly were accomplices in educational mismanagement. Rarely, have special educators refused to accept a referral from general education. Is this a fault of local special education leadership? Have special educators been unwilling to take a courageous stand for what is known and for what they believe? Is leadership weak in the face of general administrative pressure, or is it that special educators at the local levels have never been given realistic guidelines regarding their profession, its potentials and limitations? Too often we hear a special education inspector or supervisor say, "I know this isn't the best or even the right placement for this child, but what can you do in the face of administrative decisions?" Excuses and rationalizations cannot be equated with courageous educational leadership. Failure to maintain quality special education is the responsibility of special educators, and this accountability cannot be dodged. Regardless of the machinations of general educators and regardless of their motivations, if special education leadership had been firm in its acceptance of the right children into its classes, much of the present criticism of special education would be negated. The firm and educationally heroic stands were not taken, and thus special education has been used. Once the precedent was obvious that special educators would accept all referrals without argument, it is naive to believe that general educators would follow any other route but the easiest one for them.

The two factors in juxtaposition—one demanding, the other acquiescing—in large part have been effective in producing a special class system which is now under attack as being ineffective. Other elements, such as the quality of special education teacher education; the philosophical structure of special education; the inadequate, often unidentifiable curriculum employed in special education programs; unwise physical placement of

special classes within a building; outmoded or less than minimal teacher certification; attitudes of rejection, fear and guilt expressed or unexpressed by
general educators toward special classes, teachers and children separately
and together, still mitigate against quality education for exceptional children. These have been active negative influences on behalf of mediocrity for
many years.

If these are some of the factors which have produced an educational
system of poor quality, are they vis-à-vis the bona fide reasons for abandon-
ing it in favour of a policy of retention of the exceptional child in the regular
grades? Assuming that the courts of this nation will ultimately effect redress
for those children who are now misplaced in special or regular grades, what
is the situation faced by children who are accurately diagnosed as retarded,
emotionally disturbed, or with a specific learning disability? The administrator of one large city school system has publically stated to his board of
education that "current thought dictates a retention of retarded children in
the regular grades which will mean a reduction in the number of special
classes needed in the foreseeable future in this system." A less than adequate
statement could hardly be expected from a strong professional leader. Both
fact and conclusion are without foundation. A program of so-called integration is no more the answer to the educational problems of exceptional children than has been the fundamentally inadequate program of special education of the past half century.

Both integration and special class placement are more than mere administrative decisions. The failure to appreciate this will harm children.

On the assumption that diagnosis is accurate, the retention of a
child in a regular grade presupposes a climate of acceptance by the general
class teacher. Unfortunately, teachers are no more perfect than any group of
people in our society. They are characterized by the prejudices and biases of
society generally. They demonstrate the same misconceptions about disability as do their neighbors. They possess the same behaviour-determining fears
and guilt feelings as have been expressed toward the disabled for centuries. It
has long been known that it is the adult, not the peer group members, which
impresses the impact of a handicap on the exceptional child. The *adults* in
the instance to which we refer were *teachers*![2] An indiscriminate policy of integration of exceptional children into regular grades will often *face* these
children with hostile adult attitudes over which the child can have no effective control. This should never happen, but in fact it does too frequently.

Furthermore, assuming health and positive attitudes on the part of
a teaching staff, there appears to be a limit in the capacity of the best teachers truly to meet the needs of each child when those needs are spread over too
wide a spectrum. The I.Q. range in an elementary school group of 30 chil-

dren of between 60 to 130 presents educational needs of children which few teachers can adequately handle under the best circumstances. Most teachers want to do more for children than merely to monitor attendance. Faced with the range just suggested, significantly more complex in nature than here discussed, some children's needs will not be met by otherwise good teachers. One must ask, where is the evidence that integration is the superior model for either the child or for teachers?

The capacity of teachers to individualize instruction has limitations, both in terms of teacher ability and in terms of the fact that most teachers have rarely been taught what this means or how to accomplish it successfully. If these essentials happen to be present in the teachers, the frequent lack of a sufficient supply of teaching materials to encompass the individual child's needs rapidly reduces motivation and program effectiveness. No, integration is not the sole answer. Likewise, we can no longer tolerate a further proliferation of mediocre special education. What is the alternative? In reality, there is no alternative to either of these two models of education. If definition of alternatives includes quality, then that is the route education must go.

A PLEA FOR QUALITY

Quality special education is going to be hard to come by, but less than this is morally, if not legally, intolerable now and in the future. The defenders of quality in special education will be and have been easy targets of those who are satisfied with less, or of those who cannot for one reason or another match quality with personal performance. Quality special education has rarely been given a chance to demonstrate its worth. Where it has existed, few parental complaints are heard, and few, if any, consumer law suits are in the courts.

Quality special education must be founded on honest and accurate psycho-educational diagnosis and pupil evaluation. Further need not be said on this matter save to state unequivocally that the problem or its solution starts at this point. Special educators must insist on and monitor this professional function. Quality special education requires that the preparation and function of school diagnosticians and psychologists also must be monitored and must be under constant review. If accuracy in the most inclusive sense is practised at the time of assessment of the child, if adequate staffing is a routine, if parents in consideration of due process and constitutional rights are participants in decisions regarding their children, then special or general education at least starts off on the right track in an attack on children's needs.

Let us once again look at some of the basic reasons why special education is a requisite for many children and conversely why general education placement is inappropriate. We wrote of this matter two decades past, but true statements made then warrant readdress at this time in special education's history. Let's consider the retarded child first. Why is the integration of these children difficult if not impossible and unwarranted in addition to those factors previously mentioned?

The readiness age for skilful performance in those things on which society places great value is approximately a mental age of six. A child with an I.Q. of 75 at a chronological age of 6 years will theoretically have a M.A. of 4.5 years. While normal six year old children are experiencing success with a new tool, the retarded child is having a failure experience. The lower the I.Q., the greater the disparity between the retarded child and the normal children with whom he is integrated. The difference between the two groups continues to be more pronounced even under good teaching, as the gulf between the curves of CA growth and MA maturation widens over time. Maturation and experience appear as compensatory for the retarded child, but insufficiently and not in time to insure both academically and socially positive learning and adjustment to take place within his current grade placement.

Related to this is the fact that in children of normal intelligence, the achievement rate is assumed to be approximately 1.0 grades per school year. In contrast, under optimum training conditions, data of long standing exists to demonstrate that among educable mentally retarded children, the achievement rate is 0.4 grades per year. What meaning does this have for the development of positive self-concept for the retarded child in a competitive regular class? Likewise, the optimum achievement level for normals is assumed to be 12.0 grades by sixteen or seventeen years of age; in contrast, a high fourth or low fifth grade level for this group of retarded children, providing optimal educational situations exist for them. In the face of these statements, what part does the fact of integration play to minimize them, or more important, to insure that they will not be negative factors hindering the successful adjustment of the retarded child in the mainstream of community education? The uncontrolled variables in any classroom are too great to assume with comfort that the average general class teacher will be able to surmount them successfully. Finally, as the retarded child approaches the secondary school, where in any part of the present high school program are there opportunities for either realistic vocational exploration or pre-vocational training related to those jobs which in a short time he will seek to fill? This rarely exists even in special education; it is practically non-existent in general education at the secondary levels.

Let us turn to the issue of specific learning disabilities. Children with these problems have been in the regular grades, floundering and leaving school, since the beginning of required and universal education. In 1963 they were given the label of learning disability. Ten years later the child (who was always there) is returned to the regular grades, but now with a label. Is there any reason to believe that with classifications the general educators will be better equipped to meet this child's needs? If anything, the problem now is worse, for the parents of such children very often know what the child needs, but general educators as a group have not reached a similar level of professional sophistication. In this field, parents too often have read more than the teachers who teach their children. But the issue is integration! Can untrained regular teachers, adequately meet the unique perceptual and educational needs, perhaps the most complex of any of those of child development, without specialized training and when thirty other children simultaneously command attention and different types of teaching materials? We do not think so. Integration here is the wishful thinking of unknowing administrators. The literature records that this writer has often advocated a logical program of integration, particularly for the physically handicapped child. What is being witnessed today too often is illogical and defies the reasonable definition of good education in any form. This is particularly true when indiscriminate integration of the mentally retarded, the emotionally disturbed, and those with specific learning disabilities is the focus of administrative decisions. The peculiar perceptual problems now known to be related to the achievement difficulties of children labelled with specific learning disabilities are so technical that without specialized training and clear understanding, teachers — special or general — are unable fully to meet the child's needs. The regular classroom situation itself mitigates against these children. Here is a situation where with most of these children integration into the regular class is only a token recognition of a contemporary educational fad; it cannot effectively assist these children to achieve satisfactory adjustment or learning. A good resource teacher can supplement the efforts of a regular class teacher for some children. Still others, however, will need a full time skilled clinical teacher in a setting conceptualized theoretically and actually to meet the peculiar psychopathologies of the children.

TEACHER EDUCATION

We have briefly stressed two issues both of which are basic to a reasonable special class program, i.e., accurate diagnosis and prognosis, and quality in all facets of the special education program. One must look further, however, and seek other issues which need emphasis and professional concern. The issue of teacher preparation is one of these. Here too the pendulum seems to be swinging out of logical control. What is done today in teacher education will have a long-term affect on school programs. Over the past one hundred years special education has leaned more and more on medical and clinical categories as the structure for its programming. Hence, commonly one finds educational programs in operation for the mentally retarded, the deaf, the emotionally disturbed, the gifted, the partially sighted as well as for the blind, and the hard of hearing, among others. Occasionally, usually as the result of an over-zealous physician, psychologist, or educator, one finds "cleft palate classes," classes for autistic children, for dyslexic children, aphasic children, and for other more esoteric non-educational classifications. In the past few years this trend for classification in education according to medical and psychological terminology has been slowed. Non-categorical concepts occasionally are being utilized.

NON-CATEGORICAL EDUCATION

In several universities the trend toward non-categorical conceptualization of special education has resulted in revisions in the special education teacher education programs. Students whose goals are to work with handicapped children are being exposed to courses dealing with common problems related to all types of handicapped children. Students are assured that they will need a broad base of skills as opposed to learning how to cope with the specific defective parts of the handicapped children's problems. If integration is to succeed, then all future teachers, not just special educators, need these broad based skills. Special education, on the other hand, if it is to prove its worth, must produce specialists who know the fundamental issues of disability, who understand the technical implications of these issues for learning, and who know without failure how to modify or develop anew the teaching settings and teaching materials to correct, compensate for, or minimize disabilities. Special education is more than an afterglow to diagnosis. Special education teachers must have depth to their preparation. They must know and understand the implications of disability for reading, for handwriting, for mobility, for social adjustment. This writer is confounded by the superficiality of the current movement toward non-categorical teacher education which in effect produces a teacher with unsaleable competencies. Unfortunately, the unknowing employer of these products learns of the limitations of the new teacher only after two or three years of ineffective teaching have been experienced.

We have often written and spoken about the importance of non-categorical teaching and grouping of children. We have stressed the meaningless of the category "deaf" or "cerebral palsy" or others as the basis of grouping children for instruction or for teacher education. However, non-categorical education must be supplemented with something more than tender loving care. We urge educators to examine the basic problems underlying the failure of many children in different medical categories to learn to read, for example. Research is available to point up the fact that among the large majority of children with cerebral palsy, among a high percentage of emotionally hyperactive children, epileptic children, mentally retarded children, indeed of all categories, perceptual problems exist involving vision, hearing, and tactual skills. If categories are broken down, and children are regrouped in clinical teaching situations focused on the basic problem (in this example perceptual psychopathology), then progress can be made. It goes without saying that so-called "non-categorical" teacher education must include basic and fundamental preparation in diagnosis, instructional approaches, and teaching materials for meeting the perceptual problems of the children so affected. Other examples of cross-category problems can easily be identified around which teacher education can be conceptualized. This may require some re-training of college professors as well. In the rapid move to non-categorical teacher education, a vacuum has been produced which is filled with confusion rather than with an understanding of ways to reconceptualize special education and thus bring teachers to a point where deficit-oriented teaching can erase or at the least significantly minimize the basic learning problems of children. Merely to provide "supplemental help" for exceptional children within a regular grade without a specific focus of ultimately correcting the factors which cause failure will achieve little or nothing for the child, and will continue to cause the community to look with suspicion on education. We are aware that in some universities special education teacher preparation focuses, not on a child's disability, but on its consequences. That may be good. However, at the same time future teachers must be instructed in the ways of dealing with the specific consequences of disability at the expense of generalized discussions on global commonalities of self concept, vocational goals, and social adjustment. These latter are important, of course, but of greater importance are those deficits which cause the self concept problems and the failure to achieve socially or vocationally. Rather than to focus on the consequence of disability, *teachers must focus on and teach to the disability*. Colleges and universities have an opportunity to revolutionize special education if special education can be viewed as deficit oriented and if teachers can be given fundamental preparation in correcting these deficits. Global concepts of education for life and living, while high-sounding and laudable, are obtainable through special education if a deficit-oriented quality teacher education program can be implemented. Without this, special education will continue its spiral into ineffectiveness. General education, in the best concept of integration, can never effectively substitute for a quality special education program. For obvious reasons, the general classroom cannot effectively be deficit oriented. We should integrate insofar as possible. However, the school administrator who says that special education classes can be phased out by reason of integration, or the college professor who substitutes categories with global concepts rather than technical teacher education, both fail to understand the roles of education in the lives of exceptional children.

QUALITY IN SPECIAL EDUCATION

What is good special education and what is a rational relationship between special and general education? First, let us look briefly at special education per se. It consists of several elements, some of which have been mentioned here before.

1. Special education is deficit oriented, and it is the sound product of deficit-oriented teacher preparation. The teacher by reason of his training will know the meaning of eye-hand co-ordination problems, how to attack them, and what their relation is to handwriting, dressing, and eating, for example. The teacher will understand the relationship between auditory figure-background discrimination problems and how to adjust the child within an appropriate learning situation and how to bring to him the type of learning materials and training which will culminate in appropriate auditory attention skills, speech and language patterns.

Clinical special education teaching will be more concerned with the correction of specific deficits and learning disabilities in all types of exceptional children than it will be concerned with content. Content can come later, and is more justifiably the province of the general educator. Positive adjustment and social adjustment will come via the medium of motivation through success in the correction of deficits rather than as elements in and of themselves taught in ways not thoroughly understood by either special teacher or child.

2. Special education ceases to attempt to mirror the regular elementary classroom. Special education should do what it can do better than general education, namely, focus, as we have said, on specific problems related to educational and learning deficits. Special education is not the place to teach the whole child, for a whole child will never be referred to special

education. Special education must bring its technical skills to bear on a deficit-ridden child and perhaps ultimately return that child to the regular grades as "whole." If this concept is developed, the engineering focus of special education can be highlighted. Educational blueprints can be developed for the child in question, and can be instrumental in a common attack on problems of the teacher, the child, and his parents.

Special education will not be compared negatively to general education classrooms if the former fails to contain all the evidences of group motivation which the regular teacher is skilled in employing. Special education is less concerned with education for life adjustment per se than it is for the development of specific skills on which generalizations can be built later by the regular class educators. Special education will be accepted appropriately as more mechanistic and technical when it does its job well. The real contributions of special education have been minimized and lost in the frantic efforts of special educators to compete with general educators in all aspects of the educational program.

3. Special education programs for children must be based on definitive clinical diagnosis and assessment. This means that psychologists must be taught how to search for the causes of problems rather than for global characteristics of children, and they must be able to describe these and to translate them to the educator. Furthermore, it means that special educators themselves must be taught how to test for changes in the impact of a deficit on the perception and learning of children. Special educators cannot wait two or three years for a routine reassessment of a child. If special education is to be responsive to the specific needs of a child, the teacher must have up-to-date information often weekly or monthly, and then modify his instructional approaches and materials accordingly. This has implications for teacher education programs, for where else can the teacher learn these skills?

4. Special education programs must be conceptualized for exceptional children when the disparities of their mental ages are beyond the point of "easy" assimilation of the children into the regular grades and when the presence of such children exhausts the capacity of good teachers to meet all the needs of all of the children in the regular grades. This is a difficult point to define, but it can be determined by thoughtful special and general educators working in harmony without competitive feelings to reach decisions. This means the development of special classes.

Special education classes are appropriate for educable mentally handicapped children as well as for others. These classes, however, must also be focused on deficits. They must be conceptualized in terms of the occupational and social needs of the retarded as successfully adjusted adult citizens. They must contain children who are appropriately diagnosed and who are genuinely retarded as opposed to those who have experienced serious cultural or environmental deprivation. These classes might be geared to successful adult adjustment vocationally, socially, emotionally, and secularly. They must contain within the program a type of training for life which permits reasonable flexibility for the individual insofar as economic trends are concerned. Special education classes, where appropriately used, will incorporate a realistic liaison concept between the secondary school program and the first independence of the retarded individual on the job and in the community.

It has been this writer's experience that when special education is founded on an honest base and contains a realistic program in terms of child as well as adult needs, parents are fully supportive and enthusiastically applaud the efforts of the special educator teacher and administration. Parental attack on special education comes when poor placement, inappropriate labelling, inappropriate teacher preparation, dishonest programs, and faulty preparation for adult living are obvious. General education attack comes when regular class teachers realize that special education is doing on a less than satisfactory level what can be done better in the general instructional situation.

5. Special education-citizen boards of review need to be established consisting of knowledgeable specialists and selected parents to monitor teacher selection and preparation, local school placement procedures, quality and nature of the special education programs, and the referrals of exceptional children back to general education as the impact of deficits is reduced. Review boards to monitor all facets of the community education program are essential to the quality of education which the community expects of its schools.

6. Special education will receive children into its programs only after adequate screening and diagnosis for psychological and educational needs are completed and following a placement committee conference in which parents of the child under consideration have participated. Mechanisms must be effected to insure that those children who are not accepted by special education will receive appropriate experiences in the regular grades and will not become the focus of negative attitudes by regular teachers who expected to have a problem transferred. Review committees can monitor the results of those decisions also.

7. An appropriate concept of "return to the regular grades" must be adopted in special and general education, particularly with children originally diagnosed as having specific learning disabilities and also for educable mentally retarded children. One of the primary criticisms of special education programming which the courts have frequently voiced is concerned with

the performance of the special class placement. There must be a valid concept of return to the mainstream of education, and this will be facilitated by deficit orientation of programs, appropriate placement decisions, frequent teacher assessment of changes in deficit problems reflected in the subsequent adjustment of teaching materials, and by review boards which monitor child progress in the direction of re-integration. Successful special education will dictate replacement for many if not most exceptional children. Thus another question is raised. When does the exceptional child cease to be exceptional? They do, and regular educators must accept this or themselves be criticized for labelling children.

The above list is not inclusive, but it does indicate some of the things which must be done to produce a vigorous special education program. We reiterate: there is a vital and significant place for the special class if that class is well conceptualized and is staffed with a teacher who can vigorously attack the child's deficits with a broad understanding and with a full armamentarium of appropriate teaching materials and techniques. The teacher-engineer in a clinically oriented special education program can redirect children's lives toward worthwhile goals and attainment levels.

INTEGRATION AS A PROGRAM

We have indicated some of those factors on which special education must be premised. We have little faith that integration as it is being practised today can do as well. This feeling comes from some of the reasons we have already indicated; namely, the failure of good teachers appropriately to encompass the needs of children when heterogeniety within a given class is too great. Culturally and historically determined attitudes likewise have been mentioned as deterrents to successful integration of exceptional children into the regular grades. We recognize that exceptions to these statements are to be found. There are plenty of examples of good integrative experiences for blind children in the elementary and secondary grades of many school systems usually with the support of itinerant teachers. But these examples do not transfer to the wholesale integration movement which is underway nationally and locally.

If integration is to succeed, what are the essentials to this program? There are several, each of equal importance.

1. The first essential to a program of integration for exceptional children into the regular grades is that of a qualified teacher. We assume that the qualifications concerned with teaching methods, knowledge of materi-

als, and other related matters will be present in the teacher as a matter of course. We cannot assume, however, that positive attitudinal characteristics toward disability will be present, and too often we have seen the opposite to be the case. It is absurd to assume that teachers, because they are educated individuals, will accept fully those things about which they know little or nothing. The terms mental retardation, epilepsy, emotional disturbance, gifted, often have personal meaning and definition to the teacher — meanings which essentially may become disturbing factors in the relationship between teacher and child.

Although formal courses do not solve all problems, nevertheless this writer for nearly twenty years, seeing the importance of providing a rich experience and orientation to all future general educators, in one university made possible courses regarding the psychoeducational needs and development of exceptional children. A course (three credit hours) consisting of didactic lectures, small discussion groups, film viewing, observation and some participation with small groups of exceptional children or with individuals, visitations, appropriate readings of professional books as well as autobiographies and biographies of handicapped persons, individually and together provided for the future teacher a positive basis for approaching exceptional children. Individual consultation with certain students provided a forum wherein personal concerns, fears, and antagonisms regarding the handicapped could be brought to the surface, discussed, and be viewed objectively by the individual concerned. Regardless of the techniques used, a formal attack on this problem must be undertaken. In-service programs for teachers in school systems where integration is a current policy must be undertaken and can be reasonably effective. It is ludicrous to believe that a happy and positive adjustment among exceptional child, teacher, and pupils will be attained merely on the basis of an administrative decision to integrate. On the contrary, integration can indeed result in a disastrous experience for the children in question and for the teacher, if there is a failure on the part of colleges and universities or of local school administrators to provide in-depth orientation for the receiving teachers.

2. Integration must be based on an attitude which looks at the exceptional child in terms of what he is now, not in terms of where he was when he started school nor in terms of a long problem history. If the educational program anywhere in the school system has been successful in any degree, the child should be less exceptional at the time of integration than formerly. He must be given the benefit of his own progress, and he must be considered as a developing human being who is making further progress. If the accumulation of case study data on a child convinces the teacher that the pupil is more exceptional than he is a child, then the negative influences of

labelling can be transferred to the criticism of the regular class as it is of the special class. The attitudes of teachers and of the adults which surround children do impress on the children the impact of their disabilities. Appropriate adult attitudes can minimize the influence of the disability. This cannot come about, however, without the assistance of in-service orientation such as has been mentioned.[2]

   3. Integration of exceptional children must be accompanied by a related administrative decision to reduce the number of children in a given class. It is of still more importance to reduce the range which is characteristic of the class on several important variables, i.e., range of mental ages, range of chronological ages, range of intelligence quotients, and also the range in the variety of problems of exceptionality being integrated or retained in the regular grade. As we have stated before, there are human limitations apparent in the capacity of good teachers to accommodate to children and to be able to educate those children. Insofar as mental age and intelligence are concerned, the acceptable range must permit the retarded child to have a genuine success experience comparable to that of the normal children who are his companions in a given grade placement. If this criterion alone is followed, it will soon be apparent to the thoughtful administrator that integration will be effective for only a minority of educable retarded children.

   4. There must be an absolute commitment to the fact that integration must provide for every exceptional child a guarantee of an education which will bring him to the maximum level of his potential and equip him by the time he leaves the school system as a young adult with the skills requisite to appropriate employment. The courts of some nations remind us that this is the child's birth right and is a constitutional guarantee. If interaction can accomplish this without writing off generations of exceptional children, then that approach must be applauded. We have no evidence yet of any kind which can demonstrate that this goal can be reached.

   In an article of this nature, a full examination of all facets of this complex problem cannot be undertaken. We have referred to only two forms of education of exceptional children. There are others. That the issue briefly treated here is significant is apparent to many. Some of the elements of failure have been suggested here. We have no faith that the program of integration as it is now being pursued in colleges, universities, and school systems will succeed if the presently observed erratic approaches are continued. Although it is difficult to see how the program of wholesale integration, being advocated by many, can ever succeed, it will certainly fall short of its goal if the essentials we have noted continue to be ignored. We do see, on the other hand, in the mechanism of the special class a hope for many children. However, if special education programs at the local levels and in colleges and universities continue in their present misguided way and at the low levels of performance characteristic of many, it is probably better that a challenge to their existence be continued and that many be stopped. This does not mean that good special education is an impossibility. While we feel that there are limitations to the best programs of integration in terms of the growth and total development of the children involved, we do not see the same limitations in any degree in quality programs of special education, either in the special class model or in other models which supplement the special class. The issue is essentially in the answer to the question: do educators really wish to serve children? If the reply is positive, then it behooves, special educators to approach their task with a degree of honesty and determination not heretofore observed, and to create a program of such a high ethic and quality that it is unimpeachable and subject to no criticism except the best.

REFERENCES

1. Dunn, L. M. "Special Education for the Mildly Retarded — Is Much of It Justifiable?" *Exceptional Children* 35 (1968): 5–24.
2. Haring N. G.; G. S. Stern; and W. M. Cruickshank. *Attitudes of Educators Toward Exceptional Children.* Syracuse: Syracuse University Press, 1958.

LEAST-RESTRICTIVE PL

Administrative Wishful Thi...

THE ISSUE OF LEAST-RESTRICTIVE PLACEMENT for children with learning disabilities, as well as for those with other types of handicaps, is an official policy for many state and local educational systems. One state department of education, for example, has issued departmental guidelines on this problem. It has ranked several types of educational programs from "most restrictive" to "least restrictive" as follows: (1) residential or institutional programs; (2) special schools in public school system; (3) special classes in public schools; (4) resource rooms; (5) tutorial programs; (6) itinerant teaching programs; and (7) regular class placement.

There are few, if any, who would argue with the spirit of the concept of least-restrictive placement. The fact of the matter is that in terms of current educational practices, the *"least" may more often be the most restrictive* place for learning disabled children to receive their education. The decision to establish a priority list, such as that reproduced here, makes one pause to understand how such a decision was reached and how the priorities were established.

Was this an administrative decision based on thought? Based on theory? Based on research? Based on opportunism? Based on fears of parental pressures or legal threats? If all education for the handicapped children and youth of this nation were "quality," there would be no issue taken here with the concept. There also would be no pressure to rank educational placements in the way this list demonstrates. The fact of the matter is that there is no research to demonstrate that one type of educational placement is

Reprinted from *Journal of Learning Disabilities* 10, no. 4 (April 1977): 5-6, by permission.

estrictive than others. All types are needed, but all must be of high
ality.

I know the practical reasons for this unfortunate decision — a decision that is sweeping the country as a counterpart to thoughtless decisions
regarding mainstreaming. It is reflective of current fads and fashions regarding learning disability which have grown out of parents' frustrations regarding the quality of services their children have found in residential facilities,
special schools, or classes during the past several decades. A thoughtless response, such as the "least-restrictive" concept, to parental frustrations, however, will not necessarily remedy a wrong. Educational administrators and
the special education leadership cannot take any comfort to date in what has
been done through the concept of least-restrictive placement. The plan will
not, in and of itself, solve a single problem of a single child. Already a
ground swell of new frustrations is observable within regular class teachers'
groups and from parents who realize that the "least" may indeed be the
"most" restrictive, perhaps to an even greater extent than poor quality special educational programs.

An administrative decision does not correct deep-seated, underlying
causes of poor education for learning disabled children. Legislation which requires children to spend a portion of the school day in a regular class placement is a far cry from the quality educational leadership which is required.

What makes the "least" the most restrictive placement? There are
several factors, including at a minimum the following:

First, this has been a hasty and often thoughtless decision growing
from the idea that mainstreaming as a policy is unselectively appropriate.
Where, we must ask, is the definitive research to demonstrate this? It does
not exist in a form which meets a definition of research or warrants the rampant spread of public school programs of this nature.

Second, the lack of regular class teachers who have any preparation
whatsoever in serving the needs of the learning disabled child is obvious in
almost every elementary school in the nation.

Third, there is an over abundance of administrators who fail to
understand the nature of the problem and who, as a result, are unable to
genuinely support teachers who try to meet the needs of these children in the
regular grades.

Fourth, the practice of administratively assigning learning disabilities, along with special education generally, to a department of pupil personnel is widespread. Regular classroom teachers do not need more pupil
personnel services; they need assistance from experts in instruction and curriculum. Few pupil personnel representatives know how to teach a learning
disabled child. They have had no experience. The regular classroom teach-

ers, who do try to be the least-restrictive influence on the development of a learning disabled child, do not need more intelligence tests administered; they need help in modifying educational techniques and materials to the exigencies of the perceptual processing deficits of the child in question.

A child placed in a so-called least-restrictive situation who is unable to achieve, who lacks an understanding teacher, who does not have appropriate learning materials, who is faced with tasks he cannot manage, whose failure results in negative comments by his classmates, and whose parents reflect frustration to him when he is at home, is indeed being restricted on all sides.

The pendulum is swinging from criticism of the residential school to criticism of the regular class placement. I have often criticized the former for being less than adequate for many children. However, espousing a substitute on the basis of a theory and its philosophic potential without research of any type or without even minimal preparation of the general educator, is not what learning disabled children need. Hope and good intentions do not result in rewarding long-term programming. If there is failure with the present concept of least-restrictive placement, who will be to blame? The child? His parents? The teachers who tried? The administrators and educational leadership who acted without careful examination of the implications of a theoretical concept?

The child with learning disabilities deserves more than this. If the concept of least-restrictive placement is to prevail and not result in a new generation of tragedy for learning disabled children, then school leadership must attack its deficiencies with unrelenting vigor. Time is *not* on the side of leadership any longer. Teacher inservice training on a universal basis must be established. Master teachers must receive in-depth preparation under competent professors. School educators must be brought to a sound level of understanding of the complex problems of these children which at present they do not have. Diagnosis must take second place to instruction, and must be made a tool of instruction, not an end in itself. A variety of educational programs must be available for children who have a variety of needs.

There is nothing magical about an administrator's decision to foster less-restrictive placement of children unless, at a minimum, the elements we mention here are fully implemented. Even then, there is serious question whether the "best" teachers of the school can fully minister to the unique perceptual processing needs of learning disabled children in a class of 30 youngsters, all seeking their places in the sun.

PART IV

CURRICULUM

11

LEARNING DISABILITIES
AND THE SPECIAL SCHOOL

*I*T IS REMARKABLE in the face of national trends to witness and to be with you as a part of the dedicatory celebration of a new campus school building, and particularly one devoted to aspects of the education of exceptional children. This school, the Starpoint School of Texas Christian University, takes its place among a select group of private schools whose facilities and staffs are devoted to assisting children and youth with learning disabilities to find their ways toward a satisfying adult life. I say that it is remarkable to witness the opening of a new school, because two strong forces are currently in place which would daunt many less courageous people than you.

The first of these forces is the unholy economic situation at this time which surrounds public and private education throughout the nation. The history of university laboratory or campus schools during the past fifteen years has been to suffer closure at the hands of state legislatures. Sources of research such as performed in the area of curriculum by Professor John Goodlad at the campus school of the University of California at Los Angeles, and the unique organismic research of Professors Willard Olson and Byron Hughes in the Elementary School of the University of Michigan, are no longer dynamic forces which can shed new light on the significant issues of child growth and development. What of dynamic research has come from the famed Horace Mann School of Teachers College Columbus University in the past two decades? I cannot comment on the fiscal situation of your School and University other than to wish that the University in which I work were as fiscally secure and thus as able to do what you have done here.

Dedicatory address, Starpoint School, Texas Christian University, Fort Worth, Texas, 1979.
156

A second force mitigating against the creation of special schools and educational facilities is the concept of mainstreaming and normalization so rampant in the United States today. This approach to education, smooth and enticing in its sound, wreaks havoc on children and their families when it is carried out in the thoughtless and often irrational manner we see so frequently in communities of this nation. I must go on record, and have frequently done so, to state that I am not opposed to mainstreaming per se. You will find my position documented in writing which appeared in 1952. However, there is a fundamental difference between a thoughtfully planned and executed educational philosophy and the fad and fashionable mincing educational footsteps of the dilettante. While crossing the center of our University campus recently, I passed an undergraduate wearing one of the typical sloganized T-shirts we see so often today. It read: "Mainstream me Girls. I'm ready." Unfortunately the cavalier attitude expressed in the student's blazoned T-shirt reflects the educational scene as well, except that neither exceptional child, his teacher, normal children, parents of the community, school administrators, nor members of boards of education "are ready" for the experience of normalization, and thoughtless decisions are the result.

The Starpoint School takes its place today with a small and very select group of schools in the United States and abroad which over the years have performed noble services to children with severe problems of learning. It takes its place along side the Miriam Frostig Center for Educational Therapy in Los Angeles, the Havern Educational Center near Denver, St. Francis Children's Activity and Achievement Center of Cardinal Stritch University in Milwaukee, the Gateway School in New York City, the Briarwood School in Houston, the Experimental Educational Unit of the University of Washington, the Orthogenic School at the University of Chicago, and a very few others. Internationally this School has the potentials of the Children's Learning Center of McGill University in Montreal, the Evaluation Center of Children's Hospital in Birmingham, England, the Orthogenic School in Groenigen in The Netherlands. These are typical of what your School is and must be. The difference between the few mentioned here and a much longer list of schools which could be named is *quality*. The Starpoint School must always be associated with others within this fraternity where quality is the hallmark.

Most of the schools mentioned here are related to universities, and this fact alone places a different-order responsibility on those who provide services in the School and also for those who are served by it. But more of this later.

We have stressed the issue of quality. Children with learning disabilities and their families can expect and should receive no less than the best.

The problems faced by children and youth with learning disabilities are the most subtle and at the same time the most complex of all child and adolescent growth and development issues. The learning and adjustment problems of these children rarely, if ever, come as singles. Generally they meet the definition of a multiply handicapped individual. Perceptual, perceptual-motor, and cognitive problems, coupled with often-observed emotional overlays constitute in their awful magnitude issues which at most frequently defy solution, and at least still require the most penetrating thought by the best prepared personnel in the professions.

It is the issue of complexity which accentuates the necessity for competence and quality of personnel and program in a School and University such as this and in any other educational endeavor which purports to serve learning disabled individuals and their families. This issue deserves our attention today as thoughtful people move to dedicate a new building and a new program to the solution and alleviation of these human complexities. What are the elements which constitute the essence of quality, elements which must permeate every facet of the Starpoint School program? There are several.

First, this School must believe in something. It must have a philosophy around which a total program of attack on problems of learning disabilities can revolve. Piaget is great because he stands for something. Piagetian theory means something whether you agree with it or not. It is an entity which can be tested and tried. It is not eclectic. Eclecticism in the area of learning disabilities is the element which has produced the mediocrity so apparent on all sides in this country and elsewhere. This is no issue to be based on a little knowledge about a lot of things. We must believe in something and pass our beliefs on through our students. Kephart stood for a point of view, and his greatness stemmed from what he believed. Rabinovitch at McGill University held to a concept which he was able to inculcate in his colleagues and to make effective in the lives of children. Strauss and Werner believed in a concept and made it real. The fact that people attack educational giants does not minimize their contributions. Beliefs need to be examined. The strength of any educational philosophy will be enhanced by thoughtful argument. I have often said to my students, "Don't come to this course unless you wish to hear my point of view. You will not receive an eclectic survey of what others think or believe about learning disabilities. You will experience and hear only what I believe and why I believe it. You will leave here with an in-depth understanding of what one person thinks." The Starpoint School will be strong only to the extent it can be identified as believing in something, and in this belief it becomes unique. Uniqueness, alone, is not synonymous with greatness. A sound philosophical structure to your program which can be translated into everything which you do here will be the measure of uniqueness leading to quality.

Second, there must be a professional staff here sufficient unto the job to be accomplished. I hope the President of this University and his Board of Trustees understands that, while this program can add luster to the University and become one of its significant benchmarks, it is also one of the most expensive aspects of all special education if it is done correctly. To do less is to abrogate a responsibility to the families and students here being served. A professional staff, consistent and unanimous in its adherence to the philosophy and goals of the School is essential.

The faculty of a school such as this must know what it believes and be able to translate that knowledge to children and families as well as to be able to demonstrate it daily to observing students. Students must see expressed in the behavior of a faculty the essence of the philosophical structure which is the hard core of the school's program. The selection and continuing education of a strong faculty whose personal goals are well focused on the objectives of the school is a major responsibility of administration. A faculty member who deviates from the agreed-upon practice of the school can be the single element upon which programmatic failure rests. It is a truism for us all that great teachers, often a single great teacher, can provide a lifetime direction to those who come in contact with greatness. It is an administrative responsibility to see that greatness is available to all who utilize this school.

Third, the program for the development of children with learning disabilities is by the very nature of the problem interdisciplinary. This is a place where the best minds of the university must be brought together in a forum where disciplines are equals among equals and where the goal is service to children and youth and not disciplinary enhancement. It is easy to speak about interdisciplinary programming; it is quite another thing to bring it about. In my experience, however, it is not an impossibility, and when it is obtained services of a new order are available to families, services which bring a degree of realistic hope not heretofore thought possible.

Fourth, a school of this nature appropriately embedded in a major University, must be the recipient of the best of University administration. I find some of the stories my colleagues report regarding their experiences with university administration hard to believe, for in the thirty-five years of my professional experience in universities, I have witnessed such remarkable leadership. I wish every faculty member could have shared my lifetime experience of university administrators who support but do not interfere; who guide, but do not dictate; who listen, and thoughtfully make valid criticisms and suggestions; who listen, and prevent you from making mistakes; who understand the value of one's attempts to seek and to provide the necessary financial support to continue and enhance these values. These administrators with whom I have dealt for so long are not paragons of virtue. They are human, and they have often had to say "no." Like a parent who usually supports in every way possible, a "no" is recognized as something new, as an emergency, and is cause for serious pause and reflection. The complexities of a school such as Starpoint are so great that negative replies will often have to be made. For the most part, however, university administrators will meet the high demands of their offices, and will exemplify what I have so long found to be so important and forthcoming. From a selfish point of view a school such as this one is a most unique bridge between the university and the community, and as such its public relations values are self-evident. In this light, if in no other, the school deserves penetrating administrative support.

Fifth. We mentioned earlier that a different-order responsibility is placed on those who work here and on those who are served by this school. This school is unique. It is unique because it is a part of a University where research must always be a major goal. It is unique because it serves a selected segment of children. It is unique because it has resources within the city and state communities which other schools find hard to duplicate. Parents who ask that their children be accepted into this school and whose requests are granted must immediately accept a concomitant responsibility. They must willingly loan their children for purposes of research. There is little known about the learning processes of children with learning disabilities. There is less known about the same issues when adolescents are considered. We will never make advancements unless research is undertaken and research cannot be undertaken except when the children of this school are involved.

Research has received a bad name in recent years, because selfish research has been too often undertaken, research which benefits the researcher, but not those who have the problems being researched. Present day restrictions on research almost make it impossible to accomplish anything which is of value. Parents of children in this school must enter into a partnership with the university faculty, and welcome the fact that their children can participate in something which may broaden the horizons of our knowledge about these complex problems. There are many and appropriate protections for children and their families. University committees on the use of human subjects are important protectors. The first line of research is the willingness of parents and children to engage in appropriate studies. Children will not be hurt by thoughtfully developed studies, carefully screened by administrative committees, and carefully supervised by research directors. Studies in the field of learning disabilities in all aspects of learning are needed. Studies are needed in the area of human genetics and learning disabilities, in the biochemical correlates to learning disabilities, in the use of medication to control behavior of children, in teaching materials, in neuro-radiological diagnostic techniques, in neuropsychological assessment proce-dures, in early diagnosis and intervention, in teacher education, and in many other correlates to learning disabilities. It is the obligation of parents whose children are served by this school and in others like this one, to cooperate in the total research program of the institution. It is the obligation of the school and university administration to develop a research program appro-priate to this institute and appropriately focused on that which can be accomplished here, and to see this as much an obligation of a university ap-proaching the twenty-first century as any other aspect of the academic pro-gram which is espoused.

These latter comments set me thinking along a somewhat parallel line. I wonder if parents are lulled into a false sense of security in the belief that professional people have all the answers regarding learning disabilities? I wonder if parents believe that professionals know what learning disabilities are? I wonder if parents think that professionals have a unanimous concept regarding the nature of learning disabilities? If the reply to these musings is positive, then parents are falling under the spell of a misconception, some parts of which parents themselves have created.

Professional people, although they know much more today than they did three decades ago regarding the nature of learning disabilities, gen-erally still have less information and knowledge than they should have about this most complicated aspect of child development. Research is still needed in vast efforts on all fronts: neurological, nutritional, educational, psycho-logical, communication, and many other facets of human development. Re-search comes slowly, and because of this a massive world-wide search thrust is required, one which is coordinated and permits replication. This school can participate in this important endeavor.

Some professional people, with all due respect, do not know what learning disabilities are. We fail to discriminate or have never differentiated between true learning disabilities, i.e., those which are the result of percep-tual processing deficits (and in turn the result of an actual or inferred neuro-logical dysfunction), and the environmentally produced problems of learn-ing. The two issues are markedly different insofar as diagnosis, prognosis, and particularly treatment regimens are concerned. The two issues, when constantly viewed as one, create confusion at all levels of planning, and as a result little forward movement is possible. It is a true example of too many cooks spoiling the broth. Children with environmentally produced problems of learning are not learning disabilities children, if the latter are accurately defined, historically and neurologically. The confusion continues when it is believed that the situation is clarified in the minds of professionals. It is not; indeed, it becomes more confused almost daily. This school can assist in the clarification of this confusion.

I wonder if you know how many accurately defined children who have learning disabilities there are? We in the United States do not know the size of our population. To my knowledge there is not one accurate study in the world's literature which gives us information as to the real size of this problem. There are guesses and estimates, but no firm data. We have market studies on the potential sales of automobiles, radios, television sets; we have epidemiological studies relative to communicable diseases; we have data regarding the agricultural needs of world populations, but we have no data to indicate accurately the size of one of the most complicated of all developmental problems of childhood. How can governments adequately plan when we have no adequate definition in common usage and no data to indicate the vastness of the problem? Should governments appropriate thirty cents, thirty pence, thirty centimes, or should they annually appropriate three hundred million dollars, pounds, francs or yen in the solution of this problem? Without accurate data, it is little wonder to me that governments hesitate when this matter comes into their deliberations. We have the techniques for adequate epidemiological and demographic studies; there are people who would undertake this work, but funds to do the research have not been forthcoming. This school and university can contribute to this knowledge and can initiate studies in the Dallas/Fort Worth area to provide answers.

There is another misconception which bothers parents when it is mentioned. That concept, promulgated by parents in the United States for the first time in 1963, says that all learning disabilities children are of normal or near normal intellectual level. This is not so. Learning disabilities are characteristic of children of all mental levels, from the highest to the lowest. It is forgotten that the research of the 1930s and 1940s, on what was later to be called learning disabilities, was carried out with the cooperation of mentally retarded youths. This is not an issue which has a cut-off point, yet in the effort to put the child's best foot forward, the issue of low mental ability has been ignored. There are lots of intellectually normal children and youth with learning disabilities. I work with them every day. There are also many with lower levels of intellectual functioning who are not being provided an adequate education, and who indeed are being discriminated against. Modern society cannot permit this to continue to happen. This school can help to set this issue right.

I think of other problems which deter our efforts in achieving either a national or a world-wide solution to our problem, issues in which this school can share a part in seeking solutions. Perhaps it would be helpful in a short space just to list some of the more important of these for your thoughtful consideration.

1. What is the relationship of learning disabilities to either genetic or familial factors? This is a problem needing much study.

2. The relationship of artificial food coloring and additives to learning disabilities, childhood hyperactivity, and other behavioral characteristics is still equivocal. It is not a settled matter by any means, although there are well-intentioned people on both sides of this argument.

3. In large cities, is the total ecological issue, particularly that involving the constant ingestion of foul air, a factor in producing what now appears to be a larger population than in former years of children and youth with learning disabilities.

4. Dare we raise a question regarding the function of the placenta and its capacity to protect the developing fetus from "normal" medications prescribed during pregnancy to say nothing of the hard or soft drugs or alcohol which are in such common usage world-wide? Are these causes of learning disabilities in children? Research is demanded quickly.

5. Do learning disabilities diminish in their impact as the child grows older? This is equivocal. Certainly I can see hundreds of adolescents, few of whose needs are being met. These young people who are frantically trying to find their way into secondary schools and to find a niche for themselves in adult society. It is a misconception that learning disabilities somehow evaporate with adolescence. They are often minimized by carefully structured educational programs at the elementary school level. They don't go away by themselves. The learning disabled adolescent presents the current challenge to parent associations.

In recent years we have heard much about the "link" between learning disabilities and juvenile delinquency. There are those who indicate this link is as high as 75 percent. I question these data, and do so strongly. Are these data the result of longitudinal studies? If so, where were they done and by whom? What is the definition used to label these children as learning disabled? Was it a label provided after the fact when socioemotional factors served as an overlay to school achievement, or is it a label accurately defined and historically appropriate for the given problem under study? It is easy to be glib with words like learning disabilities, link, and delinquency. It is important that we really have the data before further compound labels are placed on an already confused issue.

6. There is a myth that any good teacher can solve the problems of any or all children with learning disabilities. This is not so, any more than it is true that any mechanic can safely repair the motors of a 747 airliner. Teachers may have skills which mechanics don't, but the general preparation

of a teacher is not that which is needed to meet the needs of children with processing deficits who represent one of the most complicated of all child development problems. A highly skilled educator-psychologist-engineer is needed. These can be prepared if universities are provided with the faculty who know how to do it! Parents cannot be expected to accept less.

As I re-read what I have written, I could be accused of being revolutionary. I am a revolutionist, I guess, on behalf of children. For too long now children have suffered at the hands of well-intentioned educators who simply do not know the nature of the problem being treated and who do not have the skills to modify their efforts on behalf of the complicated child problem before them. Too long those with vested interests, which are not learning disabilities, have been permitted to climb on the band wagon of learning disabilities and to confuse the issue almost beyond ability to salvage it. Too long have some children with learning disabilities and with lower capacities been excluded from the central thought of parent organizations and legislation. Too long have children and their families suffered because the educational community has not risen to meet their pressing needs. If to right these unjust situations is to be called a revolutionary, then I am pleased to be seen as that. I hope that others, discarding vested interests in those not specific to this problem, will join to make right for families those things their children truly need and must have. It is to this end that the Starpoint School must dedicate itself.

12

HYPERACTIVE CHILDREN

Their Needs and Curriculum

*H*YPERACTIVE CHILDREN by reason of their concomitant learning and management problems constitute one of the most perplexing issues to teachers and administrators and indeed to emotionally normal children within the school. Teachers as a group have long been known for their willingness and ability to serve children often far beyond the call of duty. As one talks with teachers one observes that the point at which they fine it difficult to incorporate a child within their purview is when that child by reason of learning behavior, which is too often not understood, fails to respond on any basis to instruction or when his physical behavior per se daily brings him and his classmates to the brink of catastrophe. Failure by the child to respond to a teacher's instruction and his failure to adjust within the limitations established by the teacher for group behavior constitutes a challenge to the teacher by the child which pits one against another. In this paper we shall try to analyze this educational and behavioral impasse and to make certain suggestions for its amelioration. We shall examine, first, the issue of hyperactivity. Secondly, we shall consider the essential needs of hyperactive children. Thirdly, we shall examine what the educational setting and curriculum considerations must be for children with these needs. Hyperactivity in this writer's considered opinion consists of two major aspects, both of which are interrelated. Furthermore we consider these phenomena to be organically based. The concept of the organic nature of hyperactivity is admittedly to a large extent theoretical at our present state of knowledge. Although very little has been done about the problem insofar as education is concerned, the

Address delivered at Syracuse University, Division of Special Education and Rehabilitation, 1967.

brain-injured child as a clinical entity has been known to medicine, psychology and to a lesser extent to education for the past three or four decades. We do not refer necessarily here to the grossly involved child with cerebral palsy, although many of these children do come within the scope of what we shall say. We do not include children with epilepsy, although these are all children with neurological problems and many of them will fall into the group of which we will speak. We think now of brain-injured children who by reason of prenatal, perinatal, or postnatal etiology show an exceedingly interesting syndrome of psychological characteristics. As a result they often fail to respond to learning situations with appropriate achievement. They fail to adjust as a child to a child's society within the expectancies of the adult society.

In speaking of the brain-injured child we enter into a semantic jungle out of which the profession has yet to find its way. In the current literature one can quickly develop a list of more than forty terms all used frequently and all referring to the same child. Little wonder that parents are confused; the professions are more than confused. While we will not trouble you with the total list of terms in this professional quagmire, we should perhaps mention several with which you are familiar. Perhaps you speak of these children as dyslexic, or perhaps you have heard them called children with language disorders, with cognitive defects, with maturational lag, with minimal brain dysfunction, with neurophysiological immaturity, or with chronic brain dysfunction. Perhaps you have called them hyperkinetic children or children with specific or special learning disorders. If you have heard these terms of if you have used them yourself, we are here on the same frequency. I call them brain-injured children which is what in reality they probably are, although we do not have the diagnostic instrumentation sufficiently sensitive or sophisticated as yet to make this diagnosis definitive every time. When that day arrives we shall undoubtedly see that most if not all hyperactive children have a special neurological basis to their behavior. We shall also undoubtedly learn that many children, now called culturally deprived, have a secondary neurological basis to their problem. We shall learn that many so-called emotionally disturbed children are in reality something else in addition to being emotionally disturbed. While this definitiveness of diagnosis may yet be for the future, sufficient diagnostic accuracy is available to us at present to make possible sound educational programs.

One thing we do know, and that pertains to the nature of the learning characteristics of brain-injured children. We know how they function. We know what their characteristics of learning and behavior are in sufficient detail to be able to make educational generalizations about them which are accurate and helpful in planning for their growth and adjustment. We also know that there are many children without a specific diagnosis of neurological disorder who demonstrate the same characteristics of learning and adjustment as do those children on whom definitive diagnosis can be obtained. These are often emotionally disturbed hyperactive children. To exclude these children from our consideration simply because they have been born two or three decades earlier than professional maturity would like, is absurd.

In the absence of anything better these children should be considered as if they were brain injured, as if their learning and behavior were organically based, for they will apparently respond to appropriate educational intervention if they are so considered and handled. To come full circle to our topic: brain-injury in children is chiefly characterized by hyperactivity from a psychoeducational point of view.

As we stated earlier, hyperactivity has two interrelated aspects which we have already said we feel are organically based. The first of these is sensory hyperactivity; the second, motor hyperactivity. Either of these aspects, if they are present in a child, brings the child into direct conflict with the educational program. In the case of sensory hyperactivity school achievement is directly impaired; in the case of motor hyperactivity, school achievement is also involved but in addition adjustment in the classroom and in the home becomes most difficult.

Let us examine the matter of sensory hyperactivity. One of the chief characteristics of this is that of *distractability*. As a result of what is assumed to be a lack of cortical control, the child is unable to attend to a given stimulus or group of stimuli for a sufficient period of time to be able to make an appropriate intellectual reaction, or, to state it differently, to have appropriate conditioning take place. These children by reason of their disability are unable negatively to react to extraneous stimuli in their environment. They tend to react to the unessential. They seem almost to have a compulsion to react to every stimulus within their sensory field. There was a time when we felt that this characteristic of these children was essentially a matter of reaction to visual stimuli. We now know that the problem they have involves all of the sensory systems: audition, tactual, thermal, and to a lesser extent insofar as adjustment is concerned taste and smell. The tendency of these children is to react to whatsoever stimulus comes within their perceptive field irrespective of what it is that is expected of them at the time. As normal people we tend to adapt negatively to the unessential in our experience. Advertisers recognize this and for this reason we are pommelled dozens of times a day by the same refrain in the hope that mere repetition will bring it to our conscious attention. However, most of us are impervious to most of what goes on around us. Stimuli are permitted to exist in space and in time, but to most we do not pay them the compliment of a reaction. It is this unique ability of human beings to ignore which makes it possible for us to live through a

complex day and yet to retain sufficient energy to enjoy an evening's enter-
tainment.

This is not the situation with the hyperactive child. He, for whatsoever reason, is unable to attend to the primary stimulus in his sensory field
because of the multitude of unessential stimuli in his environment to which
he is forced to attend. Any color, noise, or movement, irrespective of its appropriateness to the task at hand, may cause his attention to be distracted
and may cause him to respond. In thus responding he fails to react as the
adult would wish him to react to a specific learning assignment.

The issue of sensory hyperactivity is manifest in a number of serious
ways. As a result of the child's constant need to react, he is characterized by
an exceedingly short attention span. This writer has many times seen children whose attention span was at best no more than a minute or two. When a
child has a two-minute attention span, under optimal conditions, what is the
teacher-pupil problem when the reading lesson is planned for a twenty-
minute period? The last eighteen minutes, more or less, becomes a disciplinary hassle, not an instructional experience.

Envision for a moment a typical page out of a child's reading book.
On this page, for example, there may be 150 words, the average length of
which would be approximately five letters. Hence, there may be on the page
a minimum of 750 letters. Each letter and word has a space in between.
Thus, there is additionally a minimum of 750 spaces. Each letter forms an
angle in relationship to another letter or to several letters. Hence, there are
unlimited numbers of angles and relationships of a visual nature which are
possible. There may be a picture on the page which includes numerous details, colors, and relationships. Thus on this single page there are hundreds
of stimuli. The words are stimuli; the letters are stimuli, the spaces and angles and colors are stimuli. In this highly stimulating situation, which for the
normal child constitutes no problem, because of his ability to adapt negatively, a hyperactive child is asked by his teacher to "Begin reading today on
the first word of the first line of the second paragraph." That first word is
the *figure*. Insofar as the child can attend and not be distracted he may focus
on the first word. If he is distracted by the unessential stimuli on the printed
page, stimuli which forms for normal children the *background,* he will be
unable to attend to the essential word, the figure, long enough to make an
appropriate response. Reading specialists and psychologists tell us that these
children are characterized by a figure-ground reversal problem—a *figure-
background pathology*—which is indeed true. More basic than this, however, is the inability of the child to refrain from reacting to unessential stimuli. This results in a figure-ground problem. The end result of this situation

is the child's inability to respond orally in spite of the fact that he may know the meaning of most of the words on the printed page.

Another child is asked by his teacher or by a psychologist to assemble a block design or to function with parquetry blocks. There may be from six to twelve blocks — six to twelve stimuli. Often these may be multicolored materials. Because of the multiplicity of stimuli, the child may not be able to conceptualize the design he is asked to copy. The inability of the child to assemble the blocks appropriately is called *dissociation,* but in reality this psychological problem is likewise another manifestation of sensory hyperactivity. Dissociation, the inability to conceptualize things as a whole, is a serious deterrent to good learning.

Turn your attention to still another area of learning. How many times have teachers prepared an arithmetic drill experience for children? Let us assume that it consists of a single piece of paper on which twelve problems have been placed. Let us further assume that these consist of three-digit addition problems arranged in three rows of four problems each. On the paper are 36 numerals, 12 addition symbols, and 12 straight lines under the 12 problems. Angles, spaces, and other visual factors constitute additional stimuli. The child is likely to obtain the correct answer to problem Number One, because its location on the page brings it into relationship with two edges of the paper and a corner. This provides sufficient structure for the child to allow him to attend. Furthermore, on two sides of the arithmetic problem there is space only and no distracting stimuli. From that point on, however, as he moves to problem two, three, or four, the chances are that he will get few problems correctly solved. Extraneous visual stimuli surrounding the problems internal on the paper coupled by a third factor, the child's insecurity *in space,* constitute a major series of hurdles to successful achievement.

Oftentimes a child's attachment to a single stimulus and the pervading influence of this stimulus also will cause failure to learn. We speak of this as *perseveration.* The prolonged after-effect of a stimulus will interfere with the reception and coding of new stimuli to the end that learning fails to take place.

While we have been using examples of sensory hyperactivity which are essentially visual in nature, the same problems may characterize the child's attention insofar as other sensory modalities are concerned. Figure-background problems appear as the child attempts to sort out auditory stimuli. They are significant, although apparently not in the same degree, with tactual situations involving discrimination of figure from background. Localization and identification of gustatory stimuli is similarly affected. Auditory perseveration and dissociation are not unusual in hyperactive children or in brain-injured children. Sensory hyperactivity, then, is an essential element in the failure of the child to respond appropriately to learning situations. Furthermore, this situation quickly becomes compounded, for in the failure of the child to respond appropriately on a sensory basis, ego concepts are immediately involved. The ego concept of the teacher is also involved, for the child does not respond to her experience or wisdom in the same way as do other children. This is a threat to the adult. The inability of the child to have the reward of a success experience in terms of adult standards and norms for him causes frustration and a lessening of his tolerance level to additional frustrations. There shortly appears a significant emotional overlay to what originally was a neurophysiological problem. As a matter of fact, the term, hyperactive child, is often used synonymously with the term, emotionally disturbed child. The latter issue clouds the former completely. This clouding of what in reality is the basic problem, results in much mismanagement of these children from an educational and psychological point of view in the considered opinion of this writer.

Motor hyperactivity is the second aspect of the problem which must be considered. This more accurately is called *motor disinhibition,* but irrespective of terminology, it is the inability of the child to refrain from reacting to a stimulus which produces a motor response. Anything which can be pulled, turned, pushed, twisted, bent, torn, wiggled, scratched, or otherwise manipulated will be so handled. As some children cannot refrain from reacting to unessential visual or auditory stimuli, so some are also unable to refrain from reacting to stimuli which produce movements. These are the children who cannot sit still. Internal as well as external stimuli are significant. An epigastric sensation is as distracting to some as is a tight belt or the sensation of a shirt sleeve on the arm to others. These are children who fall out of their chairs. These are children who in a line are always pushing or pulling others around them. Some similar corporal behavior is seen in the normal adjustment of the preadolescent, and careful differential discrimination at that chronological age must be made between what is normative behavior and what is pathological. These are children who overact to certain stimuli, for example, the ringing of a fire drill bell. These are children who seem to fall apart behavioristically in the face of any tension producing social situation. A birthday party can result in tragedy for these children—the tragedy of never being invited again. The diffuse and uncontrolled *space* of the playground, the auditorium, the school cafeteria, or the school hallways constitutes a stimulus the nature of which the child and often the adult fails to understand but which violates the child's being and may preclude any possibility of his appropriate adjustment. Tensions—which are physical—which result from these experiences and from these situations in turn produce motor reactions in the hyperactive child. The combination of motor disinhibition and sensory distractability constitutes a barrier to good learning which is often unprecedented in the experience of the individual teacher and more so in the experience of the child's parents.

From this brief discussion of the nature of hyperactivity, it can be observed that the issue we deal with is one filled with psychopathology. Such psychopathology can be measured and can be described by careful psychological assessment. It is the responsibility of psychologists to delve into the nature of the child's intellectual response pattern and to ascertain the essential elements inherent in it. Without this psychological blueprint, the educator cannot conveniently, if at all, develop an educational program. The failure to adequately describe the nature of children has left educators with their only recourse, namely, to try to educate children under labels and in groups without understanding the fallacy of such grouping or the inherent implication of the label. It is possible for psychologists to so adequately describe a child in terms of the psychopathology of attention span, or figure-ground relationship, of dissociation, of motor disinhibition, or perseveration, of angulation problems, edging, immaturity, and of self-concept distortions visually, auditorily, tactually, and if need be in terms of other sensory modalities, that teachers have before them a true picture of the warp and woof out of which the child emerges. Without this, time is lost to both educator and child. Without this, a truly appropriate educational program may never emerge. Without this, the child's spiraling into further maladjustment and personal disorganization is accelerated. Psychologists indeed have a unique and significant role to play in the educational regimen for the hyperactive child.

If this be the nature of hyperactivity insofar as education is concerned, what then are the needs of the child? We must recognize that the problems of the hyperactive child are in most cases those which he has experienced for his total life. Except for those which are definitely traceable to postnatal disturbances, most of the etiology will be found in prenatal or perinatal insult to the developing organism. Because of neurological disturbance, the child may be unable to appropriately perform fine motor movements involved in sucking. Nursing then can become a failure experience from the first instance. What should have been a source of satisfaction to both the mother and the child and should be the basis of a long series of success experiences, begins as a failure experience for both. The failure to suck or to swallow efficiently is extended to delayed sitting, to delayed walking, talking, running, learning to balance, and to most other skills which are learned by normal children in the daily activities of childhood without extensive formal teaching. The child soon comes to conceptualize himself as "I am one who cannot," instead of the normal child's approach to himself of "I am one who can."

In practically every psychologist's file there are many records of children which contain drawings of persons. These drawings are oftentimes fragmatized and incoherent translations of what the child conceptualized the human form to be. When one's own fingers fail to perform satisfactorily, one can not for long claim ownership of the offending digits. When fingers fail to tie shoes, to button buttons, to "zip zippers, to pick up a glass, or to do the many other things without accidents, which are required of them each day, they tend to become divorced psychologically from the body of which they are an inherent part. When legs won't kick a ball, or arms appropriately swing a bat, or when arms together cannot manipulate a knife and a fork to the end that appropriate eating behavior is experienced, then faulty notions develop of what the human form really is. Negative self-concepts and poor concepts of body image are almost universal in appraising hyperactive children. "Why can't my hand do what my eye sees?" is a plaintive question asked of the writer on more than one occasion when a brain-injured child — a hyperactive child — tried to cooperate and to perform on visual-motor tests. This child is making a self-diagnosis of his visuo-motor problem.

Hyperactive children have had a remarkable experience with failure, but a poor experience with success. They have found few bases on which they are able to satisfy adults or to meet the standards of adjustment and behavior expected of them by adults. Since reading and writing also involve fine-motor movements, these skills, like sucking from a bottle or swallowing, are also defective. A child who dissociates will have extreme difficulty in learning manuscript writing, yet how infrequently are these children taught cursive writing when they are beginning to write. This is a time when success is uniquely important, but the child's first attempts at writing are met with failure because the method of manuscript writing itself produces failure in that it inherently involves those very concepts of association and dissociation in which the hyperactive children are characterized by pathology. The early success experience he needs is supplanted by another failure experience of which he has already had more than his share. The basic need of hyperactive children is for success — success in something in which adults and adult society genuinely believe. This need is not dissimilar to that of all children. However, most children have had their share of success. They have found ways of appealing to the ego needs of their parents and their adults. They smile politely. They parrot words and then are reported to "talk." The whole family including all the in-laws are formally notified when the child takes his first step. And when at eighteen months in his random motions he inadvertently picks up a plastic baseball bat which father has brought home, father's pleasure is almost beyond measure and the tale is related to anyone in the office the next day who will feign to listen. Children have success experiences. Through them parents have success experiences. This prompts parents to set more situations in which the child can prove himself, and when he does the basis for strong parent-child relationships are present. The hyperactive child, hyperactive for whatsoever reason, does not have this built-in insurance for strong relationships. More and more his behavior propels him outside the circle of acceptance in family, in neighborhood, in school, and in the community generally.

We come now to the implications for education of what has thus far been said. This can only briefly be discussed, for in detail the issue is a complicated one. There are some essentials however, which must be kept in mind at all times in dealing with the hyperactive child, whether it be teacher-child relationship or parent-child relationship.

First, it is necessary for the adult to find a level of achievement at which the child already as success on which to base whatever educational program is possible. Second, the educational program for a given child must directly reflect the psychopathology which is inherent in the child. Thirdly, the educational program must always be presented to the child in a learning situation and within a time span which permits conditioning to take place. Fourth, the teaching experience must always be carried out within arm's reach of the teacher. Finally, the program for the child must be structured environmentally and methodologically. Let us look at each of these five elements which are among the most important considerations in the education of the hyperactive child.

We have said, first, that it is necessary for the adult to find a level of achievement at which the child already has success on which it is possible to build toward additional successes. One of the great misunderstandings which educators continue to perpetuate is that of remedial education. There is, I suspect, a place for remedial education for certain children. Remediation, however, implies that something has taken place, something has been learned, which if modified in some form, can bring better achievement to the individual. In the case of the hyperactive child whose failure expereinces are concomitant with very early futile attempts at adjustment, there is little to remediate. In contrast, new learning is required. Initial concepts must be established. The education is hyperactive children is not a matter for the remedial reading teacher. It is indeed something else entirely.

It is essential, then, for the teacher to carefully assess the skills of the child in all aspects of his learning and to find a level of competence so primitive that success is possible, not on a chance basis, but continuously. On this primitive level then, other learnings are based. Since, unfortunately, most of these children are "discovered" for the first time officially about the time they are in the third or fourth grade, this may mean that the teacher will have to retreat with the child to preacademic levels. It is very often the case that these children are unable to discriminate between colors, are unable to recognize forms, are unable to conceptualize total puzzles from their parts, are unable to write, are unable to name body parts, are unaware of spatial relationships, are unable to balance or to deal with walking boards or other equipment which requires gross motor activities. What role does remediation play here? Something different is required. It is quite obvious to this writer that for the great majority of these children there is little possibility of retaining them successfully in the regular grades of their schools. Special class placement is required which involves a type of clinical teaching not usually the pattern at the present time in special education. This recommendation for special class placement is made by one who is known to feel that the goal of all special education is the integration of the child into the normal educational program insofar as possible and as quickly as possible. These children present too many unique differences to permit their easy, convenient or appropriate retention in the regular grade. Special facilities are required if they are ultimately to reassume a place in the normal educational stream.

It is futile for the teacher to try to build an educational program on the failure experiences of the past. It is futile then to try to conceptualize a method which is conceived in terms of the chronological age of the child or indeed oftentimes in terms of his mental age. It is mandated that the program be conceived not on failures, but at a level where success was experienced at some time. Retreat to the primitive is thus the rule. Retreat must be made to a point wherein achievements favored by both the social structures and the child can be experienced. On this success, clinical teaching will build new constructs of success and out of it will come a more perfectly organized human being.

We have said, secondly, that the educational program must directly reflect the psychopathology inherent in the child. There is little value in providing a child who is characterized by figure-background pathology with the typical reading lesson which we described earlier. If figure-ground relationship is a problem, then it goes without saying that reading materials must be provided which reduce figure-ground problems to a minimum. Instead of a reading book with many words on a single page, the reading material for this child may utilize many pages of paper with only one word at a time per page. Now there is no background stimuli for the child to confuse with the foreground figure. The figure alone is presented on the page. Twelve arithmetic problems would never be presented to this child at one time. Instead one problem per page will be given him to work, and one page at a time may be in his hand. In this procedure, problem number seven on the page of twelve problems of which we spoke cannot become confused with the stimuli of problems which surround it. Problem number seven now stands alone on its own piece of paper. The child sees it as it is without the interference of background stimuli from other problems.

The child we speak about is probably dissociating. He cannot see the whole because of the individual parts which have great attraction for him. This child must be taught to write using cursive methods from the beginning. He will not be taught manuscript writing at all. One method minimizes his pathology; the other accentuates it. Some children who dissociate may need additional help from the teacher even when in arithmetic he places one problem alone on a piece of paper. He may then enclose the single problem within heavy black lines in order that the child conceptualizes more easily the two or three digits to be added, the addition sign, and the line under it all as all being part of the same concept.

A further example of what we mean when we say that the teaching must reflect the psychopathology pertains to the hyper-responsiveness of the children to stimuli. True, usually this is a detriment to learning, but it can also be exploited by the teacher to the child's advantage. We know that the child is sensitive to stimuli and that extraneous stimuli are usually a deterrent to learning. However, in an appropriate learning environment, it is possible to increase the stimulus value of the thing the teacher desires the child to see. This can be done sufficiently so that the child will be attracted to a given visual presentation long enough for positive conditioning to take place. For example, in handwriting, instead of using a white paper with faint blue lines, the teacher may use a brilliant colored paper with many different colored lines. The teacher here is increasing the stimulus value of the line, the element he is anxious for the child to perceive as he attempts to write his name or a given set of letters or words. The brilliant colored paper serves to delineate the visual field within which the child is to write. This is using the disability to the child's advantage.

A final example of our meaning pertains to the problem of perseveration. Normally a teacher's instructional plan will be to accentuate similarities. Spelling may grow out of reading. Reading may grow out of social studies. Commonalities are stressed. With the hyperactive child who is perseverating, this is not the most appropriate procedure. Dissimilarities are stressed in order that one element not be perseverated into the next and thus confuse the child's perception of the second fact by the first. For example, reading might be followed by parquetry activities. These might be followed by motor training. Motor training might be followed by spelling. No two experiences are sufficiently similar to permit perseveration to be a significant issue. Or to put it differently, one experience follows another so different in kind that perseverative tendencies are easily displaced because of the unique differences.

There are literally hundreds of ways each day when the teacher, if he knows the disabilities of the child, can develop an instructional model for the child which either minimizes the disabilities, rules them out entirely, or exploits them to the advantage of the child and his adjustment. Unless the teacher knows the psychological or psychopathological blueprint of each child, however, what we are here suggesting is nearly impossible.

We have said, thirdly, that the educational program must always take place in a situation and within a time span which permits conditioning to take place. If a child is hyperactive to extraneous stimuli, it goes without saying that the stimuli must be reduced in the learning environment if an optimal learning situation is to be created for him. If one considers the best classroom in the elementary school in which he is familiar he will conjure up an image of a delightful situation. It is filled with things which are intended to motivate the children. It is a happy, gay, and pleasant place in which to be. The best classroom in your imagination, however, is the worst classroom for the hyperactive child. There are too many stimuli which the hyperactive child cannot avoid. These become, for him, deterrents to his education. They are elements of continual distraction.

The classroom for hyperactive children should be as free from distractions as it is possible to achieve. In an ideal classroom, from the point of view of this writer, walls, furniture, woodwork and floor covering would all be the same color. Windows would have opaque glass to reduce stimuli outside the building. The ceiling would be sound treated, and the floor would have wall-to-wall carpeting. Shelves would be enclosed with wooden doors. Every effort would be made to have the environment surrounding the learner as stimulus free as possible. The goal is to provide a setting in which the environment itself does not distract the child. To state it differently — the environmental stimuli will be reduced to the point where the child will find it possible to attend to that which is immediately within his visual field.

Another aspect of stimuli reduction pertains to the matter of space. We mentioned previously that hyperactive children experience increased tension in space over which they feel no psychological control. As space increases so stimuli increase; the converse is also true. Thus, the classroom for hyperactive children will be smaller than the traditional one and it has been found helpful to provide within the classroom small cubicles for each child. Within the small area the child finds a spatial arrangement which is unique for him and one in which he can feel that he is the master. If necessary he can actually reach out and touch the three walls of his cubicle, as one child told the writer, "to remind myself where I am." When the child is oriented to space, he can begin to organize himself in relation to his environment. He can begin to relate himself to his environment. Although the environmental area is small, his feeling of satisfaction within it serves as a springboard from which he can begin to have other types of success experiences with the things of learning and achievement — abstract as well as concrete.

We mentioned as a fourth element the necessity of the adult to carry out the teaching within arm's reach of the child. This is not always possible, we recognize. However, it is essential that as close a personal relationship as possible be established between the adult and the child. Although we are not now dealing with psychotic children, the hyperactive child, because of his tendency to dissociate and to reverse field, oftentimes has a very confused understanding of what the adult is like. His perception of the adult may be as inappropriate as are his perceptions of numerals, letters, or other symbols. The child is insecure in his relationship to his environment and to the things in it. If the teacher can always carry on the instruction with his hand on the child's arm or shoulder, the child experiences a definite and physical structure between himself and the adult. Teaching within arm's reach is not intended to have disciplinary implications. The sole implication is that of relationship structure.

Finally, in this discussion we have mentioned that the program for the child must be structured environmentally and methodologically. We have already mentioned the environmental structure through the utilization of stimuli reduction and the cubicle. In just as significant a way everything which goes on within the classroom must be structured. This is not a place for permissiveness — at least not in the beginning. How can one make adequate choices which are demanded within the permissive construct if one has never had a success experience when choice has been possible? The fundamental learning theory to which we subscribe is one of conditioning completely infiltrated with psychoanalytic concepts. In seeking to find the primitive level on which to start learning experiences as we earlier mentioned, the teacher is in effect seeking a base upon which he can provide an adequate conditioning experience. As success responses are developed, as security in learning begins to be experienced, as confidence builds up, then choice can be provided. Whenever choice is provided, the child must also always have an escape valve available to him, a feeling of permission to retreat again to a level of performance on which he knows he can succeed. When this is not understood, the child may hesitate a long while before he tries something new. To remain too long on a behavioral plateau is itself not conducive to learning either.

Structure permeates the entire teaching concept. We speak of relationship structure between the teacher and the child. We speak of program structure in the conceptualization of the school day and program. We have seen the significance of environmental structure. We help the teacher to devise structured teaching materials in keeping with the psychopathological needs of the child. For a child whose whole life to date has been one of lack of structure and failure, the externally imposed structure provides him with a concrete fabric on which to rest his life. As Rappaport so accurately states in another situation, the environment and all its components must serve as an "ego-bank" to the child who has in the beginning nothing to invest, but from which he must withdraw his total life structure. As conditioning takes place positively and as the child begins to accurately see himself in relationship to his social order, the need for the external structuring can become less and less until indeed the hyperactive child may be able to re-establish himself as a member of the normal school group—and does so in many instances.

A few words need to be said further on the matter of teaching the hyperactive children. These children are multihandicapped children in the truest sense of the word. They present the most complex teaching problems of any in the entire spectrum of exceptional children. It occurs to me that in the approach which is being suggested here and which indeed has been tried sufficiently to convince this writer and many others of its efficacy, some solution to the education ot multihandicapped children may exist. Old approaches which have been tried within the fields of both general elementary education and special education have not proven to be valuable with seriously or even mildly multiple handicapped children. We speak now of such problems as the blind retarded child, the cerebral palsy child with visual, speech, and hearing problems, the aphasic retarded child, and other combinations of disabilities.

The hyperactive child is indeed similar to these. No two hyperactive children are the same in any respect. Neither the degrees of distractability nor the relationship between characteristics of psychopathology is ever identical in these children. In one child the problem may be chiefly visuo-motor; in a second, predominately audio-motor; in a third, hyperkinesis and tactuo-motor. The concept of a *group* of hyperactive children is a figment of someone's imagination, for groups of children with sufficiently homogeneous characteristics to be considered comparable for educational purposes do not exist. Small collections of from six to eight children with relatively similar problems can be organized, but within this social structure the teacher of hyperactive children soon understands that she must constantly deal with six or eight individuals as individuals. It will be many months before she is able to bring them together for even small group activities involving two or three children at one time. These educators are forced by the nature of the children to think in terms of individual needs.

The concept of individualization of instruction and the concept of a teacher meeting the needs of a child are old. In educational history they are first discussed by Froebel, Pestalozzi, and Herbart. They become the banner and cry of the progressive educators of the 1930s. These concepts were fundamental in the thinking of Dewey and practically every great educator of the western world of modern times. But how infrequently do we see them implemented in the classroom. In practical educational situations the concept of meeting the needs of children is nothing more than a hollow cliché. It is an empty symbol of something which should be an aggressive concept.

With the hyperactive child these concepts must take on immediate meaning. The education of the hyperactive child cannot be successfully consummated unless his individual needs are identified, thoroughly understood, and until these needs become so well known by the adults who work with him that they are a constant and vital part of every educational decision which is made in the child's behalf. As a teacher I cannot work successfully with the hyperactive child if all I know is his diagnosis and his intelligence quotient with perhaps the added plus of the mental age. As a teacher I cannot meet this child's needs if all I possess is a feeling that he like all children should be considered as an individual. I do not know from this which handle to grasp first to meet his needs. I don't know what his needs are. As a teacher, I have the right to expect that the diagnosticians who assess this child will provide me with a detailed description of how this child functions mentally, of what his psychological strengths are and what is the nature of his disabilities. I must know what the length of his attention span is. If I don't, I shall violate his being a dozen times a day by exceeding it. I must know when his attention span begins to increase as the result of success experiences which I am able to provide for him. If I don't, I shall undersell him educationally. I must know if he dissociates. If I don't, I shall violate him psychologically by not providing him with the visual cues to reduce the impact of his disability. I must know if he reverses field. If I don't, I shall perpetuate his problem by providing him with inappropriate educational materials. I must know if he is a psychologically damaged child, damaged to the extent that he has little or no feeling of personal worth, for if I don't, I shall fail to provide him with those learning experiences which may give him the solidity he needs for a positive self concept to develop.

In wiring a computer after the program has been agreed upon, extraordinary care must be taken to assure that every concept is translated into the correct circuit. If this is done, it can be assumed that every idea, every measure, every desired goal will be translated electrically and mathemati-

cally into a symbol which can be understood and interpreted into a meaningful concept. So too with the hyperactive child. Those who work with him—
his teachers and his parents for the most part, for they have him for more
hours than anyone else—must have information about the child in such minute detail that they, like the computer operator, can join this child, his
characteristics, and their teaching method and materials so perfectly together that the outcome is logical and can be predicted. The educational material, the education technique, the education setting for the hyperactive
child must reflect in a one-to-one relationship the psychopathology and
needs of the child. When this is done it can then be truly said that we have
provided an educational milieu for the hyperactive child. Then and only
then can education as a profession raise its head and say we have met this
child's needs.

This seeming utopia can be achieved. We cannot do it now sufficiently often to be able to serve even a fraction of the children who need it.
The status quo prevents sound educational programs too often still from being activated. Professional educators are still too comfortable with what
they do to try to do it differently. We still teach all children by the manuscript
method! Too few administrators understand this problem to permit the too
few teachers who are prepared to practice their learning in behalf of these
children. College professors to prepare these teachers are almost non-
existent today. The situation will change in the years ahead, for the very nature of the children requires that it change. We have seen radical changes in
our *understanding* of these children since 1940. There is little question in my
mind, but that in a comparable amount of time in the future we shall see the
understanding translated into action programs and the needs of these children more nearly universally met.

PROBLEMS IN THE EDUC
OF CHILDREN
WITH LEARNING DISABILITIES
AND SOME PRACTICAL SOLUTIONS

$\mathcal{T}$HE FIELD OF EDUCATION for children with learning disabilities is undoubtedly one of the most confused problems in all of childhood education.
To trace the reasons for this confusion is a long and laborious job, and is unessential to this statement. Briefly stated, the reasons for the lack of any coherent direction and the failure to reach a meeting of the minds regarding it
on the part of professionals, are due to a number of obvious factors. Chief
among these are (1) the demands of parents for treatment programs before
large numbers of professionals were thoroughly aware of the nature of the
problem; (2) inadequate research foundations in all aspects of the complicated problem; (3) failure of universities to prepare a qualified professional
corps and its concomitance, (4) the resulting inadequate supply of well-
prepared teachers; (5) the inadequate and directionless definitions of the
problems which have appeared in the literature in the past two decades and
their inclusion into official laws or regulations; (6) the lack of any epidemiological data to indicate the size of the problem in relation to solutions; and
(7) the thoughtless fads and fashions in education, psychology and medicine
applied to this group of children which in turn have created additional confusions and misdirection. There are other reasons for this unfortunate state
which surrounds educational efforts in behalf of children with learning disabilities. Those we have mentioned will serve at least to highlight the point
we are making here. The field of education is confused and children with
learning disabilities are the unfortunate recipients of this confusion.

It is easy to point out problems. It is less easy to suggest appropriate

Paper presented at International Federation of Learning Disabilities, Montreal,
August 1976.

utions. It is very difficult, although possible, to get solutions integrated into new practices. Unless good solutions are substituted for inadequate practices, unless good solutions are seen as better substitutes for the inadequate status quo, and unless those in positions to help reform national, provincial, or state programs do so in ways which reflect correct thinking, professional education and psychology become only self-serving. The true needs of children may forever be unmet. This is what is happening in the field of learning disabilities in the United States if one reads carefully the growing literature relating adolescent learning disability to juvenile delinquency and to social maladjustment (Murray, 1976). A paper such as this can easily fall into the trap of being totally negative. In order to reach positive solutions, considerable negativism will have to be recorded. The aim here, however, is to suggest positive solutions to some of the most negative aspects we see apparent in the field at this time.

A SOLUTION LIES IN DEFINITION

One solution to the observed confusion lies in the wide-spread acceptance of an appropriate definition of the problem of learning disabilities. I have written on this matter frequently. I do so again here at the expense of being redundant, because definition is basic to everything else we say.

The term learning disabilities is recognized historically as an artifact (Hallahan and Cruickshank 1973). It is a term originally suggested by a small group of parents, agreed to be used by a still smaller group of professions in 1963 and 1964, and one which spread like wild fire by thousands of people in medicine, education, psychology, and other professions who had had minimal, if any, contact with the problem, but found it a convenient term.

As we have stated elsewhere, most of the published definitions are essentially definitions by exclusions, i.e., telling us what the problem is *not,* not what it is. One cannot develop a strong national program of education on the basis of negatives. In 1975, a strong positive definition of learning disabilities was published, the result of two years of thoughtful discussion on the part of a small national committee in the United States whose work was critiqued by many more persons who were competent to make judgments (Hobbs 1975).* The definition is worth considering for it contains the elements basic to other solutions we will discuss in this paper.

*Members of the committee consisted of Joseph Wepman, Ph.D., University of Chicago; Charles Strother, Ph.D., University of Washington; Cynthia Deutsch, Ph.D., New York University; Ann Morency, Ph.D., University of Chicago; and William Cruickshank, Ph.D., University of Michigan.

We view learning disabilities as being the result of two other factors, each equally significant and each an antecedent to the learning disability per se. Learning disabilities are the end results of perceptual processing disabilities, which in turn are the result of some aspect of neurological dysfunction. The latter may be diagnosable, or assumed to be present given the present state of neurological arts. If there is a perceptual processing deficit involving any one or more of the sensory modalities, then there must be neurophysiological involvement. The two are interrelated. If there is no perceptual processing deficit, then there is no learning disability as it is defined here. There may be problems of learning resulting from any one of several different socio-emotional or environmental factors, but these are of a different order, psychologically and educationally, from that which we consider here. The failure to understand these differences in large measure accounts for the confusion to which we are addressing ourselves here. Learning disabilities in this paper and in the definition to which we refer, are stated in psychoeducational terms, for such are the focus needed most of the time by most of the children and their families. These, then, are children *of any age* and *of any intellectual level*

> who demonstrate a substantial deficiency in a particular aspect of academic achievement because of perceptual or perceptual-motor handicaps, regardless of etiology of other contributing factors. The term perceptual as used here relates to those mental (neurological) processes through which the child acquires his basic alphabets of sounds and forms. The term perceptual handicap refers to inadequate ability in such areas as the following: recognizing fine differences between auditory and visual discriminating features underlying the sounds used in speech and the orthographic forms used in reading; retaining and recalling those discriminated sounds and forms in both short- and long-term memory; ordering the sounds and forms sequentially, both in sensory and motor acts . . . ; distinguishing figure-ground relationships . . . ; recognizing spatial and temporal orientations . . . ; obtaining closure . . . ; integrating intersensory information . . . ; relating what is perceived to specific motor functions.

To these characteristics of what the child *is* can be added also such elements as dissociation, resulting in part from closure, mentioned above; short attention span, which may account for several of the factors previously listed; perseveration; and of ultimate significance, an inadequate body image and self-concept. This is what learning disability *is,* and, although never called by this name, is to what Goldstein, Strauss, Werner, Wepman, Kephart, Frostig, I, and many others referred long before the term "learning disabilities" was conceptualized per se. In these statements there is the core of a positive understanding of the problems, and there is also contained therein the core of several other solutions. We will refer to the definition again.

When this definition is commonly accepted and implemented, a giant step toward the solution of the total problem will have been realized. Until that time, problems of childhood learning having no relationship whatsoever to perceptual processing will creep under the umbrella term and create more confusion, misunderstanding, and impossible programming.

A SOLUTION LIES IN QUALIFIED UNIVERSITY PROFESSORS

Prior to 1963, when the term learning disabilities was essentially foisted without serious thought on the professions, the number of qualified professors, whether in research or in training, was less than minimal. This was certainly true in the United States, and as well characterizes the professional thrust in this area in most of the other developed countries of the world. In the United States, prior to 1963, the primary leadership constituted something in the realm of two dozen persons in all the professions. This is hardly the requisite number on which to base a national crash program, as was requested by the parents in 1963.

There was no real precedent on which to base a program. There were waiting along the sidelines, many persons ready to call themselves experts overnight or who had an absolute minimum of training. Many of these functioned in all good faith, not realizing the technicalities of the problem they were facing, and not having faculty members or resources in nearby universities or colleges who had had experience, training, research capacity, and clinical experience which would be helpful. As I see the issue of the education of learning disabled children, there will be no significant movement away from the chaotic situation observable in the schools until there is available a qualified corps of professorial personnel in universities and colleges in departments or schools of education, psychology, and related disciplines. For some years before his death, Dr. Newell Kephart and I had been discussing this problem and we had a solution, it appeared to us.

In a short time a single approach cannot completely solve the problem, but it can go far. We here suggest that there be national or international commitments to the preparation of a qualified corps of professors in the area of learning disabilities.

It is recommended that one hundred faculty members from existing colleges and universities be selected carefully on the basis of their abilities and their commitments to a long association in the future with professional education.

These personnel would be split into two groups of fifty professor-students and assigned to one of two universities (speaking here nationally for the United States). Similar patterns could be effected in many other countries. Who would be the faculty members in these two universities? Presently available, but carefully selected leadership in the field of learning disabilities who combine long-time practical experience with these children, research experience, clinical experience, writing, and related skills would be identified and asked, as a reflection of a national emergency, to seek a two-year leave of absence from their places of employment and become the faculty. For one year a group of six or seven faculty persons would be located in one of the two universities; for the second, in the other. Matters of financing the professor-students and the faculty are significant details, but these are of less importance here than some other issues. In the long term, the costs would be less than that now being expended for short-term, inadequate programs of teacher education, the products of which cannot meet adequately the existing need.

The recruited faculty members would represent the needed variety of disciplinary backgrounds sufficient to be able to provide a total program. Since the student group essentially would be post-doctoral personnel, time should not have to be spent on elementary concepts of learning, teaching, or mental health. The professor-student group would be submitted to an intensive eleven-month-per-year program which would include, among other things, the following essential knowledge and skills deemed essential for the leadership in whose hands the preparation of future teachers is to be invested:

1. knowledge to develop competence in the area of neurophysiological systems of the human organism, particularly for the chronological period of pre-natal development through eighteen years post-natally;

2. knowledge to develop competence in the area of perception and perceptual processing in all sensory modalities;

3. knowledge, clinical experience under supervision, to develop competency in the areas of both quantitative and, more important, qualitative, assessment of children and youth in the areas of perceptual processing deficits;

4. knowledge and understanding to develop competency in such concepts as perceptual-motor match; psychoeducational match; the relation between academic readiness, prolonged preacademic training, and perceptual-motor training;

5. knowledge and understanding to develop competency in the area of intersensory information processing and its relationship to instruction and learning;

6. knowledge and understanding to develop competency in the re-

lationship between perceptual processing deficits and socio-emotional growth and maldevelopment in the child or youth;

    7. knowledge and understanding with respect to the role of structure in the life development of the human organism and the especial relationship of structure to those with perceptual processing deficits;

    8. knowledge of the relationship of perceptual processing deficits to all levels of intellectual function and the meaning of this with relation to all other points of emphasis above;

    9. in-depth experience under supervision in psychoeducational diagnosis and subsequent individual or small group practical experience with children with perceptual processing deficits;

    10. knowledge and understanding of cognitive structure and its relationship to deficits in perceptual processing;

    11. in-depth and long-term counseling relationship, under supervision, with a family or group of families in which learning disability is a factor in familial adjustment between and among members;

    12. knowledge and understanding of the available research and theory relating learning disabilities to chemotherapy agents, to environmental and nutritional deprivation, to biochemical imbalance, to genetic or familial factors, to food additives, and to other seemingly related factors.

    A nation would not need to rely solely on these two university programs. These would, however, insure an initial supply over a two-year period of highly competent personnel who would return to their own universities and colleges, the nation being assured that quality products could be developed for the classrooms. The programs of the two would serve as models for other major teacher preparation centers in the country. Obviously, the details of this solution must be developed. They can be developed with ease. However, until expert university and college professors are installed and until these well-prepared professors have developed sound programs of educational preparation for teachers, the needs of children with learning disabilities in the schools cannot be met adequately. The day of the instant specialist in the field of learning disabilities must be put behind us as part of an unfortunate bad dream.

A SOLUTION LIES IN QUALIFIED PSYCHOLOGICAL PERSONNEL

As the definition of learning disabilities molds the nature of the program for the preparation of college and university personnel, so it does also for the preparation of psychological personnel who will function in the schools with these children and youth. For years there has been an unholy marriage between psychological tests and psychologists. The rigidity of the profession can be seen in the examination of the files of almost any school system. Adherence to intelligence quotient concepts has been farcical in situations almost too numerous to catalogue. The inadequacies of quantified measures of mental ability have been overlooked in the attempt of school psychologists to meet the demands of administrators to test all children. Parents and the courts have brought this frantic, thoughtless effort to a sudden halt, fortunately. Perhaps there will be time now to practice what we and others have been advocating for a long time; namely, the careful, on-going, qualitative assessment of children with perceptual processing deficits (among others). Someone has referred to this as *continuous evaluation,* wherein educators, psychologists, parents, and others maintain a constant, penetrating inquiry into the learning needs of these children. The child's level of intelligence or mental age are relatively inconsequential. What teachers need from diagnosticians is a careful analysis of the child insofar as visual and auditory processing are concerned. They need to know about the length of the child's attention span under normal conditions of learning; about issues of eyedness, handedness, footedness; about memory span; tactuo-motor perceptual processing; midline problems; conceptualization abilities; and other significant elements which go to make up the definition we have discussed earlier. Does a child in question dissociate? perseverate? have figure-ground disturbances and under what circumstances? What is the concept of his body as he understands it, and is he oriented insofar as body is concerned to space, time, and location?

Universities and colleges in their clinical and school psychology training programs do not emphasize these diagnostic areas and their needed skills in sufficient extent or depth to produce effective diagnosticians. Furthermore, little of the graduate student's training is spent on assisting him to understand how to translate his skills and his findings into educationally usable concepts or vocabulary. In the reverse, educators are not helped to understand how to translate their observations of these children into psychological concepts or how to use psychological information effectively to the benefit of the child. Diagnostic information which merely lies dormant in the files of a school or agency is hardly worth collecting. Information which can be translated into a dynamic management plan for the child who has been examined or observed is vital information for all who work with the child and his family.

We are not here asking for the creation of new information, for a new type of university professor, or for anything beyond the reach of the immediate knowledge. We are asking that new emphasis be placed on the preparation of the new young psychologists so that they are more effective in their first independent employment. We do not need more testers. We need more people more understanding of the developmental needs of children and who know how development is modified by perceptual processing deficits. We need psychologists who understand how to evaluate these problems qualitatively, and how to translate their observations into realistic recommendations, instructions, or advice which is immediately usable by other disciplines; i.e., educators, language and speech pathologists, occupational or physical therapists, or others. Give us not more WISCs, WPPSIs, Binets, Leiters, IQs, or MAs. Give me substance in terms of the basic factors included in the definition of learning disabilities. There is no educational or curricular potential in an IQ score and little more in the MA. There is everything needed, if psychologists observe how children function, in the discreet processing characteristics inherent in the definition we have presented. Out of this information can come dramatically effective educational programs of high quality for the children and youth who need them.

TWO SOLUTIONS LIE IN THE QUALITY OF THE TEACHING STAFF

The needs of children with learning disabilities are complex. The complexity of the problems which they present requires different educational models with which to meet them. Although there are several different plans which one encounters in schools, each conceived to meet some or all of the needs of these children, only two will be considered here: the plan of integrating the child into the ordinary classroom, i.e., normalization, and the plan of the special clinical teaching station. There are others which we only mention; namely, resource rooms and itinerant teachers or tutors, for example.

If the perceptual processing problems in a particular child are at all severe, the likelihood that he will be able to succeed in other than a specialized clinical teaching program is doubtful. It is this type of teaching program we shall consider first. The program for these highly specialized educators must be premised both on the definition of learning disabilities and on the availability of high quality teacher education programs in higher education. Less will not produce the needed professional educators. The nature of the program for teachers of children with perceptual processing deficits and resultant learning disabilities will not be greatly different topically than that sketched for university professors. The depth of instruction may vary, but not the scope.

Teachers of these children need understanding of the neurophysiological system of the organism, but only in sufficient depth to understand the locus of the problem itself. In like manner they need general background in the historical development of the field. They need generalized information, sufficient for them to participate fully in an interdisciplinary team, regarding medication, psychological evaluations, language development, motor development, and other items closely related to their professional work. Teachers need to be selected for their anticipated ability to function as an equal among equals on the interdisciplinary team.

On the other hand, they need in-depth understanding and skills in many aspects of learning disabilities. Too often teachers leave the college or university program as they came into it, with little or no understanding of such matters as cognitive structure, the meaning of intelligence, or basic learning regarding perception. Too often the teacher leaves the professional training program with little or no knowledge of how children learn or of theories of learning. Each of these topics for the teacher of children with learning disabilities must be approached in depth. Each is fundamental in the approach which the teacher must make to the child if effective learning is to take place in the child.

It is when the issues of perceptual processing deficits are approached that heavy emphasis must be made in the teacher preparation program. It is not my contention that there is an exact one-to-one relationship between the perceptual processing deficits, perceptual pathology, and teaching techniques, but there are many ways in which the educational plan for the child must mirror the characteristics of perceptual processing which are uncovered by the diagnosticians. This is the fundamental notion behind the concept of the psychoeducational match, about which I have written frequently. For these reasons, I want the teachers who work with children with learning disabilities to possess certain basic understandings which can be illustrated by a few brief examples.

Teachers of these children must know, for example, the intimate relationship between short attention span, distractibility and figure-ground pathology. They must be able to assess how figure-ground disturbance varies under different environmental settings. They must be able to provide the child with learning materials which minimize the need to differentiate figure from ground until such time as he has had success experiences. They must be able to provide materials with a gradation of background difficulty in relation to figure discrimination until such time as the child, through conditioning and success experiences, is able to function with a standard textbook, to differentiate figures from the normal environmental background of a classroom or landscape, or to function in this area of perception without difficulty.

Teachers of these children informally must be able to assess almost daily the duration of a child's attention span. They must subsequently be able to provide learning experiences for the child which have a successful beginning and end within this known attention span. This is another aspect of the psychoeducational match.

These teachers, through diagnosis, observation, or other means, come to learn that the child dissociates, has closure problems, or in other terms is unable to conceptualize the development of new ideas from the joining of parts. The teachers must know what this means in terms of teaching handwriting, drawing, and successfully completing puzzles or peg boards. They must understand through knowledge, practicum experiences, and reading during their preparatory years what these psychological phenomena mean in terms of learning to lace a shoe, button buttons, assemble toy models, set a dinner table, or complete the building of a new classroom aquarium. Success in the latter skills will be dependent upon how completely the teacher plans for experiences which minimize the dissociative tendencies of the child and result in success.

These teachers must be taught the meaning of the impact on the child of his over-responsiveness to extraneous and unessential visual and auditory stimuli, and what, as a result, must be done to reduce the environmental hazards to his learning. What indeed does environmental structure mean? How does one structure space to the profit of the learner? From this the teachers must be helped to understand the total concept of structure in all its essential parts, not only environmental and spatial structure, but human relationship structure, programmatic structure, and the development and use of appropriate structured teaching materials.

It is of great concern to me whenever I hear a university professor say that he teaches his students an eclectic approach to the education of children with learning disabilities. This tells me that either the professor doesn't know very much or he has no concept of what these children really are and how teachers must meet their challenges. There may be more than one way in which human beings learn; if so, I fail to understand more than one. Or is it that professors today are afraid to teach what they really believe? I do not care if all professors do not see this problem as I see it. What I do care about is that their graduates, who will be the ones to face the children, know an awful lot about at least one way to meet these children. I do not want these children exposed to teachers who know a little about a lot of things. In the former state, teachers are secure in the knowledge that they know how to manage the teaching situation; in the latter, insecurity on the teacher's part is observable from the first moment. The children sense this immediately. What these children do not need is another experience with insecurity. Their whole life has been one of failure and insecurity. The teacher, as Sheldon

Rappaport so wisely says, must become the "ego bank" for the child. The child for many years may draw his total strength from the teacher. To be able to provide in this manner for children, one must know whereof he speaks and acts. He cannot be hesitant, insecure, or random in his thought or actions.

The definition of children with learning disabilities contains in and of itself almost a total teacher-preparation program. I would be content if teachers only understood the definition in all of its ramifications, but I would want that understanding to be complete. Obviously, there are other things which specialist teachers must know in order to fully address the problems of the learning disabled child. These children present some of the most complicated of any learning and teaching problems seen in the development of children and youth. Thoughtful leadership cannot afford to provide for these children an untrained or poorly prepared teacher.

Normalization

We mentioned that two types of teacher education would be discussed here. The second pertains to teachers who function within the concept of normalization so frequently, and often so thoughtlessly, established in schools. The concept of retaining the child in the regular or ordinary grade of his community school is the goal. There are many arguments for and against this point of view; few today would argue against the concept. However, in its present method of implementation there are many who see it as almost completely disadvantageous to the children it purports to serve. Without going into arguments for or against normalization, [these having been discussed elsewhere more fully (Cruickshank, 1974)], let it merely be noted that something much more than now being done is going to have to be effected if the concept is to succeed. Success may be a doubtful outcome at best in light of the peculiar learning needs of children with perceptual processing deficits. Although I do not fully subscribe to the idea that integration of the child with perceptual processing deficits into the ordinary classroom will be to his advantage, let us for a moment assume that this is a valid decision. The capacity of the teacher to understand the problem, to modify teaching materials and environment, and to provide success experiences for the child is an absolute essential if it is to work at all.

In the United States many, many communities are employing the concept of normalization with learning disabled children without any formal or informal in-service training for the teachers who are falsely assumed to be knowledgeable. Where the teachers are to obtain the necessary expertise is apparently of little concern. No exposure to these children or to their complex learning needs is provided in pre-service training programs. Somehow it is assumed that the teacher of the ordinary class will be able to meet the needs of this group of children simply by reason of being a teacher. I cannot subscribe to this fantasy.

If a child is diagnosed and is found to have perceptual processing problems, he is in need of highly developed skills insofar as his teacher is concerned. Actually, much of that which normal children need in the teaching situation is contrary to the needs of the learning disabled child and exacerbates his already significant problems. What he needs in terms of his unique characteristics is often contrary to the requirements of the majority of his classmates. If normalization as a plan is to be adopted with respect to learning disabled children (or for any other type of handicapped child for that matter), teachers of the regular classrooms must be given considerable preparation for teaching these children.

The self-concept of children with learning disabilities will not develop positively if they are faced with continuing failure in the regular grades of the school and in the presence of a teacher who does not understand how to provide an adequate educational experience for them. The ordinary classroom then becomes the most restrictive placement for the child. A solution to this problem lies in a widespread in-service training program for regular classroom teachers and for other professionals who work in neighborhood schools, including all administrators. Without this vast effort, the concept is doomed to failure. Another aspect of the solution, of course, is that all pre-service students in colleges and universities must likewise have a thorough understanding of this problem, if they aspire to become teachers of elementary or secondary education.

OTHER PROBLEMS NEED SOLUTIONS

There are several other problems which should be mentioned, but time does not permit their thorough examination. One I wish to highlight; the others we will mention here only to record their importance.

Early discovery and initiation of developmental programs specific to the needs of very young learning disabled children are required. In the State of Michigan, for example, in 1973 mandatory legislation was enacted requiring local school districts to provide for the educational needs of handicapped children between the ages of birth and twenty-six years. The demands on schools for services to children between birth and the previously customary age for school admission are great. This problem needs solution. It is not an impossible one to solve.

The extent to which teachers are assisted to function as educational diagnosticians in order to be able to respond more quickly to the changing characteristics of children with perceptual processing deficits is a problem open to argument. I feel strongly that a major solution to the development of excellent teaching programs for these children is in the extent to which teachers are able frequently to diagnose the child's learning problems and make immediate responses to them.

The place of gross motor training in the educational program of the schools presents a problem to some. Theoretically and practically this is extremely important. Its full acceptance and solution, however, lies not only in the special or ordinary classroom, but also in the extent to which physical education personnel are able to provide non-competitive, developmental, motor training on a regular basis. Most physical education personnel have no training or understanding of the impact of perceptual processing deficits on gross- or fine-motor skills. Inservice training is required here.

A complete catalogue of problems and their solution is inappropriate here. Suffice to say that if schools are to respond adequately to the needs of children with learning disabilities, solutions to the problems we have mentioned, and others which are apparent on all sides, must become a high priority for school administrators.

THE ADOLESCENT

There is one additional problem which must be mentioned, and this pertains to the demands which are starting to be made on secondary schools by youth with learning disabilities. Learning disabled children do grow up and they frequently reach adolescence with perceptual processing deficits still active as handicaps.

To meet the needs of the learning disabled adolescent, solutions are at hand if courageous educational administration is willing to try them. Adolescents with learning and perceptual disabilities have essentially the same needs as their younger counterparts insofar as perceptual training or prolonged pre-academic training is concerned. Hence, among other things, we recommend that teachers prepared as elementary educators accompany the youths into the secondary school levels. Recognition of their social needs as well as their learning needs is reflected here. One cannot rely on the usual corps of secondary teachers to meet the needs of these youths. Secondary educators are more concerned with content than they are with the developmental needs of children, particularly if they are unusual needs. Solutions for the education of adolescent youth with learning disabilities lie in the degree to which prevocational education can be provided them, to the extent to which physical and social education can be made appropriate to their needs. These youths also need extensive information, discussion, and education in the area of human sexuality. Driver education must be a vital factor of their secondary school experiences. No one of these items is beyond the realm of reality, and all can and must be integrated effectively into the school-life experience of the learning disabled youth between the ages of twelve and eighteen years. This educational problem should be seen not so much as a problem, but as a realistic challenge. It does not defy solution.

CONCLUSION

The practice of education for learning disabled children is unfortunately not supported by adequate research. Schools of the several nations were required to respond to parental demands before research was completed in any satisfactory degree. There must be a significant thrust in all facets of research. It exists now as a confusion. It is misunderstood and often seen only as remedial education. In truth it is a developmental problem intermixed with perceptual pathology. Research is required of a long-term nature. We do not need more studies of six or eight heterogeneously characterized children for three weeks for a few minutes a day in two learning climates to determine whether or not a cubicle is satisfactory or unsatisfactory! The conclusion to that type of research is known before it begins. We need long-term controlled studies on almost everything we have mentioned in this paper. Research in biochemistry, in perceptual pathology, in learning theory related to processing deficits, in motor training and learning potential, and in a myriad of other specific and general topics is needed. It must be completed before we can state in actuality that solutions exist to the learning and classroom problems of these children and youth.

REFERENCES

Cruickshank, W. M. "The False Hope for Integration." *The Slow Learning Child* (Australia) 21 (July 1974): 67–83.

Hallahan, D. P., and W. M. Cruickshank, eds. *Psychoeducational Foundations of Learning Disabilities.* Englewood Cliffs, N.J.: Prentice-Hall, 1973.

Hobbs, N., ed. *Issues in the Classification of Children.* San Francisco: Jossey-Bass, 1975, Vol. 1.

Murray, C. A. *The Link Between Learning Disabilities and Juvenile Delinquency.* Washington, D.C.: American Institute for Research, 1976.

PART V

ISSUES AND MYTHS

14

SOME ISSUES FACING THE FIELD
OF LEARNING DISABILITY

𝒯HE FIELD OF LEARNING DISABILITIES is today a complex, confused conglomerate of ideas and professional personnel. It is at a point in its growth where careful assessment of all of its aspects must be undertaken. It is easy to say that something is at a crisis stage. It is my considered opinion, however, that of all of the aspects of the psychology of disability and special education, the field of learning disabilities is in the most crisis phase. The field is at a point where it cannot continue as it has in the past decade without the expectancy of failure and without bringing down on the heads of children professional frustrations, political hostility and parental antagonism. There are many reasons for the situation as we see it today, but one factor of significance is the precocious maturation of the idea of learning disabilities.

Learning disability as it is understood today is of relatively recent origin. It is true that during the decade of the 1920s and 1930s such people as Grace Fernald, Samuel Orton, and Maria Montessori, among others who could be named, were developing new insights into children and were valiantly attempting to translate their understanding and information on to others. Little if any concerted or organized efforts in behalf of these children was apparent, however. The impact of the basic work of the individuals we have mentioned was for many years minimal because of the status quo attitude in which they were working, a characteristic experience shared by many who operate at the cutting edge.

It was in the late 1930s that the issues of perception and perceptual

Reprinted from *Journal of Learning Disabilities* 5 (1972): 380–88, by permission. Address delivered at Learning Disabilities Symposium, National Rehabilitation Training Institute, Miami Beach, Florida, October 26, 1971.

motor development began to be studied in the United States in an organized way with consideration simultaneously being given to their educational implications. This work, first aimed at the exogenous mentally retarded child, was not translated into research dealing with intellectually normal neurologically handicapped children until approximately 1948. The results of this work did not find their way into publication until approximately 1952. It was as late as 1957 when the first efforts in the United States were expanded to translate theory into an educational program with hyperactive brain-injured children. This work aborted due to change in federal funding procedures, but was nevertheless published in 1961. Thus only ten years ago the first organized attack on the education of a small group of these children was reported in the literature. The first efforts at considering the competencies of teachers needed to work with these children appeared in literature in 1966. The first report of any organized attempt in this field at teacher education per se was published in 1969. We are within two years of today. In essence, prior to 1965 little if anything relating to the application of psycho-medical findings of these children to the educational scene was undertaken.

The Association for Children with Learning Disabilities is still not ten years old. The term learning disabilities in its present popular sense is less than ten years old. In the late 1950s and early 1960s, however, the publications which did begin to appear in professional literature fell on extraordinarily fertile ground. Parents of tens of thousands of children in the United States knew what they had, even if professional educators and psychologists and pediatricians did not. With the early appearance of articles dealing with brain-injured children, with dyslexic children, and with perceptually handicapped children, parents began to respond with the offer of their child as a subject for study. It soon became apparent to them that hundreds of their neighbors had similar problems which heretofore had not been discussed publicly.

The growth of the Association for Children with Learning Disabilities, both at the national and state level, is of historic significance. Rarely has an organization grown with such rapidity and with such volume. National, state and local meetings of these groups habitually produce more participants than auditoriums are capable of holding. Professional people have responded in a variety of ways to this outpouring. Academies of pediatricians now devote frequent meetings to the consideration of these children. Universities and colleges recently have developed programs to prepare teachers in the area of learning disabilities. Psychologists organize themselves and consider these problems at almost every professional meeting. Disciplines often not normally associated with the educational process have likewise sometimes changed their direction in behalf of this group of children. Chief among these is the optometric profession, but occupational therapists and physical therapists have often followed suit.

In almost every community some teachers bring themselves to the attention of the professional and lay groups as teachers of children with learning disabilities. Divisions of children with learning disabilities exist within national professional organizations composed of young instructors in colleges and universities as well as of representatives from the public schools who are concerned with this problem.

The growth in this visible image, however, has been disastrous insofar as the development of a coherent professional attack on the matter is concerned. School superintendents under pressure have responded by organizing classes without themselves thoroughly understanding the implications of this problem. Psychologists have examined and diagnosed children within the public schools without thoroughly understanding the nature of the basic problems of perception and their implications for a learning situation. Teachers who are well intentioned have been placed in classes for these children without any formal training or often times informal training. An expressed interest has often been enough to create a specialist overnight. Colleges have organized courses around university professors who themselves have had no experience with these children, who had experienced no research activities with these children, and who indeed too frequently do not themselves understand the implications of the problem they seek to solve or teach about. Teacher education in American universities generally in the field of learning disabilities is in an abysmal stage. In attempting to face the gigantic problem of providing services with inadequate financing and inadequate personnel, the efforts of national leaders have been dissipated to the point where concerted thought and efforts have been seriously and effectively minimized.

While there are many vital issues to which we could direct our attention in this arena of child development, three have been selected for some consideration here. These are not necessarily presented in an order of their importance; each is vital to the eventual solution of the problem.

WHAT IS A LEARNING DISABILITY?

Let us take a look at the issue of terminology as applied to these children. In the literature, as we have reported elsewhere, more than forty English terms have been used which essentially all apply to the same child. This issue of variance in nomenclature is in itself a significant barrier to the development of a coherent program. While other fields of disability face the same issue in lesser extent (for example, cerebral palsy and mental retardation or the gifted), sufficient common knowledge of term utilization is available to obtain a meeting of the minds. In the area of which we here write, however, not only is there an overabundance of terminology but no common denominator of understanding. Furthermore, some people utilize certain terms to provide themselves with untouchable territorial baronies. For example, in an eastern state the term dyslexia is legally used to apply to these children and was inserted into the law at the urging of several reading specialists who needed to protect their professional point of view. In another state two groups could not agree, so two terms appear in the education regulations, neurologically handicapped and educationally handicapped. The duality which is insufficiently defined produces misunderstanding, confusion, and poor programming so obvious at the public school level. So too in other states the terms minimal cerebral dysfunction, perceptually handicapped, brain-injured, special learning disorders, *ad infinitum,* appear often as the pets of small groups without thought being given to the fact that state and county lines are artifacts, and that what is needed is a meaningful national consensus.

The term learning disability also is inadequate. In the normal course of my professional activities during the last two years while speaking about learning disabilities, I have kept a record following public lectures of the types of children about whom people from the audience have asked me under the impression that their child was one I was speaking about. In total slightly more than 300 different inquiries have been received. Included in this number have been more than half where the combination of neuropsychological factors brought the question within the arena of the topic on which we earlier had spoken. However, parents attending a lecture on learning disabilities also have seen fit in a public forum to question me about their child who stuttered, who teased the family cat, who could not deal with geometry in the 10th grade but who otherwise was getting along well in school, who had night terrors, who was diagnosed by the family psychiatrist as depressed—all of these under the label of learning disabilities. I have had parents question me on the failure of the child of nine years of age to be able to swim, another who could type, but not write legibly, still another who masturbated, and still another who didn't like to go with girls. Parents in their concept of learning disability have talked with me about nail biting, poor eating habits, failure of the child to keep his room neat, unwillingness to take a bath, failure to brush teeth. Teachers have questioned me about disrespectful children, children who will not listen to the adult, children who cry, children who hate, children who are sexually precocious, children who are aggressive—all in the belief that these are learning disability children.

One parent asked me if the fact that his college-aged son who wore long hair and whom he "suspected" of living with a girl outside his dormitory was the result of a learning disability!

One can go from the sublime to the ridiculous in this situation. Indeed, many of the behaviors observed by parents which are reflected in these questions may be related to learning disabilities. Many are not, but the fact that they are included within this undifferentiated umbrella is a factor in confounding the confusion in this important area of child growth and development.

"Minimal cerebral dysfunction," a term proposed by the National Institutes of Health a few years ago, is generally unacceptable to educators and to parents. The problem is certainly cerebral and dysfunctions exist, but the issue is not minimal. The term "minimal" refers to lack of gross motor dysfunction, but on first blush it is not understood in this manner. Neurologically handicapped, brain-injured, hyperkinetic, and other similar terms are not satisfactory to parents or to educators, although they may be much more accurate words in describing the children. Dyslexia is too specialized and narrow a term, if it is employed correctly. Learning disabilities is too broad a term and permits too much variation in diagnosis and in performance. This accounts in part for the poor programming we see.

We do not propose to create a new term. We would like to suggest, however, that, irrespective of the presence or absence of diagnosed neurological dysfunction, learning disabilities are essentially and almost always the result of perceptual problems based on the neurological system. Visual-motor problems, basic to recognition of letters, numerals, writing, reading, and arithmetic, are equally accurately described as visual perceptual-motor problems. Auditory-motor problems, basic to attention, language production, and response to the auditory environment, are more accurately described as audio-perceptual-motor problems. Tactual perceptual problems, related to learning through feeling and physical sensation, are essential in understanding these children and their areas of dysfunction. Perception and perceptual dysfunction in relation to a motor response to a stimulus, perceived or misperceived, are the bases to the great majority if not all of the learning problems of these children. If the unfortunate term, "learning disabilities," is too deeply ingrained to be soon changed, we would certainly recommend at least a modification to the term, "specific learning disabilities." "Specific" here refers to specific and diagnosed perceptual problems in any one or all sensory modalities. If freedom to adopt a more accurate term is permitted, then I would strongly urge that the concept of perceptually impaired, perceptually handicapped, or perceptual lag be used. Historically the first lay group in the United States concerned with these children was called the Fund for the Perceptually Handicapped in Illinois which antedates ACLD by many years. It is to be hoped that this organization's name will ultimately be used more widely. Classes for perceptual development in the public schools could then be organized with a specific goal in mind; teachers could be given a background of professional preparation specific to the needs of the children to be served. The issue of nomenclature must be refined and more specific and accurate terms be employed.

The confusion surrounding the term learning disability is nowhere more evident than in the definitions of the problem. The Council for Exceptional Children's definition, the definition used by the NIH Task Forces, as well as those quoted in briefs prepared for legislative hearings, generally resort to statements of inclusion and exclusion while trying to define the problem. This is to be expected when such an all-encompassing term is utilized to describe children. The failure to produce a reasonable clear-cut statement of definition of the issue will be minimized and avoided when less inclusive terms and more refined concepts are used in terminology.

THE QUALIFIED PROFESSOR

Another issue to which we address ourselves is that of the professional person and his readiness to adequately serve this cause. The ultimate provision of quality service to a perceptually impaired child requires a teacher who understands the nature of the problem and how it is to be solved. The presence of a quality teacher at the educational firing line requires a source of professional preparation of unimpeachable quality and stature. This means university faculty members who *know* the problem. If one refers to authority, the primary definition of the word *know* means to be able to perceive directly, to recognize, to discern the character of something, and hence to recognize it as distinct from something else. A tertiary meaning of the same word says that to know is to be more or less familiar with the matter. University and college instruction for this problem today is in the hands of those who function on a tertiary level not a primary level.

The fact that the first college courses for children who are perceptually impaired were taught in universities after most of the present crop of college instructors was born is indicative of the fact that our present instructional group has had minimal experience, little or no formal instruction in the problem, no opportunity for research to test, and almost no direct psycho-educational clinical activity. One sees a former student one year at a national convention as a professor of the education of mentally retarded in a certain college as he was prepared to function; the next year at the same convention, his badge reads "Director, Learning Disabilities Program." Teachers who have graduated as good teachers of elementary education, but who have had no formal education since, re-introduce themselves three years later as the "learning disabilities teacher" in their school system. "I didn't study in your department, but I guess they know I graduated from Syracuse University where you were and I would know about this problem." Students who have had one three-week seminar in the summer in the gross area of learning disabilities return to their school systems in September as consultants. This is a reflection of the tremendous pressure on the part of school officials to do something to meet the gigantic thrust of parental-community need. It has resulted in one of the most confused professional situations in all of education. Further, to meet the pressing need, the United States Office of Education has for several years fostered a program of training grants in the area of learning disabilities both during the academic year and summer sessions. These grants have gone to some universities with good programs, but they have also gone to hundreds of teachers in institutions of higher education which offered immature instruction, inadequate clinical programs and a poor conceptualization of the problem.

We have made a suggestion to federal agencies on which no action has been taken but which has merit. A significant key to the solution to the problem we face is in the creation of a corps of well-prepared college professors. Without this there can be no adequate group of teachers or future college professors prepared. We have suggested that for a three-year period there be declared a moritorium on all scholarship, fellowship or traineeship support at the national level for teachers or other types of service-oriented personnel in this field. Ride on with what we have, inadequate as it is, for a period of time longer.

On the basis of a national educational emergency, an appeal would be made by the U.S. Commissioner of Education to carefully select and recognize leaders in the psycho-educational development of perceptionally impaired children in the United States asking them to take a two-year leave of absence from their present employment. Ten to fifteen mature leaders could be identified who in any list would represent the finest thinking in this country on this matter. A year of planning would be required during which curriculum and course of study would be prepared. These leaders would then be assembled at two sponsoring university centers to become the faculties of an intensive professor-preparation program in the area of perceptual impairment.

Fifty professors would be granted two-year post-doctoral fellowships following a period of careful selection. Each of these fellowships would be awarded in conjunction with a memorandum of understanding between the U.S. Office of Education and the president of the university from which the faculty member was to be given a leave. The memorandum of understanding would declare that upon completion of the two years of study the faculty member, without loss of time in rank, salary, or promotion privileges, would be reassimilated into the university to head up the program of professional instruction in this field.

What would the program consist of for these two groups each of twenty-five persons? Remember this is the potential leadership group for the nation. These are mature men and women with a life career commitment to special education. These are not going to be dilettantes. These are the future Orton's, the future Montessori's, Frostig's, Werner's and Strauss'. These are fifty persons selected *to know* this problem in the primary sense of the term. Without going into great detail, for it would be inappropriate here, the skilled faculty assembled for this crash two-year program would provide among other things basic knowledge in perception, fundamental knowledge related to psychopathology of perception, extensive and in-depth knowledge pertaining to the relationship between physical maturation, perceptual development and gross and fine motor controls. The student-professors would be provided with the best information available on the confused issues of dominance and laterality, and this based on an appropriate understanding of neurophysiological growth and development. As professors of special education these students would need also to know about psycho-educational tests of diagnosis and continual assessment. They need to know the interrelationships between test and item performance, psychopathology, and implications for educational structuring of all types. Environmental design modification, its purposes and psychological dynamics, would be given a thorough explanation. The student-professors would attain a useful understanding of the role of drug usage in public school children to control behavior as well as of alternative methods to accomplish the same thing. Psychopharmacological concepts must become a part of this preparation. These professors must learn how children learn, i.e., from the basic, step-by-step growth of a child's recognition of line segments on to the formation of numerals and letters, words, sentences, and problem solutions.

Formal instruction must be supplemented or interrelated with long-term clinical teaching experience with a child and a group of children. The student-professor must throw off his cap, gown, and hood, and be willing to confront the perceptually impaired child where he is and how he is. Until the student-professor is himself comfortable with the fluctuations in child behavior before him, with outbursts of uninhibited but frustrating temper, with language of a hair-curling nature, with physical punishment which these children can often deliver with skill, with a sobbing appeal for help and rescue, with primitive behavior not yet self-controlled, and all of this with a warm detachment which makes possible a mutual transfer of respect and love, that ultimate professor is not going to be able to instill within his students those qualities and understandings which will in turn make it possible for them to function appropriately. In-depth, long-term clinical teaching experience is required.

It goes without saying, I suppose, that the student-professor will need to learn the specifics of gross-motor training, and be able to evaluate the several published programs pertaining to this important aspect of child development. This strand would be included in the instructional program throughout the two years coupled with practicum experiences. Without continuing this recital indefinitely, permit me merely to list a few other issues of significance to the student-professor and his later effective function. He must know concepts of cognitive structure and the impact on cognition of emotional and physical stresses. He must know about behavioral disorders, their etiology, and concepts of treatment. He must have experience in an interdisciplinary group with pediatricians, speech therapists, psychiatrists, psychologists, and others and know how to organize these teams in relation to the best function of a teacher and the children in her charge.

One can readily see that this is more than a summer's time investment. It is also a costly investment. It will be far cheaper in the long run to make this investment with the guarantee of qualified teachers in the foreseeable future than to continue to award endless traineeships for between six and thirty-six weeks in settings where the end cannot be guaranteed and where less than the rights of children will be insured. I believe that the entire two years, plus the year of planning, the cost of the faculty and the support of each student-professor at an average of $50,000 per year, including secretarial support for each student and overhead charges, could be achieved for something less than three-quarters of a million dollars. The magnitude of this investment is too small to be other than a high priority on the national economy and in educational planning.

The long-term solution to the problems of children with perceptual impairments is essentially that of the educator. This is primarily an educational problem. To accomplish the task, however, the intervention team must include pediatricians, psychiatrists for some children, neurologists for others, psychologists, social workers, speech and language personnel, physical educators, and others. Each of these has a non-traditional and important role in the total picture and a specific relation which must be understood to the teacher and to the educational program. It then follows that what we have said for the preparation of teachers must be considered for the other disciplines we here have mentioned. The nature of the preparation normally provided to these groups, however, is closer to the problem at hand than that usually provided in education. Hence, we do not see the need for such an intensive crash program other than in special education. Other procedures can be employed to produce what is needed.

CONSTITUTIONAL ISSUES

We turn now to another matter of immense proportions in the education of exceptional children which is directly relevant to specific learning disability. The names Hobson, Sprangler, Diana, Covarrubias, Stewart, and Arreola may be strange to some, but these are names which students in special education will come to know well in the years immediately ahead. These are names which may indeed and hopefully will change the face of special education.

While these names to date have been linked primarily with the education of the mentally retarded, it is no leap of logic to appreciate their relationship to the perceptually impaired child with specific learning disabilities or to other children submitted for some reason to special education. Hobson, Spangler, Diana, Covarrubias, Stewart and Arreola are plaintiffs in very recent legal cases, specific or class actions, each of which has challenged one of the sacred cows of educators and psychologists.

Three issues are involved in these suits all pertinent to the education of the children being considered here, namely, (a) educational placement and labeling, (b) psychodiagnosis, and (c) parental involvement in the educational process. On these three significant issues the plaintiffs have found dissatisfaction with the schools, and state that psychologists and educators have been in violation of the Due Process Clause of the 14th Amendment to the U.S. Constitution and have deprived citizens of the equal protection clause under the laws.

In 1967 Judge Skelly Wright held illegal in *Hobson v. Hanson* the method of achievement and ability testing of the Washington, D.C. public schools which were used to place children in both special and regular classes. The court stated (269F. Supp. 401.1967, P. 514):

> The evidence shows that the method by which track assignments are made depends essentially on standardized aptitude tests which, although given on a system-wide basis, are completely inappropriate for use with a large seg-

ment of the student body. Because these tests are standardized primarily on and are relevant to a white middle class group of students, they produce inaccurate and misleading test scores when given to lower class and negro students. As a result, rather than being classified according to ability to learn, these students are in reality being classified according to their socioeconomic or racial status, or — more precisely — according to environmental and psycholgical factors which have nothing to do with innate ability [p. 514].

Other circumstances interact with and reinforce the language handicap. Verbalization tends to occur less frequently and often less intensively. Because of crowded living conditions, the noise level in the home may be quite high with the result that the child's auditory perception — his ability to discriminate among word sounds — can be retarded. There tends to be less exposure to books or other serious reading material — either for lack of interest or for lack of money [p. 481].

These comments directed at education for the retarded are relevant to children with specific learning disabilities. In a center city elementary school in one of the large metropolitan systems, 73 percent of the children were classified "learning disability." How was this determined? By group tests including the statement that all children had been "Frostiged" and had received the California Test of Mental Maturity and the Stanford Achievement Test. The latter was one of the tests which Judge Wright specifically considered in the Hobson case and rejected as invalid for the purpose used. Neither the Frostig materials nor the California Test of Mental Maturity were appropriately used in this cited instance either.

Following the *Hobson* decision, the Federal District Court of Southern California found in the Pasadena School District discrimination as a consequence of grouping students. Thus *Spangler v. the Board of Education* and *Diana v. State Board of Education* in California contended a deprivation of citizens rights to an equal education and demanded special testing of minorities.

Covarrubias v. San Diego Unified School District for the first time sought damages for a conspiracy to deprive citizens of equal protection under the laws, and Covarrubias sought an injunction against all special class placement until placement procedures were modified.

Parents are saying that the concept of special education is contrary to equality, and they further are stating that the procedures utilized to place children within the schools are unsatisfactory. Moreover the plaintiffs in Hobson, Stewart, and Covarrubias state that the administration of tests is performed incompletely, that public school personnel who administer tests are not adequately trained to do so properly. In Hobson the courts agree with the plaintiffs.

A damaging argument by the plaintiffs against special education placement is that special education programming itself is inadequate. Ross and his colleagues[1] say that, "once a child is improperly placed in a . . . class, there is little chance that the student will leave it. Insufficient attention is given to the development of basic educational skills and re-testing occurs infrequently if ever. Contributing further to the lack of . . . mobility is the student's self-image which is formed by improper placement and creates a self-fulfilling prophecy of low achievement." The courts agree.

Finally it is stated that "parents are not given an adequate opportunity to participate in the placement decision". This is a fundamental argument in Arreola, Diana, and Stewart, in California and Massachusetts courts, an argument based on the Due Process Clause of the 14th Amendment to the U.S. Constitution.

Citizens do not generally complain to school officials unless they are disturbed that something is basically wrong with the system; that their child is suffering in some fashion; or indeed that their child in other cases is being permanently damaged. In terms of the total school population the number of complaining children and parents represents a small percentage. Fear prompts many to eat their dissatisfaction. Those parents who feel sufficiently disturbed at the quality of education are applauded by the more timid citizens when justifiable complaints have been made to authorities.

Educational officials, however, too often have neither listened to the citizens nor to their leadership colleagues who have rarely been timid in pointing to defects in the system. The practicing educational establishment too frequently has considered itself untouchable, and has warded off complaints and warnings with self-assured omnipotence in all educational matters. The normal channels have not worked, and since 1967 we have seen the unusual phenomenon in the U.S. of the judicial system being asked to determine for the educators what is bad and to a lesser extent what is good in their special education programs. Educational and psychological leadership is on the verge of losing control of its own system. The courts are placing it right back where state constitutions generally place it, and by failure to mention it specifically where the Constitution also places it, as a right reserved to the state and delegated to the citizens. What an awful indictment of educational leadership at the local level! Courts would not have been asked to intervene if special education always had been fair, appropriate to client needs, and had held hope for the child and his future. Special education's frequent mediocrity, its sterility, its failure to possess a dynamic quality, its position of guilt ridden rejection produced by attitudes of general educators toward it, and its willingness to be used by the very people who reject it, its acceptance of every child general educators refer to it knowing that it is undesirable for many—these and many other indictments are the things which bring parents to the courts. The courts apparently agree.

It is interesting to observe that only in *Hobson v. Hanson* has the case actually gotten into a court of appeals for a decision. There, however, public schools have not been willing to appeal to higher courts. In the other cases (as well as apparently in two new cases, *Quadalupe Organization v. Tempe Elementary School District* and *Simpkins and Washington v. Consolidated School District of Aiken County,* South Carolina) school systems apparently see the illegitimacy of their programs. The systems, not wanting a court decision, are seeking to settle out of court as in *Diana*. This timidity on the part of superintendents and boards of education appears to be based on a fear that if the matter gets into the supreme court—a step parents are now quite willing to take—special education and much of psychological practice has a significant possibility of being declared unconstitutional!

To reiterate, let it be again stated that parents do not complain if they believe their child's needs are being met. Today the needs of most children in programs labeled "learning disability" are not being met. There is little need here to dwell on the negatives; they are obvious in every visit to any public school program. Suffice to say that poorly prepared teachers are a primary reason for this situation, and as we have said this is in large part due to our national policy of inferior teacher education in this field. An uninformed public school educational leadership regarding this complex issue is another reason for program failures. Unsophisticated school psychologists, still married to a mental age and an intelligence quotient, instead of qualitative diagnostic blueprints of child capacities, produce sterile information which assists no one, teacher or child or parent. Specialized clinical teaching material is unavailable to the teacher. Environmental modification is looked upon as the idle thinking of an ivory tower college professor. Educational practice in direct relation to psychopathology in perception is a concept not understood. These are the cornerstones of a vital program, however, and their application will bring satisfaction to teachers, gains to children, and applause from parents.

Education for perceptually impaired children with specific learning disabilities cannot afford to go the route of another field of special education. Community warnings are here for us to read. There is an urgency around us today for quality programs for these children. If we ignore them we commit professional suicide; if we recognize them and do something about them in behalf of children we reach the apex of professional responsibility and function.

REFERENCE

1. Ross, S. R. Jr.; H. G. DeYoung; and J. S. Cohen. "Confrontation: Special Education Placement and the Law." *Exceptional Children* 38 (September 1971): 5–12.

15

MYTHS AND REALITIES
IN LEARNING DISABILITIES

$\mathcal{T}$HE ISSUE OF LEARNING DISABILITIES in childhood and youth is one of the most interesting phenomenon which has occurred in education. Its history has been well documented on more than one occasion so that no further reference will be made to it here (Hallahan and Cruickshank 1973; Weiderholt, 1974). The field is frought with misconceptions. It is ill defined in the minds of most educators and psychologists; certainly it is not understood by physicians who have only recently become interested in the problem. Its implications are neither understood nor adequately conceptualized by the majority of school administrators. The hopes of parents are not being realized because of these facts. It is essential that serious thought be given to this matter and that more appropriate directions be initiated.

A recent volume indicates that the field of learning disabilities was developed coincident to the development by Kirk of the Illinois Test of Psycholinguistic Abilities (Haring 1974). This is the first myth which should be considered. Kirk's work, uniquely important, nonetheless had antecedents which he recognizes. The ITPA itself is based on the earlier conceptual framework of Osgood, but the additional and perhaps still earlier stimulus for whatever Kirk did in the ITPA came, he says, from personal contact with Ruth Monroe in Chicago and later from Strauss, particularly when he and Kirk were both working in Wisconsin. A still earlier stimulation of Kirk's direction undoubtedly came from his direct association with, and exposure to, both Strauss and Werner in Michigan. There is no effort here to minimize the work of Kirk. The fact of the matter is that he, along with several others, was working simultaneously in various institutional and university settings

Reprinted from *Journal of Learning Disabilities* 10 (1977): 51–58, by permission.

along somewhat similar lines. With the exception of Monroe and Grace Fernald, to whom Kirk also gives credit for the stimulation of his thinking, most of these investigators were, directly or indirectly, his colleagues at an institutional setting in Michigan, i.e., Newell Kephart, Sidney Bijou, Bluma Weiner, William Cruickshank, Ruth Melcher Patterson, Charlotte Phileo, and others who followed.

The reality of this situation is that Kirk was one among several who moved to understand the complexities of children who were *later* to be called learning disabled. Kirk took the route of Osgood and the ITPA; Kephart, the conceptualization of perceptual-motor matching and training; this writer, the concept of the psychoeducational match and structure. Bijou branched off into behavior modification, others into other areas of child growth and development.

But then there were others who have made significant contributions to the field presently known as learning disability, and these were not related to the original Michigan group. Their thinking added much to the understanding of this problem, and is represented by the work and writing of Marianne Frostig, Belle Dubnoff, Sheldon Rappaport, and others whose orientation comes essentially from concepts of ego psychology and introspective clinical orientations. There were still others. All of the initial contributions of these individuals antedated the publication of the ITPA and the term "learning disabilities." No single person is responsible for this field. The thinking and conceptualization of the individuals to whom reference has here been made is, however, astonishingly similar. There are few points of disagreement among them. There is difference, from time to time, in the vocabulary employed; but, if careful analysis is made regarding the meanings of words used, it will be observed that underlying concepts are basically similar.

During the 1974 annual conference of the Association for Children with Learning Disabilities, I chanced to hear a speaker state, "The field of learning disabilities is an old one, one with a long history and many precedents." Let us consider Myth No. 2. The field of learning disabilities is perhaps the most recent development of any aspect of exceptionality in childhood. It has few precedents. It possesses an inadequate research base. It is characterized by an inadequate professional corps in colleges and universities, and, therefore, by an inadequate supply of appropriately prepared teachers to serve the complex needs of these children.

What is the reality of this field? Weiderholt has traced the beginnings of this field of interest to Gall as early as 1823, but with discrimination, he points out that the phenomenon of learning disability per se is a contemporary issue. The Michigan group, to which earlier reference was made, had its origin and did its greatest work, however inadequate from present day research standards, in the late 1930s and 1940s. The first extension of this original work which was done on high grade mentally handicapped boys, was initiated and completed in 1948–53 with a population of intellectually normal cerebral palsied children. The first investigation into structured educational programming for these children started in 1957 and was reported in 1961. Kephart's initial publication appeared in 1960. The first publication dealing with the competencies needed by teachers of these children appeared in 1966 and the first report of a coordinated program of teacher education in 1969. The ITPA first appeared in 1971. With the exception of Gall, every person and date mentioned in these few paragraphs falls within the life span of the conference speaker referred to above and is contemporary with him.

This is a new field insofar as its formalization is concerned. As a credit to Kirk, he certainly tried to give impetus to its non-categorical implications, an effort which others at the same time and earlier had also attempted. It has become categorized as an aspect of child deviance in ways that most of us hoped never would happen and, in effect, have worked hard to prevent. It is easier, however, to speak in terms of groups than it is to speak in terms of concepts. It is easier to classify than it is to attempt to meet the peculiar needs of individual children with learning and teaching materials and techniques germane to the problems directly at hand. It is easier to conceptualize groups than it is to envision the variety of developmental needs of children within a group and to address each appropriately.

The newness of the field in part accounts for the ill-prepared professional and teaching corps which are to be encountered at every turn in professional education. The conference speaker to whom I have referred simply did not know his facts, but his position is frequently shared by school officials who are likewise uninformed. This produces frustrations in teachers and disappointments in parents as they see children continuing to flounder without adequate understanding or appropriate educational efforts on the part of school service personnel.

What is learning disability? There are those who would view this term as a synonym to "remedial reading" or to educational remediation in general. This is completely fallacious. Remedial reading teachers, consultants or specialists, by these or any other names, are not overnight appropriately converted into specialists capable of working with the problems of the learning disabled. This is Myth No. 3 to which we wish to address ourselves.

It is important to trace the concept of learning disability back to its neurological origin. Learning disability, specifically defined, is a manifestation of a perceptual processing deficit. It is important to differentiate between sensory perception leading to normal vision or hearing from the concept of processing of a perceptual nature, which not only involves the appropriate recognition of form or sound, but also includes the attachment of learned meaning or appropriate motor responses to whatever stimulus is received. This is the essence of the ITPA; it is likewise the basis of the concept of task analysis which Junkala (1972, 1973) discusses in terms of input and output concepts. There are numerous other ways than the ITPA, however equally effective, to qualitatively assess the capacity of the child to process that which he perceives. Regardless of the tools used, it is an absolute in considering the concept of the psychoeducational match that such evaluation and assessment be done in order that teaching materials and the learning environment can be matched with the specific processing needs of the child under consideration. If the child's disability involves perception or perceptual processing, it logically follows that one is dealing with a neurological dysfunction of some sort. Thus learning disability would, from a practitioner's point of view, be conceptualized more accurately as a *perceptual processing deficit* resulting in a specific learning problem of some sort, involving one or another or all of the sensory modalities. Definitions of learning disabilities which ignore the concepts of either perceptual processing or the neurological base are misleading. Such is not to state that the specific neurological dysfunction can always be identified. From the psychoeducational point of view, the specificity of the neurological deficit (if it could be determined) many times would be helpful, but it is not a requisite to good programming.

While those concerned with remedial reading, or other forms of remediation, frequently may need to employ techniques utilized with children who have perceptual processing deficits, remediation is in no way the solution for all the problems of the so-called learning disabled. One must differentiate between problems of learning and perceptual processing deficits resulting in specific learning disabilities. In the former, i.e., problems of learning due to initial poor teaching, problems of mother-child separation in early childhood, or due to other similar types of problems, remediation undoubtedly has a significant role. One does not, however, remediate a vacuum, and this is essentially the case in the child with perceptual processing deficits. In this child, appropriate learning has not taken place because of neuro-perceptual processing problems. A technique of education has to be developed which will provide the child with the necessary initial skills, regardless of chronological age, and which will give him a sound base for the acquisition of more complex learnings later. This is not remediation; it is new learning.

What is an adequate definition of this problem? In 1974, there appeared an appropriate and a logical definition (Hobbs 1974) which merits thorough consideration and adoption. It is a thoughtfully prepared document, the result of the combined thinking of several people with long experience in this field plus the critique of a much larger field of experts who know the problem well. It is a definition stated in appropriate perceptual terms. The authors define the problem in terms of its "psychoeducational reality." It is stated that this problem refers "to those children of any age who demonstrate a substantial deficiency in a particular aspect of academic achievement because of perceptual or perceptual-motor handicaps, regardless of etiology or other contributing factors. The term *perceptual* as is used here relates to those mental (neurological) processes through which the child acquired his basic alphabets of sounds and forms. The term *perceptual handicap* refers to inadequate ability in such areas as the following: recognizing fine differences between auditory and visual discriminating features underlying the sounds used in speech and the orthographic forms used in reading; retaining and recalling those discriminated sounds and forms sequentially, both in short- and long-term memory; ordering the sounds and forms sequentially, both in sensory and motor acts . . . ; distinguishing figure-ground relationships . . . ; recognizing spatial and temporal orientations; obtaining closure . . . ; integrating intersensory information . . . ; relating what is perceived to specific motor functions . . ." The definition ends here, but to this could be added such things as an inadequate ability to conceptualize parts into meaningful wholes; the sometime presence of perseveration; the inability to refrain from reacting to unessential environmental stimuli; and the resulting immature or faulty self-concept or body image. Actually contained within this definition is a total program of teacher preparation as well as a total concept of service to children with such problems in the public schools of the nation.

It is immediately obvious that one is dealing with a complex developmental problem, not a problem of remediation. It is also obvious that students in colleges and universities are not being given the appropriate preservice experiences to meet the challenges of this definition nor of the children who present these characteristics.

A continued reading of the definition provides us with a further concern and with Myth No. 4. The committee which prepared this definition, of which this writer was a member, does not go far enough, although there is an important allusion to the relationship of intelligence to processing deficit resulting in learning disability as we are defining the problem. *The reality of the situation is that learning disability is a matter relating to children of any intellectual level.*

Numerous definitions of this problem define learning disabilities by exclusion, i.e., what it is not. It is stated that this is not a problem of primary mental retardation or sensory defect. I would agree. The crucial word is *primary*. This, however, is often overlooked by the non-discriminating professional person. Indeed many definitions of learning disability to be found in state and local regulations speak of children with learning disabilities as having I.Q.'s above 80. The implication is that the problem is a different one below the 80 level. This is an arbitrary statement absolutely without a basis in fact. There are reports by parents of mentally retarded children that they have been unwelcome when they expressed a desire to become a member of the local association of parents of learning disabled children. The reality of this myth is that learning disability is a respector of no intellectual level. Perceptual processing deficits are to be found in children of every intellectual level and are respectors of no given intelligence range.

As a matter of fact and history, practically everything which is known about the nature of perceptual processing deficits was discovered initially from studies completed with exogeneous mentally retarded children of the educable levels. Certainly this was the orientation of the basic initial studies which were undertaken by Werner, Strauss, and their associates. Recently the author was informed by a representative of a state department of education that the problem could be defined by the state in any manner desired. This may be technically correct, but it is professionally irresponsible. It indicates a lack of knowledge or appreciation of what the problem actually is.

The adherence to a concept of IQ 80, itself an alogical, arbitrary cut-off point, serves to deprive thousands of mentally handicapped children of appropriate understanding and programming, and indeed, in many instances, it results in the worst type of discrimination. One does not have to travel far in any direction to find classes for the mentally retarded being essentially black; classes for children with learning disabilities, essentially white. The IQ concept does not have an appropriate relationship to this problem, although it may take class action suits to bring the matter to a reality base for many state and local educators. Under the present myth, thousands of retarded children with perceptual processing deficits resulting in learning disabilities are being misclassified and are in effect being denied an educational birthright.

One does not have to look far to find Myth No. 5. This has to do with incidence and prevalence. From time to time it is stated that the problem of severe learning disability accounts for one percent of the elementary school population. From still another source it is stated that learning disability is a matter of 12 percent of the same population. More frequently in lay groups the figure of 20 percent is used. An outstanding elementary school principal stated to this writer that 83 percent of her center-city elementary school pupils functioned as if they were perceptually handicapped. Somewhere between these extremes lies the truth.

The reality of the situation is that we do not know how many such

children there are in the schools of this nation. There is absolutely no adequate data of either an epidemiological or demographic nature to give us a
base for adequate programming. At the present time adequate data do not
exist, and this results in the horrendous guesses to which we have referred
just now. The absence of data constitutes the basis for confusion in state and
federal legislative houses and, as well, means that local school administrators must respond to parental and community pressures with inadequate information. The collection of this information is an absolute requisite for national planning of all types.

In what we have thus far said, it appears that there is a reason for
the crazy-quilt manner in which this field has developed. Originally we point
out that the underlying processing deficits and an obvious matching of them
with teaching materials and environment could provide an outstanding clinical teaching program for the children who needed it. We at Syracuse University in the 1950s and 1960s had learned that what the investigators of a decade
earlier had discovered regarding the learning problems of exogenous mentally retarded children also applied in full force to cerebral palsy children of
all intellectual levels. Others of my students and colleagues learned that this
was also the case with deaf children whose deafness was of an organic nature, with aphasic children, an observation of Mildred McGinnis of long
standing; of some epileptic children, of some blind children, and of many, if
not most all, of the so-called hyperactive emotionally disturbed children.
This latter group has been studied more carefully by Haring, a student of
mine, and Phillips. The essence of the matter, however, is one of clinical diagnosis of a penetrating nature. The medical, psychological, or educational
category or terminology is meaningless and completely unnecessary. The essential thing is the penetrating evaluating of the child in terms of the psychological processing problems we mentioned earlier inherent in the definition.
As these are identified, they must be matched by equally as carefully considered learning and teaching techniques so that new learning will result and the
child will be started appropriately along his developmental route. Although
Kirk, and many of us before and after him, urged that a new category of
special education not be created, that very thing has happened. Once again
we see children be assigned to classes rather than to see educators be concerned for the child's uniqueness and educated in such terms.

Let us look at Myth No. 6, which is related to the nature of the professional relationships to the problem of perceptual processing in children
leading to specific learning disabilities. This is basically a psycho-educational
problem, not a medical problem. It is only recently that pediatricians, for example, have become actively aware of this problem of childhood. Nowhere
in the preparation of the physician, however, is there provided training

which would permit that discipline to assume major direction of the life management plan for these children. True, medicine has a place in the interdisciplinary attack on the problems of these children. It reiterates once again, however, that the long-term issue is not one of medicine, be it pediatrics or neurology, but is of education. This writer takes no issue with the medical profession, except when that profession enters into arenas for which it is not prepared or is ill-prepared. There are a few medical personnel who are performing outstanding services to these children, but they are doing so generally in conjunction with educators and psychologists who are skilled and experienced with the problem.

We hasten to point out, however, that in instances of research, it is important to have neurological colleagues join the interdisciplinary research team. Neurology is first to state that it does not have all of the refined skills needed to isolate the neurophysiological problem basic to the processing deficits. However, the skills of this discipline can go far to refine the diagnostic effort, and this will result in a somewhat more homogeneous population for study. We here, however, are talking about the learning situation. In this arena, the educator is and must be predominate. Learning disabilities is not a medical problem; it is the problem of numerous disciplines bringing their skills and expertise to the educator, who in the long run must be the only implementor. Experience over many years has demonstrated the wisdom and validity of this approach.

Myth No. 7 deals with the efficacy of medications in the management regimen of children with specific learning disabilities. There is an appalling lack of adequate research pertaining to the utilization of medications for the control of behavior in elementary school children other than minimal research stated as having been done by commercial drug companies. This, in my mind and in the minds of others, is not sufficient to warrant the widespread utilization of medications by physicians with these children. There is evidence to the effect that in some classes of children with learning disabilities, medication is a part of the daily intake of 40 percent of the children. In at least one institution known to this writer, 90 percent of the total population was on some sort of medication.

The reality of the situation is that, if there is an adequately structured educational program with adequate matching of teaching materials to problem and with built-in success experiences for the child, medication will often not be required at all. Medications are poor substitutes for good educational programs, are often a resort which parents must seek when good programming is unavailable and when teachers are ill-prepared to meet the unique features of the child with specific learning disabilities.

There is a myth which is no myth at all to parents whose children are

being served by ill-prepared teachers. Myth No. 8 deals with the reality of
the instant specialist in colleges, universities and public schools who present
an aura of quality, but in reality have only the veneer of the specialist. The
newness of the field accounts for the lack of a well-prepared corps of university professors in this field. As such, it differs from some of the other areas
of special education, mental retardation, for example. The latter field had
been visible since about 1918, when Charles Scott Berry started summer
teacher education courses at what is now Eastern Michigan University. In
the interval between then and the late forties when the parent groups began
to organize, quite a large number of persons experienced with mentally retarded children began to write and later to teach in colleges and universities.
A body of knowledge, although limited, was available. Professors with an
orientation both to retardation and teacher preparation were available in
small numbers, but in sufficient numbers to prepare others adequately when
the 1963 so-called Kennedy legislation became a fact. The field of specific
learning disability was not a reality until after 1963. Before that, it was a
matter of exploration, theory and clinical research done by a very small
number of persons. There was no precedent of teacher education in this
field, except for small programs at the University of Illinois and at Syracuse
University which began about 1945.

When the parent group organized in 1963, there was the general assumption that sufficient dollars would provide the treatment services their
children needed, and that all was known which needed to be known in order
to provide quality programs. Indeed less was known about the problem than
was known about it, a situation which continues today in large measure.
There were no formalized teacher education programs, nor were there college faculty members with experience to staff them. In contrast to the response which universities were able to make to the Kennedy legislation, which
resulted in a splendid new group of university faculty members in the field of
retardation, practically no personnel were available in the field of learning
disabilities to be able to turn out young faculty members for teacher education institutions. The few who were available often resorted to the mechanism of summer seminars, which were a far cry from what was needed. There
has never been a national policy espoused by the U.S. Office of Education or
by state departments of education which was focused on the production of a
qualified corps of university professors in this area of child development.

As a result, we have in this area what Kirk long ago called a cafeteria
approach to teacher education. A little of this and a little of that does not
produce good professors or good teachers. Although university faculties in a
certain state were given more than two years of notice to submit programs of
teacher education in this area, most universities did nothing about the mat-

ter until a few weeks or months before the deadline. As the deadline neared, there were frantic efforts on the part of faculties in special education in the universities and colleges to put together programs. These consisted essentially of utilizing old course titles, since time did now not permit the development of new courses appropriate to the problem. To these old titles were appended new course descriptions. Since few, if any, of the universities possessed faculty members expert in this field, the nature of the conglomerates which were developed were a far cry from that which was in reality needed. To my knowledge, every one of the patchwork programs was approved by the board of higher education in that state, and teachers today are being prepared through them. The response of the mature students in terms of critique is sad to hear. They realize what they are being given is not appropriate to the need which they face in the classrooms of the public school systems.

Where did the professors come from to staff these several programs? In one instance, a good professor of the education of the emotionally disturbed overnight became the faculty leader in the area of learning disabilities. In another instance, a faculty member in the field of school psychology becomes the more or less self-appointed expert in the field of learning disabilities. In other instances, similarly sad situations prevail. A parent turned educator heads the program in one of the facilities. This is no way to guarantee a solid teacher group in the state under consideration. But this state is not unique. Until the national leadership provides a program for the preparation of college professors, and until the program which they experience is one of depth, as has been described and suggested elsewhere, no quality is going to be observed in this confused field. In my considered opinion, the situation is one of the saddest in the total field of professional education. The myth that colleges and universities can presently produce a solid teacher group is being negatively demonstrated on almost every side throughout the nation.

The final myth I wish to highlight here, Myth No. 9, pertains to the current unfounded fad that children with specific learning disabilities can and ought to be educated in the regular grades of the community. Parents supported this position for many years, because they were disturbed with what they oftentimes saw their children receiving in the special classes. General educators, teachers and administrators for years declared that the better place for handicapped children was in the regular grades. Often there was almost an inquisitional program launched by general educators against special educators, and at best special educators frequently were granted what amounted to second-class citizenship in the public school system. Special education was placed, and still often is, within the administration of departments of pupil personnel. Special educators did not need more personnel approaches; they needed instructional assistance, something their supervisors were unqualified to give and general instructional personnel did not provide because of their own lack of background with atypical children. Against this poor situation, parents saw integration, mainstreaming if you must, as a way out. The general educators supported this, and some of the special education leadership also advocated it on the basis of a few case studies, not on the basis of any adequate research. Today we see a backlash developing. We better be prepared to meet that backlash with some powerful educational tools.

Children with perceptual processing deficits resulting in specific learning disabilities have needs which the general elementary or secondary educator cannot provide in the normal classroom setting. Probably some integration for short periods each day could be valuable, but until genuine success experiences are integrated into the child's self-perception, either through the medium of well-prepared teachers working in resource rooms or in special clinical teaching stations, the capacity of the child with anything short of a very mild learning disability is going to be less than that needed to function in a normal or ordinary classroom situation. Unless general elementary educators understand the nature and needs of the problems of processing deficits and know how to adapt the learning situation and teaching materials to the child's needs, the potential for continued failure on the part of the child is present. It is more than unlikely that preparation of elementary general educators will include this emphasis in the foreseeable future. In the meantime, what of the children who are physically, but neither educationally or psychologically, integrated?

In my considered opinion, the status of learning disabilities in the public schools of this nation is one of educational catastrophe. We have too many instant specialists in positions of leadership, positions which because of their lack of preparation or knowledge, they must defend with the pretense of expertise. This can be rectified if a hard line is assumed. There is sufficient knowledge available to put together overnight a splendid program of university professor preparation. Within two years, a corps of well qualified professors could be read which, with some national support to universities, could result in the beginning of a steady stream of qualified teachers being released to function in the public schools. We do not have all the research needed in this area, as we have stated, but we have enough to turn around the field of education for children with specific learning disabilities from a position of chaos to one of logic and satisfaction to the professional educator and parent-consumer alike. It will take guts to do this, but unless strong stands are immediately taken, the chaotic situation we see nationally, as evidenced in the mediocre local school programs, will continue unabated.

16

LEARNING DISABILITIES

A Charter for Excellence

*I*N September of 1972 we wrote in the *Journal of Learning Disabilities* (Cruickshank 1972) an article concerned with fundamental issues facing the education of children with specific learning disabilities. Therein we focused attention on the confusion in the field due to the lack of an appropriate educational definition of the problem. We noted that, since learning disability has become both a fad and a scapegoat of the decade, we see in public education almost everywhere programs functioning without direction and at a high level of mediocrity, the exceptions being startlingly few in number. We also focused attention on the quality of the corps of college and university professors which purports to function in this field.

It is indeed difficult to continence what one sees in the education of children with specific learning disabilities in the schools of this nation today. In my opinion it is of unprecedented poor quality. But we are not writing today to grumble about the failures of the past decade or the ineffectiveness of learning disability education today. We wish rather to look at the stance we must assume in behalf of good education for these children in the years immediately ahead. Obviously, however, we would not be so concerned about futures if the present were in anyway nearing a satisfactory state of affairs. This field of professional education is so lacking in anything which could merit the characterization of quality or excellence that we are faced with class action suits and court intervention. Against this backdrop, how can we move to serve children in terms of both quality and excellence?

Reprinted from *Learning Disabilities: Selected ACLD Papers,* edited by S. A. Kirk and J. McCarthy (Boston: Houghton-Mifflin, 1975), pp. 103–17.

TEN PHASE PROGRAM

If the profession is going to accept seriously its responsibility, some rigorous stands are going to be required. We are not speaking of a mere motor tune-up; we are talking at the minimum of a complete overhaul if not the replacement of the old with a new motor. There are several components to the rigorous attack which we feel must be taken, and these, although interrelated, we propose to examine separately thus highlighting each. Each one is important if quality education is to be achieved.

The Professor and Teacher Education

In a very large measure the quality of public school programs is founded on and reflects the quality of teacher education and thus it reflects the quality of college or university professors. The total field of education of children with specific learning disabilities is essentially a product of the last decade. Granted that research efforts on a very modest scale began in the latter part of the decade of the 30s and that the interests of such people as Grace Fernald, Ruth Monroe, Samuel Orton, and a few others then and earlier were concerned about children who could not learn, little was known or conceptualized about these children in an organized way. Facts nevertheless record that suddenly in 1963 the term learning disabilities burst on the scene and became the popular educational vehicle of the decade.

The demand of services by parents and the subsequent attempts by school superintendents to meet the parental demands brought a problem to colleges and to universities for which they were not at all prepared. The lack of definition of the problem, the research void, the lack of any content literature, perplexed educational faculties. A professional vacuum truly existed. Into this vacuum stepped young, often well-intended persons who possessed an absolute minimum of professional preparation and practical experience.

In 1963, at the time of the learning disability explosion, several persons were active in the field who had in a sense grown up with it. Among these persons can be noted such people as Samuel A. Kirk, Newell C. Kephart, Charles Strother, this writer, Helmer Myklebust, Sidney Bijou, and a few others who, often by happenstance, had been associated with multiply complex problems of brain-injured children and their concomitant perceptual pathologies. These people through association with Monroe, Strauss, Werner, the clinical work of Kirk Goldstein, Bruno Kopfer, Samuel Beck, through experiences with war injured men who suffered neurological damage, and from fortuitous experience accrued practical experiences, some research orientation, and excellent theoretical foundation. On these few persons, almost all of them psychologists, fell a responsibility of establishing educational training programs to meet the demands of the public educational requirements. Relatively reputable but short-lived programs were developed at the University of Illinois, Northwestern University, Purdue University, and Syracuse University among the few universities which can be identified. Out of these universities has come another relatively small second generation of fine young psychoeducators who through personal contact with their professors have extracted most of what was known plus what was occurring to that date. Among these can be cited Barbara Bateman, James McCarthy, Norris G. Haring, and John Junkala. Samuel Clements and Sheldon Rappaport, again psychologists, joined this small group from other directions. The professional educators, other than Elizabeth Freidus, Jean Lukens, Laura Lehtinen, Marion Tannhauser, and a few others who truly know this field, are almost completely unrepresented.

Into this demand-laden field, nearly void of personnel, stepped many unprepared persons who almost immediately, with little or no professional preparation or experience, became directors or professors of programs for teachers of learning disabilities. This unfortunate situation can be documented many many times over. The products of these programs, teachers accepted into service, unsuspectingly represented much less than the best preparation. This is obvious when one assesses classroom programs.

For some time this writer has been advocating a strong and aggressive stand to correct this situation. Let us examine it, and assess its implications. In the first place we must recognize that much of what is going on in the field of learning disabilities is exceedingly ineffective and of poor quality. We point to the unprepared college professor as the first point where logical criticism can be placed. With this in mind, we recommend that we move to correct this situation as rapidly as possible. Funds should be spent at once to provide the basis of one or two national training programs for professors in service. Of what would this consist?

1. First, there would be assembled into the training centers, the national leadership, each on a maximum two-year leave of absence from his position, to serve as faculty members. This faculty would consist of those who have long been associated with this problem. The logistics of developing a faculty are difficult, but in no sense do they defy accomplishment. If there were two centers, the faculty could probably rotate between the two locations in order to make the core personnel available to both student groups.

2. Second, fifty or sixty college professors now in service would be selected by a review panel to become professor-students in this program. Each of these would be placed on a two-year leave of absence from his uni-

versity or college. A written contract would exist between the funding agency and the university to the effect that the two years away would be considered in terms of promotions, salary increments, and that upon completion of his program the professor-students would be reinstated in his position at the university to undertake teacher education in the field of learning disabilities. These professor-students would be recruited from any age bracket and from any professorial rank. Proof of commitment to education, general or special, would be required. These would be people with a professional career already indicated in higher education teacher education. Their admission into the program would include full pay plus cost of living allowances, since often two homes would have to be maintained; travel; book allowances; and secretarial assistance. The host universities or centers would receive their usual overhead costs as well as other reimbursements for direct costs. While it is probable that these programs would be housed in a major university, there is no reason why that is a mandatory factor.

3. What, in brief, might the programs be for the professor-students? It would not be a restating of what should have been learned earlier. This is not a remedial program for professors. The basic skills would be ascertained at the time of selection of the person into the program. The selection program would be rigorous and in depth. The actual learning experience would consist of a number of significant things, some of which are detailed here.

Sometime ago authorities in the area under discussion made available an in-depth statement of the competencies needed on the part of teachers of these children (Cruickshank, 1966). These competencies must be provided to teachers essentially through the medium of university instruction, hence they become even more critical as a statement of competencies of college and university professors. They are as valid today as they were a few years ago when they were initially published, and in some instances, as the result of certain social and economic factors, they have become even more essential. The professor-student, about whom we now speak, will be provided with learning experiences to help him develop his instructional competencies in the following areas:

1. He must know and understand the psychoeducational definition of his field. He will be able to define and defend these children from the point of view of perceptual definition, perceptual-motor definition, and motor definition; and he will understand the differences, subtle and gross, between these issues. He will understand the neurological and pseudoneurological characteristics of these children as well as those characteristics which are developmental in nature. He will understand that the term learning disabilities *per se* is meaningless, and that it serves only for the gross identification of a large heterogeneous population.

2. The professor-student, as he presents deficiencies in his own background will develop those competencies in areas of general teaching of reading, of mathematics, handwriting, spelling, and other areas of basic elementary education.

3. The professor-students will need specialized information on the development of cognition and cognitive structure. Specific attention must be given to the effects of neurological dysfunction on attentional processes, on memory formation, on ability to categorize experiences, on control of motor responses, and on the development of attention span.

4. These professor-students will receive input concerned with the development of visuomotor skills in relation to academic performance. The concepts of the perceptual-motor match of Kephart, prescriptive teaching developed by Peter, the education-perception match as we have discussed it, each and all, require a thorough understanding by the professor-student in order that implementation can be rationally undertaken.

5. The professor must have a basic understanding of perception, *per se*. He must know the difference between perception, perceptual-motor, and how attention and attention deficits modify both.

6. Although most of the work is theoretical and yet to be conclusively demonstrated, much of what goes on in the education of children with specific learning disabilities today, involves motor training programs. The professor-student will be given training in these programs in sufficient depth that he can evaluate them carefully and thus to be able later to bring to his students rational concepts based on known evidence, theory, and practice.

7. In the same non-definitive manner, issues of handedness, laterality, finger localization, and cerebral dominance still escape conclusive data. The professor-student must have what information there is well enough in hand, however, to deal with it logically in the face of frequent reference to these issues when presented as supposedly known fact and as supposedly the controlling elements in educational or psychological methodology.

8. The professor-student must become sufficiently expert in the use of some psychodiagnostic techniques that he can instruct teachers in their uses. Children of the categories about which we are concerned will require frequent, albeit not necessarily indepth assessments, of many aspects of their learning characteristics. Experience has demonstrated that teachers often can do this as well if not better than many school psychologists. They can certainly do it with the frequency which is required, something that psychologists can never hope to achieve so as to provide the basis of good daily instruction. Teachers need to have professors who understand this and who can provide the needed instruction.

9. Although the issues of the education of children with specific learning disabilities are essentially psychoeducational, the teacher needs

some background to enable her to fit into a total professional experience. Several items stand out in this regard. The professor-student must have instruction in the area of neurology and neuropsychology in particular so as to understand the literature. He must have instruction in the area of clinical psychopharmacology, and understand the few positive and the many potential negative gains in reliance on medications. He must understand the pay-offs for these children of education *per se* without medication. Most of these children will present themselves at the school door with emotional overlays; hence, teachers and professor-students must have a thorough background in the dynamics of emotion and emotional maldevelopment. Communication problems and communication disorders are a frequent characteristic of these children. The professor-student will receive background in this area of human growth and development in sufficient depth to know both what the teacher needs and how to deal with his colleagues in other disciplines so as to achieve this and all of the instructional inputs which others must teach to preservice teachers.

We have spent more time on this matter than we will some other points because the lack of a corps of well-prepared teacher educators is so blatant, and because this is the group on whose shoulders the quality of education for these children will rest for the next several decades. It is an issue which cannot be further ignored. Poorly prepared professors must be by-passed, and must be replaced by those who know the field from the point of theory, practice, and organized knowledge and experience. The total cost of this program, while great for the two-year period and for a year of planning, would probably not exceed the sums invested by federal and state governments in traineeships for teachers attending inadequate programs of higher education and who later enter public practice as ill-prepared educators. Fifty or sixty professors, and a mechanism to provide a continuing supply, will not have the political visibility as do hundreds of teachers being given summer scholarships. But this is no time to be concerned with politics. The lives of thousands of children are in balance as are those of tens of thousands of their brothers, sisters, and parents whose life experiences are twisted because of their presence of the handicapped children in their midst.

Problem Complexity

In the reference to the aforementioned article (Cruickshank, 1972) in which we posed certain fundamental issues facing the field of learning disabilities, we once more stressed professional confusion in the absence of adequate definition. While we do not claim insight greater than those who have considered this problem before, we are prompted to examine the matter further, and hopefully to conceptualize both a definition and the basis for a definition.

The field of learning disabilities today is a conglomerate of different types of problems. It did not start out in this manner, but in more recent years problems of a widely diversified nature which appear unsolvable to general educators have been classified as learning disabilities and placed into special classes or programs under teachers generally ill-prepared to deal with the complex problems of most of the children. The issue of hetrogeneity is with us, much as we may dislike and oppose it. The problem is to examine the issue and try to deal with its variations logically and in a more homogeneous manner.

There are three basic elements in conceptualizing the field of learning disabilities keeping in mind that we view this term as one which is broadly used to encompass a multiplicity of childhood problems. The three significant variables are (a) perception, (b) motor characteristics, and (c) intelligence. We present our thinking essentially from the orientation of the educational system thus consciously ignoring the psychological and medical systems which admittedly have a relation, but are not the central core insofar as long-term effort is concerned.

In the paradigm, perception is noted on a spectrum in degrees from normal to "severe" disability; motor characteristics likewise are noted on a separate axis from normal to "severe." Intelligence is noted on still a third axis, and is shown in a traditional quantitive scale from very low (zero measurement) to very high (infinity).

Perception is understood as a mental process through which the qualities or the nature of an object are recognized. We consider perception to be comprised of a multiplicity of characteristics which, through the relationship of memory with the special sensory systems of the body, brings the object to a conscious level. Perception, since it involves cells and sensory systems, is viewed as neurological. From the point of view of learning, it is recognized that numerous factors, some neurological (accident, disease, injury), some possibly developmental and others environmental, may distort or disturb both the cellular system and the normal function of one or more sensory systems. In the paradigm, complexity prevents the writer from noting that there are different perceptual systems relating to the several sensory modalities characteristic of humans, namely, vision, audition, tactation, etc.

Due to any one or combination of factors, the sensory systems may be affected completely; partially, but each in different degrees; or not at all. Why this occurs, is not fully understood. Differences occur between and among sensory systems to say nothing of between and among individuals and is a matter of fact. These deviations in neurological and sensory systems, however, are measurable — at least qualitatively — and to these measures are attached such labels as association or dissociation, memory, sequencing, discrimination, figure-ground differentiation, sensory and motoric hyperactivity, prolonged aftereffect of a stimulus (perseveration), closure problems, and other related psychological characteristics, each and all possessing great implications for the learning process. Each of these characteristics appears to be typical of each of the three major sensory systems, although admittedly definitive research is lacking. Each can be described on a paradigm if one is working with something more than a three dimensional cube concept.

Motor characteristics, noted on another baseline axis on the paradigm, must be conceptualized from two points of view, i.e., sensory-motor characteristics and gross or fine-motor characteristics. The latter have traditionally been classified by neurologists when treating children with cerebral palsy, for example, as *normal, mild, moderate,* or *severe.* Sensory-motor activity has not generally been viewed in the same fashion, but here for the sake of our definition we view the uncontrolled motor activity of the individual, whether gross, fine, visual, auditory, to be of similar degrees and probably even more an inhibitor of learning. Characteristically children with these problems have been viewed by practitioners as hyperactive (or when gross motor factors alone are involved, as hyperkinetic). The diagnostician, however, must keep in mind that the motor factor noted in the paradigm is very complex and varies widely in terms of degree, nature of the motor problem (i.e., sensory, gross, or fine), and in terms of the localization or generalized nature of the handicap.

Another factor cannot adequately be described on the paradigm, namely, the interrelationship of the two forces we have briefly considered. The impact of perceptual function or dysfunction on motor learning and activity is recognized, but not specifically understood. Thus the child in block "A" in the paradigm is a perfectly normal child of high intelligence, child "B" is a severely handicapped child, perceptually and motorically, and is of very low intelligence. Child "C" is moderately handicapped perceptually; of normal motor ability and of "normal" mental ability.

It is with the interrelations that the categories of perceptual-motor disabilities develop, i.e., eye-hand coordination, ear-hand coordination, tactual-motor activity, *ad inf.* In dictating a spelling lesson, for example, the teacher is requiring the child to employ both audio-motor and visuomotor systems simultaneously.

Intelligence has to be indicated on the paradigm, for it will be a controlling factor in the child's ability to learn, to self-control his own problems, and it will be a factor in logical educational placement. There is nothing mystical about this statement. It is made by this writer in the full knowledge of the complexities of measuring intelligence in these children and of the fact that both perceptual and motor problems may affect intellectual function as measured. As a controlling factor, however, intelligence must be recognized.

A positive definition of this problem thus concerns itself with an individual (a) who is characterized by a quantitatively or qualitatively measurable deviation from the normal in total perceptual function or in any one or more of the sensory systems related to perception, (b) who is characterized by a deviation in motor abilities in either gross- or fine-motor activities or in sensory activities related to perception, (c) who may be further handicapped by the abnormal interrelationship between perceptual and motor systems, and (d) whose intelligence may be of any quantitative level.

A Diversified Program is Required

When one contemplates the tremendous variability possible in terms of the oversimplified paradigm, and much more pronounced in real life, it becomes obvious that no single educational solution can be applied within a community school program. The child's clinical needs, his educational program and his placement will be determined essentially on the basis of qualitative assessments of a psychoeducational nature. On the basis of these data children will be provided a vital educational experience, not merely assigned to undifferentiated "learning disabilities class", a meaningless and unproductive term. The child will be placed in a clinical teaching situation, one of several types conceived as the most appropriate for a given child's needs. The educational perceptual match partially takes place at this point. Some of these children will be retained in the regular grades with understanding teachers where both teacher and child receive guidance and instruction from skilled itinerant teacher-clinicians. Other children, probably quantitatively in greater number will spend varying amounts of time each day in a resource room where through one-to-one teaching situations or in very small homogeneous groups, the deficits of the children will be treated. Still others whose perceptual-motor problems are pervading and severe will require a full-time clinical teaching station for long periods, perhaps years, until through training and/or maturation they are equipped to return to the regular grades fully or with resource of itinerant teacher supports. The mechanism we suggest is not new. The refinement in ascertaining the primary learning deficits, the educational placement in terms of severity of the problem and the homogeneous groupings of children in terms of the type of perceptual motor problem, although not a new concept either, is new in terms of what good practice requires. Implementation is a requisite now and in the immediate future.

Quality Teacher Education

Qualified professors, prepared in depth to understand and implement the real issues in specific learning disability will in all likelihood produce qualified educators. We have spoken and written so often on this problem that it is redundant to do so again. Certain conclusions from thirty years of work in this field are appropriate, however.

1. The field is so complicated that it cannot be treated in any satisfactory manner in three to six week summer courses. Were we again to undertake the organization of a bona fide teacher education program for resource, itinerant, or special class teacher-clinicians, it would be done on the basis of a sixty-hour master's degree encompassing 18 to 24 months. The details of such a program have been delineated elsewhere (Cruickshank, Junkala, and Paul 1968).

2. If retention of some of these children in the regular grade is a part of the policy, then *every elementary and every secondary teacher in the nation* must have a thorough orientation and understanding of the impact of specific learning disabilities on the learning process. If teachers do not understand and if they fail through ignorance to teach adequately, these children are hurt.

3. Every administrator as a part of his minimal certification, requires a full understanding of the child with specific learning disabilities, the nature of programs of training, and the criteria for selective placement within a program.

4. The education of children with specific learning disabilities is not synonymous with remedial reading. Many children who need reading assistance may profit from methodology appropriate to that employed with some types of specific learning disabilities. Much of the failure of educators to deal appropriately with the learning disability issue is due to the administrative decision which suddenly assigned the learning disability program to the remedial reading program. The education of these children must go far beyond the best concepts of reading instruction.

Adequate Psychological and Diagnostic Services

The concept of the match between educational methodology and the specific learning disability must become the focus of assessment. Kephart speaks of the perceptual-motor match as a basis of his motor training program. We extend the idea of the match to education and perceptual-motor disabilities.

This concept is teachable to psychoeducational diagnosticians. The focus of diagnosis must be on those functions which are basic to learning the skills of reading, mathematics, handwriting, and spelling. The diagnostician seeks evidence of the intactness of such processes as have long been recognized as fundamental to perceptual-motor problems, namely the child's status relative to discrimination, attention span, memory span, selective attention, figure ground relationships, and other crucial factors. From some quantitative instruments, but mostly from qualitative test situations and clinical skills, the next generation of diagnosticians must be taught how to build the perceptual blueprint of a child. From this, the qualified educator makes the educational match to child placement, learning environment, teaching method, and teaching materials.

Courageous Special Education Leadership

Special education has been much less effective than it could have been because it has too frequently bowed to the wishes of general educators and administrators regarding the placement of children. Special education has been used in a very indiscriminate manner to relieve the regular class of problems which the general educator could not solve. Special education leadership has aided and abetted these actions and has rarely refused to accept a child even though transfer was known to be inappropriate. As a result of this, because unteachable situations were created for teachers, special education is under attack. In the courts and in the community we hear these facts stated and restated.

Special education directors, supervisors, consultants, and departmental chairmen (a) must find for themselves large quantities of intestinal fortitude and use it appropriately in behalf of children; (b) must be prepared to seek court action if need be to protect children from unwise decisions regarding school placement; and (c) must match this in terms of its own appropriate action. Placement of a child in a clinical teaching situation is a serious matter, and the decision must be made thoughtfully and with all pertinent educational facts available.

Return to the Regular Grades

We have often spoken of the care with which children should be placed into a special classroom and of the structured procedure which is helpful in organizing the special class group each fall. We have seen the value to both an individual child and the total group when the school administration adds one child at a time to a class, and carefully structures the total situation until the entire group of children is assembled.

Just as care must be taken in developing a special class or in assigning children to a resource room, so equal care must be taken in returning the child to the regular grades when it is felt he can cope with the less sheltered situation. It is indeed a major decision which now has been reached in considering return.

First, it must be agreed that upon return the child is able to compete at age in grade to the degree at least equal to the medium achievement level of the receiving group. Secondly, the decision must be reached early enough to permit the special class teacher, in cooperation with the regular class teacher, to undertake and accomplish an acquisition of the content material which the child will experience in the receiving classroom.

Thirdly, care must be taken in selecting the regular grade room into which he will be assimilated. If there is a choice of multiple sections of a given grade level, our experience suggests that a general rule would be to select the teacher among those available who is more comfortable than others with structure and who might be characterized as a traditional teacher — an adult accepting of children, but one who approaches the teaching situation with topic, class, and the individual child well in hand. The child in whom we now have an interest is one who generally finds difficulty in permissive situations and with a teacher or other adults who themselves operate in a very unstructured manner.

Fourth, the child must always know that in the event he needs to return to the special teaching situation, he may do so. There must always be an escape valve for the child, a prearranged procedure through which he may retreat with honor.

Supplies, Material, and Teacher Aides

It should be a truism that educators know how to select appropriate teaching materials. However, too often this is not so. Newell Kephart (Kephart 1971) has written wisely regarding the perceptual-motor match. Peters (1965) speaks of prescriptive teaching. We have stressed the importance of the educational and perceptual match. Each of these concepts strongly implies that the child's specific learning characteristics along with other considerations will be matched with specific teaching materials to compliment one another. It is infrequent that sufficient care is taken in purchasing educational material, and too frequently mass purchasing leaves the teacher instructionally helpless and the child further vulnerable to poor teaching.

As we look forward to the future and to a degree of excellence yet to be attained in the education of children with specific learning disabilities, three issues remain to be discussed.

Well-Informed Parents

Never before have parents so quickly become so well informed about the problems of their children as have parents of the children about whom we here write. Unfortunately, parents were often misled in assuming that professionals knew what needed to be done and that all which was lacking was a sufficient supply of dollars to provide the needed treatment and educational facilities. This is another story, but nevertheless is true. In the course of their efforts these parents became exceedingly knowledgeable, and subsequently exceedingly helpful in many communities in the development of educational facilities. But a well-informed parent group is not enough. Information alone is insufficient.

Our experience convinces us that the great majority of parents of children with specific learning disabilities come to a realization of the essence of the problem of their child with deep-seated frustrations, misunderstandings, of guilt feelings of their own, and often with unrealistic expectancies for the child. If this happens, the problems for and surrounding the child are often more than either he or the family together can handle. When counseling, often of an obligatory nature, has been included in the educational process for the family—parents and the siblings—the role of the learning disability in the dynamics of family living takes on a significantly different flavor, and the course of progress for the child is smoother. Psychiatrists, social workers, psychologists, guidance and counseling personnel, clergymen, and others, understanding both the counseling process and the learning disability problem, have been able to play unique and extraordinarily important roles in bringing family members to a new level of group integration. Residential facilities or private day schools which serve children with learning disabilities should profit from the experience of those which require this experience as a part of the acceptance of the child into the school program and which cover the costs of this additional professional activity within tuition and fee structures. The public schools which will continue to serve the largest numbers of these children must in cooperation with parent groups work out mechanisms whereby the same benefits can be accrued to families and children within the local communities. The issue of specific

learning disability is so complex that a twenty-four hour approach is required. The impact of the disabilities is to be seen in dressing, eating, and
general behavior in the home and neighborhood as well as in the school.
Thus parents must be as well prepared to provide structured educational experiences in the home as teachers are to do the same in different areas in the
school location. The future must include this consideration for a total program of educational service.

The Para-Educational Support Team

The teacher of children with specific learning disabilities will require
assistance depending upon the degree of severity of the child's problems.
Support teams of specialist personnel have been used for many years in varying ways to assist the child and the teacher. Two factors are significant in re-
emphasizing this important aspect of a total program. First, it is essential
that all members of the support team have a common point of view regarding the learning of children with perceptual deficits. These children require
structure; they cannot easily adjust to different approaches as they meet
teacher, speech therapist, psychologist, or other professional person. Common points of view and common approaches to the problem must be practiced by all.

Second, a different way of utilizing support personnel may be required for many of these children. It is generally the practice to send a child
from the classroom to the specialist. Many children cannot tolerate this
movement, cannot adjust to new situations quickly, and become tense simply by reason of walking through school corridors. As a result, the time with
the specialist is not utilized as an optimum, and time is required upon return
to the home classroom to readjust from the tension of the earlier movement.
Experience has demonstrated to us that with children possessing severe perceptual problems, it is better to have all or a major portion of the support
personnel input made to the child via his teacher. The number of personali-
ties to which the child has to learn to adjust is then minimized, and all inputs
are assured of being presented in the same way and within the same theoretical structure. Administration has to provide opportunities for the teacher to
meet with support personnel to receive their suggestions and directions for
working with the child, and support specialists have to be provided with time
to observe the child in the classroom so as to be able to provide the teacher
with up-dated information and directions. Good programs logically conceived in terms of the child's limitations and needs, however, bring the skills
of the specialists into the daily program in an appropriate way and at times
when they are needed.

Review Boards

As a final element in the development of a quality program of education for children with specific learning disabilities, I would like to discuss a technique on which we have written once before (Cruickshank, 1972), namely, the establishment and use of review committees. The quality of education for these children we have stated is poor. It is absolutely imperative that a program be conceptualized and made operational nationally in which we can have pride. Nothing should escape the spotlight of healthy scrutiny. The quality of the professorial corps and the teaching corps is not of a sufficient level of excellence to insure to the child and his family the psychoeducational experiences he requires to bring the child to the level of community participation society expects. The issue of quality requires attack not only on the factors pertinent to the educational arena *per se* for children with specific learning disabilities, but also on both the total area of psychodiagnostics and psychological training and on general education as well.

As a drastic step toward the excellence we seek, we strongly recommend that at all levels of education there be established review committees to monitor the quality of excellence of the programs. Educators will object to this as being interference with traditional concepts of academic freedom. Academic freedom is indeed a right to be cherished. However, academic freedom does not give educational professionals the concomitant right to ignore their obligation to provide quality education to the very society which supports them. Medicine and dentistry, and to a much lesser extent psychology and some of the other disciplines, through their own professional mechanisms monitor and review the professional performance of their membership. This type of review is essential in those areas of service delivery where the general public cannot be authoritative. Society must rely on internal monitoring of the profession to guarantee high quality of personnel preparation, institutional efficiency, and service delivery.

There is, however, a problem with education and the schools. In these fields we are faced with the feeling that everyone is a specialist in both how schools should be run and how children should be taught. Everyone is an authority. That the schools are open to public inspection and education, is a right reserved to the state and delegated to the local community. Intraprofessional review is difficult to come by and to operate. This fact, however, does not minimize the need for professional standards and their constant monitoring. It only makes the problem a more challenging one.

Citizen or judicial review panels are upon us if the professions do not immediately move to establish their own monitoring systems. We have previously stated that education is often just as cruel to children as are police reported to be when on occasion they mishandle university students, members of minorities, and both those awaiting trial and those committed to prison terms. It is a difference of style not fact. As citizens of many communities are taking a stance to demand review boards to monitor behavior of individuals and quality of programs for public protection, so citizens, joining with professionals, appear to be needed to establish review panels to monitor that which goes on in the name of education. It is essential that professional educators and psychologists move to assume this responsibility and establish quality programs before either citizen review boards or the courts of the nation assume that responsibility for educators.

REFERENCES

Cruickshank, W. M., ed. *The Teacher of Brain-Injured Children: A Discussion of the Bases for Competency.* Syracuse: Syracuse University Press, 1966.

Cruickshank, W. M.; J. B. Junkala; and J. L. Paul. *The Preparation of Teachers of Brain-Injured Children.* Syracuse: Syracuse University Press, 1968.

Cruickshank, W. M. "Special education, the community, and constitutional issues." In *Special Education: Instrument of Change for the 70s,* edited by D. L. Walker and D. P. Howard. Charlottesville: University of Virginia, 1972, pp. 5–24.

Cruickshank, W. M. "Some Issues Facing the Field of Learning Disability." *Journal of Learning Disability* 5, no. 7 (1972): 380–88.

Kephart, N. C. *The Slow Learner in the Classroom.* Columbus: Merrill, 1971.

Peters, L. J. *Prescriptive Teaching.* New York: McGraw-Hill, 1965.

17

ADOLESCENTS
WITH LEARNING DISABILITIES

$\mathcal{T}$HE ADOLESCENT WITH LEARNING DISABILITIES is one for whom little or no planning has been done in any coordinated manner — nationally, at the state level, or locally. Some few programs are in operation, but these are sporadic, often short lived, and many times opportunistic. A very few are good or long-standing in nature. The learning disabled elementary school children of the late thirties and forties are in some cases grandparents now; those of the sixties should be in the fullness of their lives. Whatever their status, particularly if it is positive, it is very likely *not* because of their school experiences, but in spite of them. If their lives are not being spent optimally, it is largely the responsibility of ineffective school programs, for even at the elementary level educators have hardly scratched the surface of the problem with meaningful and appropriate programming. At the secondary and college levels, almost nothing has been accomplished.

WHAT YOUTH TELL US

Few have concerned themselves with groups of learning disabled adolescents. There are some exceptions to that statement, but generally this is true. In my own professional practice, this is certainly the case, yet recently we have gone back over many folders of children and have been able to select quite a large number of those who now are junior-senior high school students and a much fewer number of students in community colleges or other

Keynote address, The Adams School Conference, New York City, April 22, 1978.

types of higher education. Others are now employed in their communities. There are also many more examples of those who did not succeed in any of these avenues of education or work.

It is dangerous to use examples, for one can appear to prove most any point from a single example. However, we shall write briefly about some examples, and see what these young people tell us. From these statements we can attempt to make some generalizations and to suggest what is needed educationally.

A seventeen-year-old male is known to his friends by the name of *Luke*. His intelligence level is normal. He presents many perceptual processing deficits, although by no way are they as severe as six years earlier when he was first seen. He has failed his driving examination once, but anticipates that with tutorial help he will pass it on the second trial. "We can't get into driver education, you know," he reminds me. "They [the public school personnel] don't trust us. The driver school will take us, though—anything to make a buck. I am sure that I can do it the second time. The guy at the academy says that the driving examination is written at a third grade level, and I can do that." "How do you get around," I ask. "My pal has a car, and he drives. We do OK, or I guess I should say I do OK." Is driving an important issue for adolescents insofar as their psycho-social adjustment is concerned? Is this a matter which should be of concern to educational planners?

On another occasion Luke's case notes are of interest in a different sphere. We were visiting with him about the residuals of the perceptual-motor problems with which he and the clinic staff were working, and somehow the discussion veered to Luke's girlfriend. "Hell, I got problems I know," said Luke. "I've had those problems all my life and I guess I always will. Susie doesn't seem to mind. I mind, but Susie doesn't. She's a swell gal. I'll have to bring her in to meet you. You know, Dr. C., I don't have any perceptual-motor problems when Susie and I get into the back seat of John's car—what a gas!" Do these two vignettes, when generalized to the larger group, indicate concepts regarding the content of curriculum for adolescents who also have learning disabilities?

Alec is sixteen. He has been seen periodically in a good diagnostic facility since he was six years of age. He is a classic example of a child with perceptual processing deficits severe enough to have required that he receive individual tutoring for two years, that he be placed in a special clinical teaching program for three years, and later that he be assigned to a resource room through his so-called junior high school years. In high school, however, Alec was "mainstreamed," as his principal states in a letter to the clinic director. As a fourteen-year-old student, moving along in terms of social promotions, Alec demonstrated three years ago that he was functioning with a fourth-grade mathematics achievement, strong third-grade total reading scores, and an estimated intelligence score in the low one hundreds. While he had made a good social adjustment in the more sheltered situations, he started to deteriorate markedly concomitant with the mainstreaming experiences of the upper secondary school. At sixteen, where is he? He has had three severe brushes with the police. He is on marijuana and other drugs. His academic achievements are at a standstill. He had no genuine success experiences within his recall. He says to me, "It's like I don't exist in those god-damned teachers' classrooms. Mr. Carver didn't even say 'pardon me' when he stepped on my foot the other day. He just glared. I go to school only to please my dad and mother. To hell with the rest of them."

When one compares Alec and his present achievement levels, his progress, his attitudes, one sees a completely different individual than when he was in elementary, or even in junior high school, programs. He is lost. He has no basis for genuine achievement in the programs of the non-adjusting high school. He is receiving no attention from teachers, for they consider him as a failure and as a block to their content-oriented teaching. They do not understand him, and they do not want to be bothered to do so. Our questions are: Is mainstreaming a valid concept with the severely learning disabled? Is Alec, as representative of hundreds of others in similar situations, to have his life spoiled, his parents distraught, because of a fad of mainstreaming which is based on not one iota of valid research? Who indeed is the culprit — Alec or the educational establishment?

A third example consists of fifty sets of parents with whom the author has worked. These are all parents of male learning disabled children older than fourteen years of age. They are asked, "What are the hopes you have for your children?" What are their answers? In order of priority, the parents say:

1. I want my child to be able to get and hold a job.
2. I want my child to be socially and emotionally happy.
3. I want my child to be able to make appropriate decisions.
4. I want my child to have a girl friend. This later was expanded to a girl friend or a boy friend, since three parents stated their sons were undoubtedly homosexual.
5. I want my child to have the opportunity to enter the armed forces.
6. I want my child to have good sexual experiences.
7. I want my child to be able to function properly in the community insofar as purchasing, banking, and related matters are concerned.

These seven wants were the responses of the ten or more parents to each of the above-listed items. There were thirty-three other wants covering the total spectrum of adolescent-young adult adjustment and learning. A valid question is: Is there a curriculum obvious here in these "wants"; i.e., vocational or prevocational, human sexuality, social achievement, and academic?

Karen is a sixteen-year-old young lady with whom we have had contact since she was four. At four Karen was the bane of her family's existence. Characterized by hyperactivity and all of the psychological attributes by which children with perceptual processing deficits are described, Karen was a classical so-called learning disabled child. The community in which she lived was small and had no facilities for nursery school, preschool, or significant individual adaptations for troubled children at the elementary school level. Already a child with emotional problems as an overlay to her basic perceptual difficulties, adjustment problems were intensified when Karen was placed at six years of age with an aunt in a neighboring large city where university clinic facilities were available for her. She was enrolled in a clinical teaching situation at the university for four years until she was ten. Significant strides were made in terms of perceptual-motor reorganization, in the acquisition of basic learning skills, and in social adjustment. At ten she was placed in a neighborhood elementary school on a part-time basis, still living with the aunt and seeing her parents only on infrequent weekends or holidays. The trial placement in school appeared to be satisfactory; at least the school could tolerate Karen's problems and worked with the university program to maintain her positive growth. By twelve, Karen's primary problem was social and emotional. Her parents did not really know her and were pleased to write her off to her aunt. This did not help Karen, although the aunt was more than genuine in her interests in Karen. The aunt remarried at this juncture. Karen entered puberty and also faced the problems of adjusting in a junior high school. While academic success was sufficient to support her in elementary school, it was not sufficient to carry her into the junior high school with success. The change in the life pattern of her aunt, the physical changes of her own life, the inability of her academic experiences to provide success acceptable to her and her peers, and the inelasticity of the junior high school to support her with that which she needed accentuated her emotional problems. These were further complicated by the time she reached fourteen in a rampage of sexual activity which gave her a reputation throughout the school. She was socially labeled to the point of no return. For her, success experiences had been achieved. However, adults had other plans. It appeared wise to return her to her parent's home and into a new social climate not ladened with at least the former sexual cues, and where a different reputation might be created. Frequent trips to a therapeutic setting were initiated. The small high school into which she was entered in her parents' home community was traditional and had no member on the staff who understood or truly accepted the problems of children in need. College placement was the school goal, and the percentage of graduates who went on to college was high. Others dropped by the wayside.

Now at sixteen, Karen is hopelessly lost. Her sexual success patterns were begun again, and are well established. Therapy has a minimal influence. A discrepancy of six years exists between chronological age and academic achievement age. Perceptual processing deficits are not now a major factor, although even without the social and emotional situation she experiences, Karen would need assistance in order to improve her academic success rate. The question is: Who is at fault in the general ruin of Karen's young life? The state, which provided no support for services she needed as a child? The parents, for not having moved to a larger community and thus maintaining a wholesome relationship with their daughter? The university program, for isolating her from the realities of an elementary school program? The inflexibility of the secondary school programs? The aunt who unfortunately got married? The secondary schools for not having provided total guidance and counseling to Karen when she arrived in its classrooms? None or all of the above?

The day before *Jeff* arrived at a clinical teaching classroom as an eight-year-old, he had been permanently excluded from the Boys' Club facilities in his city, because he had ripped up three pool-table covers. With that evidence added to the boy's already growing file, the public schools likewise excluded him. The relationship between the two actions is possible to see, but cloudy at best. For three years Jeff prospered in varying degrees in the clinical teaching program of a nearby university. The first year was more than difficult for both Jeff and the staff, but progress through careful nurturing, a highly structured teaching program, parent involvement, and well-prepared teachers paid off, and Jeff gradually turned failure into success experiences. At the end of three years, a part-time trial placement was undertaken in the community schools with supportive resource facilities available. The educational program for Jeff continued within the frame of reference of his previous special class experiences. His achievement continued. His social adjustment did not regress, except for the usual problems of a preadolescent child's adjustment. Jeff was continually promoted on a chronological age basis through the junior high school years. Always he was given one-to-one support either at the university clinic on an out-patient basis, or with carefully supervised university students on either an outreach or practicum basis. As he reached sixteen years he was transferred to a vocational high school where the status quo *maintenance* of his academic achievement was the only goal in that area of his development, but where prevocational testing and training was the primary concept. He was given a variety of community-based, supervised, prevocational experiences. Often there was failure, because this once-classical perceptually handicapped boy still was characterized by a residual of processing deficits, although his understanding of his problem was complete and his compensatory mechanisms were plentiful. There were frequent contacts for purposes of guidance from the high school to university personnel, and the parents were fully supportive. Jeff had his problems; there is no denial of that. He sowed his wild oats in a variety of adolescent ways. The security of his home and the closeness of his relationship with one of the university faculty members was a great support as he experimented with fast driving, beer, girls, marijuana, more fast driving, the police, and with aggressions against adults generally. The goal was to keep what may be considered normal adolescent behavior separated from the perceptual processing deficits and his learning problems in the minds of all who worked with him.

A prevocational placement in supermarket employment, the second in this type of activity, appeared to be a success. The manager asked if he wanted to work full time during the summer. Jeff was eighteen by then. He was told that if he did accept the job, he would be counted on to be on time, courteous, clean, off beer during working hours, and more important, be expected to build his skills with numbers, for he would be doing stock clerk and inventory work that summer. Fortunately, this was a success. He started going with a girl. His job continued into the fall. He dropped out of school. He and his girl started to live together. A baby arrived. They decided they could and should marry. Parent support was evidenced throughout. At twenty-two Jeff is still with the supermarket chain. He is now assistant night manager. His wife helps him with those things he needs to know and read where his skills remain deficient. The food chain knows something of his background from the original school placement. The manager sees no reason why in the future he should not move at least one step further up the employment ladder. Interestingly, his relationship with the university faculty member has always been maintained — originally as a professional in his special teaching situation, later as an anchor in times of trouble, and at the moment, although several hundred miles separate them, still as an anchor, but also as a good friend.

Greg is nineteen, a young man whom the author first knew as a boy of seven years of age. He has completed his junior year in a high school in a large middle-class community. When Greg was smaller he had dozens of problems which brought him into conflict with the teaching staffs of two schools. He made great strides during the three years he was in a clinical teaching situation in the nearby university clinic, and he was later transferred back to the public schools. Although currently he has a diagnosis of dyslexia, he was earlier seen as a child with most of the classic symptoms of perceptual and learning disabilities which we have described here. Greg was always an appealing boy, one who could attract attention by his good looks. His behavior soon belied his otherwise cherubic outward expression, and he was in constant conflict with teachers or other authorities. His early case record reads like a horror story.

However, Greg had achieved the rudiments of learning skills by the time he was eleven. He prospered in the public schools, although with a tremendous amount of effort on his part and that of his parents and some teachers. Junior high school was a real crisis for Greg, for the inability of the schools to adjust to his needs plus the onset of normal adolescent growth and behavior mitigated against him. It was sometimes touch and go. However, he made it, and completed the eleventh grade. Mathematics ability was at least at grade level if not above. Reading was at a minimal eighth grade level.

His twelfth grade program was to be planned. At this point two things happened. First the guidance counselor of the high school insisted that his records from his seventh and eighth chronological years be submitted for study. It is difficult to understand the reason since there was no need for these records. In the hands of an uninsightful person, these records could only do harm. The fact that exceptional children do often cease to be exceptional was completely ignored by this guidance counselor. The relationship between Greg's needs at seven years of age to his needs eleven years later is hard to understand. The clinic director wisely refused to release the records. The guidance counselor responded by saying that they were not needed anyway, for Greg's fifth grade records had been found "tucked away" someplace, and these would serve the desired purpose. The desired purpose was never specified.

Secondly, Greg and his parents were told that Greg could probably be granted a diploma at the end of the twelfth grade, but that it would be stamped "Dyslexic." What in the name of conscience this would accomplish is hard to understand. Furthermore, in many states such labeling of such a document is illegal, and suit could be instituted against the Board of Education, the superintendent of schools, and the building principal. More such suits ought to be initiated in defense of children and youth who have struggled and succeeded. When challenged regarding this potential action, the reply by the high school principal was "Well, Greg's a fine boy and has done a good job, but I couldn't possibly give him one of my diplomas without somehow noting all the problems he has had." Advocacy has a place in every community. In Greg's case, still not fully resolved, advocacy against such bureaucratic attitudes and possessiveness is certainly warranted. Such, however, are the problems that well-intentioned adolescents with learning disabilities must often face as they attempt to succeed within the secondary school arena.

RESPONSES TO YOUTH'S NEEDS

We have described a set of children with learning disabilities. Grown into youth and young adulthood they present a variety of problems, some sad and as failures, others modestly successful, and at least one with the potential of reasonable adult adjustment. What generalizations can be made?

In spite of the commonly held statement, not all children with perceptual processing deficits grow out of them as adolescence appears. Some may, but we have no broad-based data to illustrate that this is a firm and general rule by any means. We hope that all will outgrow their deficits, but in the face of reality, thousands carry their problems into adolescence and adulthood. Maturity seemingly does have a leavening effect, however. Adult insights which can be developed in the youth assist in the individual's adjustment.

In going back over the comments made by the young people referred to here, what are their specific concerns? Several are immediately apparent: a need for driver education; a need for human fulfillment; a need for success experiences; a need for techniques to provide positive social acceptance; a need for freedom under appropriate adult monitoring for social and personal experimentation; a need for pre- and ongoing vocational evaluation and training; a need for personal security in social situations; a need for training and education at interest and capacity levels; a need for information regarding marital responsibilities and child growth and development; and a need to be able to be an adolescent without misinterpretation.

If these needs, not an exhaustive list by any means, are logically grouped, three major categories become apparent: (1) human fulfillment, (2) educational, and (3) vocational. Let us examine them in this order.

Human Fulfillment

It must be understood from the beginning that the handicapped are not asexual beings. There is an absolute myth held by many parents and a large segment of society in general to the effect that human sexuality is something which does not affect the handicapped. "Thank God. I don't have to worry about my son and his virginity," said a father to the writer on one occasion. "He'll always be one. He can't walk." It's only wine and song for my boy," commented a mother. "He'll never have to worry about the women in the verse. But then, he doesn't have that need, what with his handicap." "Do perceptually handicapped people have normal sex drives?" writes a parent. These comments and questions reflect ignorance.

Perceptually handicapped youth and adults do have sex drives, of course. They also have more than the need for the mere physical relationships in sex. Human fulfillment or human sexuality encompasses the totality of the concept of love in its broadest definition. Human fulfillment means a parental and social concern for the physical well-being of the youth, for his emotional and social well-being, and for freedom to grow normally into these spheres of human behavior. The security of two parents who are accepting, and the satisfactions learned by the youth through the structure of a good early childhood and elementary education, make it possible for the young man or woman to experiment, to test this dimension of human experience, and to broaden his or her own horizons of experience. Parents often must worry, must hold their peace, must exert self-control as well as extend a minimum of specific direction for the adolescent. The extent of parental worries about their children's behavior will be a reflection of the depth of the dialogue which has existed between and among family members from early on. All that one would wish between parents and normal children must also prevail between parents and youth with learning disabilites.

It must be recognized that in our society the child of eight is an independent, voting adult a decade later. From the point of physical maturity, the learning disabled is not different from any other youth of comparable age level. That youth, whether man or woman, has needs on occasion to experiment with his body, to push it to the point of physical exhaustion, and to learn pride in his body and what it can do. The youth has need, depending on circumstance, to engage in sexual behavior of his choice with the security of knowing that he is ready for it, is intellectually prepared, and is supported in his actions by an accepting society. Like Jeff, the young man with the severest of perceptual processing deficits, the learning disabled youth with the support of family and friends must move unhesitatingly into marriage, if that be *his* or *her* desire, and be able to engage in the totality of a married life including the rearing of his own children. Is this asking too much of society? The role of the schools appears obvious. Can society, by whatever dimension, arbitrate that youth with perceptual processing deficits be denied those things which go to make up a full life? Years ago Professor Franklin Bobbitt of the University of Chicago used to speak of human fulfillment as the attainment of "the good life." He was ahead of his time by four decades at least.

Where are the essentials of the good life learned? First they are learned through the modeling of two secure parents. In the greater number of instances they are learned through the total program of the schools — a place where today human fulfillment and all it implies is usually ignored or vigorously avoided.

Perceptually handicapped and learning disabled youth have all the needs of all youth. The home and, particularly the schools, cannot disenfranchise handicapped young people in this area of development. The schools need to face this challenge and the parents must support these areas of learning. Human fulfillment cannot be left to chance, to the gutter, to word of mouth, to fear. Nor by avoiding the issue do parents or the larger society have the right to impose on these young people fears, guilt feelings, psychological impotence, or other negativisms which are controlling and self-defeating. Youth with a history of perceptual and learning disabilities have had enough of such life tones. They do not need now to warp their lives further. The learning disabled youth and young adult has a human right to the beauty of human sexuality in its richest forms.

Educational Needs

The fact that youth with these problems exist means that something must be done about them at the junior-senior high school levels, and, for a smaller number, in the community college or other types of higher education programs. This will be difficult because the educational settings are content oriented rather than individual oriented.

The fact that the secondary schools are not presently receptive to the individual differences of children presents a totally new and somewhat different challenge for parents with youth with learning disabilities. It is essential, from my point of view, that parent organizations, having begun a reasonable program for young children, again muster their energies and begin a national, state, and local attack on public educational facilities to open up the secondary schools to youth with perceptual processing deficits.

What must be available in the long term for these children? First, there must be sensitive teachers and administrators who understand or who are brought to understand the unique individual differences of this population of youth.

As we have already stated, secondary school teachers are generally content oriented, often to the point where their view of the *learner* of the content is blurred or completely lost. Certification programs for secondary school teachers contain a maximum of subject matter courses and a minimum of information about human beings, their childhood and adolescent development. Concepts of individualization of instruction are read about but rarely integrated into a way of a teacher's life or practical application. College preparation is a goal, even often a nonverbalized goal, held by many of those teachers who work in center-city schools or with disadvantaged populations of youth. The focus of all too many teachers is on the number of their pupils who pass the New York State Regents examinations, earn Merit Scholarships, who enter the university directly out of high school, or obtain high scores on the SAT! To recall a high school graduation is proof. Scholars are rewarded. Even some athletes are recognized for their prowess. Where is the recognition of the learning disabled youth who, by sheer dint of a good education, of supportive parents, a unique teacher, and his own persistence, has achieved a high fifth-grade reading ability and success in four prevocational experiences? That youth's diploma, if there were one, should be embossed in gold and he should be given a standing ovation. Who in the schools ever genuinely rewarded Jeff for becoming an assistant manager of the night shift in the grocery store? Educators speak of meeting the individual needs of children, but rarely do they or the schools they work in demonstrate this point of view. If the learning disabled child is to be accepted into the secondary schools, the schools must be characterized by administrators, teachers, and programs which are truly responsive to the nature and needs of the youth they purport to serve. What is the point of this?

If secondary educators are to meet the needs of a large number of youth with learning disabilities, at least three things must be accomplished. First, teacher education programs must provide a thorough understanding of the nature and needs of young people who arrive in junior and senior high schools still characterized by educationally and socially debilitating perceptual processing deficits. Preservice teachers must have a broad orientation to all types of exceptionality, but since this book is focused on the perceptual processing deficits and the learning disabled child, it is this group to which we give consideration now. Secondly, teachers in service must receive or be given the opportunity to learn about these young people and to understand ways in which they can be assisted. Mainstreaming without teacher orientation will definitely be a failure.

Finally, if the youth arrives at the secondary level with perceptual processing deficits which are functional to his disadvantage, his total educational achievement level also will probably be limited—reading, number concepts, and related areas of school learning. If this be the case, it is logical that there must be included within the teaching corps of the secondary schools some elementary educators who, by reason of their specialized training and preparation to work with children characterized by perceptual processing deficits, can meet effectively the continuing needs of such youths. The needs of learning disabled youths, *if the processing deficits are still present and apparent,* is for exactly the same type of educational training activities as used with younger children. Obviously these have to be adjusted to a higher social interest level, spoken vocabulary, and to the youth's greater experience.

The author is reminded of a twenty-eight-year-old first sergeant in his hospital during World War II who could not sign his name, who found it difficult to judge distances, who was originally in a special training unit set by the Army for high-grade retarded soldiers, and who needed his company clerk to read orders, regulations, and other items which arrived on his desk. He had taught himself techniques of adjustment, and he succeeded. Others are not so fortunate.

Don is a twenty-three-year-old married man who was referred by his employer for assistance. He was in charge of a large department in industry. He could not write or read. His wife assisted him and he did well on his supervisory job. In the clinic his perceptual-motor skills were at times below expectancy for an early childhood level. How he reached maturity as a well-adjusted young man almost defied logic. He willingly entered into private therapy which began at a reading readiness level and included color-form sorting; recognition of the meaning of line segments, forms, and shapes; recognition of letters and numerals; and perceptual-motor training of a very primitive level. Motivation, of course, was high and played a role. Within a two-year period this man was reading at a strong third-grade level, was signing his name to his own handwritten checks, and was emotionally elated at his progress. His personal irritation related to his anger at not having been given the opportunity to advance a decade earlier.

It is this type of radical educational adjustment which must become one of the characteristics of the educational program for learning disabled youths in high schools. The secondary schools must make available highly individualized learning and teaching programs which are geared to the residual needs of the youth and which will — when he is an adolescent — provide him with genuine success experiences seen as such by both him and his parents and accepted as such by his less handicapped peers. This means that Gallagher's tutorial concept will follow these youth into the secondary school, along with the special teaching program as may be required for small groups, the resource room, and a healthy and appropriate program of integration where possible. We reiterate that if these individual educational adaptations are required at the elementary level, we must face the fact that they may also be needed in some cases at the secondary level. The provision of each and all of the techniques which we have mentioned will mean that youth with needs characterized from extreme to mild may be served. The cost of this can only be offset by an understanding and real appreciation of what the failure to provide will mean in terms of life span, lowered tax payments, welfare costs, delinquency manifestations, police and jail costs, psychiatric fees, and unhappy lives which damage the whole community in the long run.

Vocational Education

A focus must of necessity be placed at a minimum on at least the type of prevocational education, community trial placement, and vocational placement which Jeff experienced. The technical or vocational school concepts so often found in community schools is little different from content-oriented English, history, and science teaching. There are many such facilities which have a rigorous admissions policy, sometimes more restrictive than college-oriented academic programs.

Simply stated a mechanism has to be found whereby exploratory prevocational and vocational experiences can be provided to youth who retain significant perceptual processing deficits. These young people are important. Their needs must be met. Prevocational and vocational educators must be found whose interests and values can be directed to this population of adolescents. There must be a close working relationship among all educators who have direct contact with the child who retains perceptual processing deficits. There are more things which many of these young people can accomplish— driving a car included for some-than there are those which are unobtainable. This is an area which is almost completely unexplored by educators. It cannot remain in this ignored status longer.

Not one of the items briefly discussed here is beyond the reach of a society which cares. Since it does not always care, private organizations will have to provide pressure. Professionals are not strong enough to do this alone.

It is absolutely necessary that youth with perceptual processing deficits be seen for what they are. What is normative in their growth and development and what is specific to their learning disability? Normal growth and its adolescent problems must be separated from the processing deficits by those who work with these children and youth. As Luke reminded us, he has few if any perceptual-motor problems when he is out on a date with his girl friend. He functions then as a normal man. Yet the very fact that Luke must remind us of this is his way of saying he would like to be able to talk about it with someone who can help him put this aspect of his life in perspective. There is most frequently an emotional overlay observable in the young people about whom we speak, a carryover from childhood as the result of a life history of failure. This is a learned response to a failure experience. It is not an inherent characteristic of perceptual deficits. If this adjustment is carried into adolescence and is mixed with the daily emotional tensions of adolescent-adult growth, then another type of support is involved. Somewhere in the community there must be available to these youths an adult friend or a counseling service which understands their needs. This does not always have to be a formal service. A buddy system is often successful. A big brother or sister concept works well in many instances. A school counselor may be helpful. We could go on. The point we make is not to describe such a program, but to insist that it be planned into the life of the youth in some manner.

In the preceding pages we have emphasized our long-standing opinion that structure as a tool of instruction is a vital and necessary factor in the learning and development of children with learning disabilities. The confusion which the child experiences as a result of the unpredictability of the perceptual processing problems can only be offset by the thoughtful and intelligent structuring of his learning environment and program. With the onset of puberty and the child's growth into adolescence, emotions, physical development, and social expectancies regarding him constitute further sources for confusion and tension. Although the specifics of structure must change and accommodate the older youth, the necessity for a structure which will provide him with the security he seeks (but often also rejects) must be provided. Here the art of parenting or teaching becomes obvious. The capacity to provide freedom to explore and to develop within the adolescent peer culture must be granted the youth while at the same time leaving him with the knowledge that an adult structural base is constantly available to him which he can use as a yardstick for his learning, growth, and behavior.

Adolescence has often been described as a period of contradictions — simultaneous love and rejection of adults; emotional stability and moodiness; fastidiousness and complete disregard for personal cleanliness and care of possessions; charm and gross vulgarity; desire to be wanted and complete rejection of those who would attempt to own or control. Within these dimensions, each with a pendulum which may swing with a different speed, the adolescent often finds himself in a vortex of misunderstanding — misunderstanding of himself and of the social situation around him. The need for structure, an external framework which he can use to learn and experience an orderly pattern to life, is greatly accentuated during these years.

The Lukes, the Alecs, and the Karens of this nation — representative of thousands of youths and young adults — are not going to grow like Topsy into acceptable adults except by chance. This nation cannot afford such careless planning. We are at the point where the plank in our national charter for these children guarantees life-span planning. Nothing less is acceptable.

PART VI

THE FUTURE

18

A TIME TO REVIEW IN TIME TO ACT

*W*ith the opening of the *Inferno* Dante says, *Mi ritrovai per una selva ocursa che la diritta via era smarrita* ("I found myself in a dark wood where the straight way was lost"). An old-fashioned, but more recent proverbial saying reminds us that "We're not out of the woods yet." The more popular statement lacks the dignity of Dante's sentence, and it is that to which I wish initially to address myself in this paper. For in learning disabilities we are in a very dark wood, and the straight way is indeed lost, at least temporarily.

In 1980, it is slightly more than forty years since less than a dozen researchers and clinicians began their work at a small institution in Michigan — work which ultimately led to the vast field of interest in children, youth, and adults with learning disabilities. It is 178 years ago this date when Gall began his superficial explorations in the field of phrenology in England, a step which stimulated a few neurologists, psychologists, and some additional persons of other professions to have an interest in the complex issues of learning and adjustment of those who are now called learning disabled. It has been seventeen years since parents, frustrated by the inactivity of the schools in behalf of their children, appalled by the lack of understanding of their children by physicians, educators, psychologists, and by the majority of individuals in most other professions, organized, frankly, to become a pressure group to effect optimal services for their children and their families by all disciplines which should have a concern for the problem. We are at the point now when much is known, and much is apparent, which, while not definitely known, is on the periphery of our knowledge. It is appropriate in

M. Sam Rabinovitch Memorial Lecture, Fifth Annual Convention of the Quebec Association for Children with Learning Disabilities, 1980.

1980 that we examine the known, the suspected, and the unknown, to ascertain the directions in which efforts must be made to insure that total services are available in appropriate form for all children and to insure that no additional generations of children be permitted to slip through professional fingers and end up leading partially or totally ineffective lives. It is time to plan for these eventualities.

The field of learning disabilities in 1980 often reminds me of a great orchestra a few minutes prior to the arrival of the concertmeister and the conductor — each instrument being tuned irrespective of the needs or wants of the neighboring musician, whose tones must be louder than those of the first in order for the player to be able to hear himself. It is a true example of cacaphony — a cacaphonous confusion with no sense of cooperative ensemble, in which no purposeful music emanates from the 110 musicians. Even the eight bassists standing in eminence to the right above all the other musicians emit rumbling chaos instead of the glorious comparison to the sixty-four foot pipe of the great cathedral organ. The concertmeister appears, and a common tone quality is effected. The conductor assumes responsibility, and music of a glorious form replaces the discordance of moments earlier.

If one examines the field of learning disabilities it is easy to discern the many individuals who are tuning their instruments without thought of others, with little concept of harmony, with less concern or knowledge of the roots of their profession or of an appropriate methodology for those they purport to serve. In the field of learning disabilities we lack the conductors. Perhaps it is safer to say that we have a few conductors, but each plays the tune to his own beat. There is today no universal attack to the symphony of the child and its problems. Then too, there are some conductors, who in this complex symphony cannot even read music and the result for the listener, to say nothing of the child and his family, is meaningless dissonance, cacaphony of the worst order. This is learning disabilities, 1980. From this point we have three obligations during this presentation, namely, to look back from whence we have come (and that only briefly as a review); to analyze the present situation and the reasons for it; and finally to look ahead to the next few years to determine what actions are required and must be insisted upon in order to bring to the learning disability children and to their families their total birthright.

A TIME TO REVIEW

Wiederholt (1974) has done a fine job of outlining the antecedents of the field of learning disabilities, tracing the history of this field from Gall in 1802 to Kirk, Frostig, Myklebust, myself, and some others. I do not propose here to repeat Wiederholt's work, nor to look at this field prior to about 1935. It is true that the work of Broca in 1861 still plays an important role today in our understanding of some children with learning disabilities. Bastien in 1869; Wernicke in 1861; Marie 1906; Orton 1925; Goldstein in 1927; and a few others contemporary to these and preceeding them were significant. They were exploring, and the disciplines were too unsophisticated, while the equipment was either lacking completely or was too unreliable to use extensively with human beings. Hence, little was really accomplished, except that theoretical concepts were laid down, and this was indeed important. Psychology was just born. Binet and his colleague Simone were asked by the French government of Paris to devise a method of excluding mentally retarded children from the schools as late as 1905. The Division of Clinical Psychology in the American Psychological Association was formed immediately following the second World War, and is still in its infancy. The field of neuropsychology is not yet a decade old, and the first basic book relating education and neurology will be forthcoming within the year under the authorship of a Canadian, your highly respected Dr. William Gaddes of the University of Victoria. This, in spite of statements of some of the neophytes in the field, is a new area of professional investigation, but basic to learning disabilities.

I place the beginning of formal attack to the problem in about 1935 when, escaping from the Nazi holocaust, two German-Jewish professional men, Dr. Heinz Werner, one of the world's outstanding developmental and genetic psychologists, and Dr. Alfred A. Strauss, seen by his German peers as one of their outstanding young neuropsychiatrists, escaped with their families from Germany by various routes and eventually landed in the United States where they found a comfortable reception at the Wayne County Training School for high-grade mentally retarded young people, located outside the city of Detroit. I stress this latter, for whether parents today accept the historical fact or not, learning disabilities as an aspect of child deviance had its beginning in research with the mentally retarded, and there are as many if not many more mentally retarded learning disability children in our countries than there are those of normal intelligence. But more of this later. Strauss and Werner immediately established themselves as a working team, and attempted to determine why some children in what was a remarkable institutional facility did not profit from the splendid program which was provided the residents. Their research is widely published, criticized, and critiqued. There is no reason for repeating it here. Suffice to say that by 1950 they had distinguished two very important separate problems, among others, in the field of mental retardation: namely, on the one hand the endogenous type of retardation, i.e., the familial, hereditary, or genetic type of retardation, and on the other hand the exogenous type of retardation, i.e., those in whose case history there was no evidence of hereditary factors for at least three generations back, but in whose case history there were evidences of accident, injury, disease, illness of a prenatal, perinatal, or postnatal nature which could be directly related to the neurological system of the organism, and to which we have later made direct relationships (as did they in a clinical manner) to perceptual processing deficits. These were the mentally retarded learning disabled youth, for they were working with young people between the ages of twelve and eighteen years, approximately. It is from this work, sometimes crude as it was, out of which the total field of learning disabilities has arisen; not just because of these two giants, Werner and Strauss, but because of a second set of factors which was of equal importance.

The Wayne County Training School was a unique institution, no longer functioning. In the many years it operated, until about 1950, it was headed by a remarkable superintendent, Dr. Robert Haskell, and by an equally remarkable Director of Research, the giant Norwegian psychologist, Dr. Thorleif Hegge. When there are good people in a leadership role, good young people are attracted to learn and hopefully to carry on the work of the older researchers. This is what happened at this school between about 1936 and 1948. Let us take a look at the partial roster of young people who then by chance or by invitation were attracted to the Training School and to Hegge, Strauss and Werner. You know many of them, for in the United States they constitute the second generation of workers in the field of learning disabilities since 1935. Samuel A. Kirk was then a young and budding psychologist. He was there. He did not become vitally interested in the exogenous child until several years had passed and until both he and Strauss were in Wisconsin. Then he caught fire, and out of his earlier exposure to the problems of these children there developed the Illinois Test of Psycholinguistic Abilities, which has become an important diagnostic tool in the hands of those who truly know how to use it. Dr. Maurice Fouracre, later head of the Department of Special Education at Columbia University, was there. His work lead him into a related field of study, i.e., cerebral palsy, but that is closely related as we have subsequently found. Dr. Bluma Weiner, now of Yeshiva University in New York City, was a significant staff member at the School. Dr. Ruth Melchior Patterson, late of the Columbus State School, Ohio, contributed much basic research to this problem during her years there. Marcella Douglas, following the leadership of Strauss and Laura Lehtinen, translated psychoneurological findings into educational practices on an experimental basis.

Newell Kephart was a young psychologist working with Frances Yoakley at the Training School. Together they published an article which caught the attention of Strauss and Werner when they finally arrived from Europe, and from this relationship more than a decade of significant research and theory developed. Kephart and Yoakley observed that a large group of their subjects did not respond to normal educational methodology or social adaptation training: these they later found to be exogenous, brain-injured mentally retarded young people. Kephart and I were closely associated at the Training School, and it was the unannounced decision of Strauss and Werner that we two young men were to be the focus of their attention as scientists. Psychologically and gastronomically they were proselitizing us to follow their leadership and guidance. Both Kephart and I were so poor, had so little money, that if the Strausses and Werners had not fed us regularly we would have followed no one. But they did provide intellectual and dietetic sustenance, and we followed, remaining close working friends and colleagues until Kephart's death a few years ago. But more of this still later.

The Second World War came on and was finished. After that I moved to Syracuse University, in New York State. It was there that a young student asked me for suggestions regarding a doctoral dissertation, and I suggested that she replicate all of the Strauss-Werner research, but with children of normal intelligence on whom specific neurological dysfunction was known. Miss Jane Dolphin undertook this task with a group of cerebral palsied children and youth, a small group and one which was largely heterogeneous. It was not then known that the various sub-types of cerebral palsy differed one from the other in their psychological characteristics. However, she found with statistical significance exactly the same types of processing deficits in this group of neurologically handicapped as Strauss and Werner had found with the mentally retarded exogeneous children. When Dolphin's articles were published in 1950–52, the concept of intellectual normalcy for the first time entered the literature in connection with this problem in children. Later Dr. Harry V. Bice, our student associates, and I made intensive studies of 400 athetoid and spastic cerebral palsied children of normal intelligence and 100 physically and intellectually normal children as a control group, and found that Dolphin's studies were essentially accurate. It was on the basis of these sets of studies that I undertook the first educational experimentation with intellectually normal and also retarded learning disabled children in the Montgomery County (Maryland) Public Schools in 1957, and published a partial report in 1961 regarding this work. It is out of these studies that the concept of learning disabilities and normalcy of intelligence grew.

THE INTELLIGENCE FACTOR

By 1963 the parents were seriously concerned about the lack of facilities for their children. I have no idea how many reprints of papers I sent to parents who asked for them, but it was in the hundreds, if not thousands. My incomplete 1961 book on the education of hyperactive and brain-injured children, along with Kephart's book, the *Slow Learner in the Classroom* (1960), sold so rapidly that reprints after reprints were prepared. The parents were far better read than most professional people regarding this problem. When representatives of nearly twenty parent groups met in Chicago in 1963, they arrived with a firm intent to modify the situation. They asked Dr. Samuel A. Kirk to address them at their dinner meeting. Sam did, although he was the first to admit that he, like most of the others who were working in this field essentially on a part-time basis, did not know the answers, and Sam struggled to formulate his comments. He said one significant thing, and the parents picked it up erroneously or misinterpreted it and therefore perpetuated a problem. Dr. Kirk stated that these children were not of the "primary mentally retarded" type, were not "primary blind or deaf." Rather they were educationally handicapped for one reason or another. The audience was not listening carefully, for instead of hearing him say that the children were not of the *primary* mentally retarded type, they "heard" him say that they were not primarily mentally retarded children, a completely different issue. In a letter dated January 10, 1980, Dr. Kirk wrote me as follows: "I think, however," he said, "that the various psychological problems of perception, etc. are being greatly neglected in learning disability programs. These are the areas we worked on earlier with the mentally retarded, but I am afraid that the current generation has completely forgotten the origins of what we now call learning disabilities and the problems that children encounter, especially at the younger ages." Nothing could be more to the truth. It is this that I have been urging parents and professionals to consider for years. The "origins" of which Kirk speaks were the mentally retarded brain injured children.

On January 11, 1980, I received a second letter from one who will go unnamed, but one you all would know if I were to mention the name. He writes me stating "Many of us feel that we must reserve the term 'learning disabilities' for perceptual and linguistic processing problems in those with potentially average to above average intelligence. In other words, we do not link 'learning disabilities' directly to 'perceptual linguistic processing deficits', but rather reserve it for only those whose primary problem is in perceptual and linguistic processing." This is pure gibberish, and doesn't even make sense. It illustrates a lack of basic understanding of the problem entirely. It is a paragraph talking in a circle, and is not good English. However, when national leadership speaks this way, it is easy to understand why the vast membership of parent organizations follow along with mistaken ideas. It would be interesting to know what a "perceptual linguistic processing deficit" is and how it differs from other perceptual processing deficits, a term which I believe I used for the first time in a book I revised in 1977. Since perceptual processing deficits were first recognized in the population of exogenous mentally retarded boys in 1932 about which I earlier spoke, this group falls directly within the population of which my ill-informed correspondent speaks.

I believe it may be helpful to examine this situation a bit further. Intelligence is an elusive characteristic, at least in human beings. Under varying conditions, it can be measured along a continuum. The continuum has limitations to it. I suspect there may be something like an IQ of zero, although I have never seen one. The lowest I have ever personally measured was an IQ of 6 in a youth of approximately sixteen years of age. At the opposite extreme, intelligence quotients of 160, 170 or higher have been reported, and there are frequent instances wherein the individual being examined has exhausted the test being used. The fact of the IQ per se is not so important to our argument here.

Let us take two children, both aged twelve years. Both experienced cerebral anoxia at birth. One has an IQ measured accurately at 135; the other, 65. Now at *every* intelligence level one finds psychological characteristics which are basic to learning. In youths such as these two who possess the residuals of birth trauma, we seek to ascertain to what extent these psychological characteristics have negative values and thus deter learning potential. In the boy with the high IQ there is found the presence of dissociation as noted on the Kohs Block Design Test and on the Rorschach Test. The second boy with the lower intelligence also shows dissociation. Both youths thus have difficulty in forming letters, making puzzles, and putting things together in new relationships. Boy No. 1 has a figure-background problem; so does Boy No. 2. Each thus has difficulty with reading, arithmetic, and spelling. Boy No. 1 has sequencing problems. Boy No. 2 has sequencing problems. Both boys have difficulty forming appropriate sentences, dressing appropriately, and following instructions. Boy No. 1 with the high IQ has visuo-motor problems; his counterpart with the lower intelligence also in addition to mental retardation has visuo-motor problems. We could continue further with this list of malfunctions. At any intelligence level, with no exceptions, perceptual processing problems or problems of perceptual pathology may occur and may interfere with learning up to the capacity of the intellectual level involved. To believe otherwise is to think contrary to basic scientific facts which professional persons daily encounter. Not only does the individual who rules out Boy No. 2 from appropriate educational and clinical services as a learning disabled retarded child, but also that person is contributing to the most heinous type of discrimination, particularly in large communities or in rural areas in which there are large groups of minority pupils. In one city, for example, classes for learning disabled children were 100 percent white; classes for the mentally retarded nearly 100 percent black. This is not a chance factor, and parent groups or professional educators who continue to espouse this definitional fallacy indeed are committing crimes of human decency to which the law is preparing to address itself. Once again we shall see courts of justice dictating how education is to be operated. It is certainly both a time to review and a time to act.

Obviously one can define learning disabilities any way he wishes, but accuracy is required. A Ford car is defined by Mr. Ford in a certain way as opposed to all other cars, and we may not wish to buy it. An intellectually normal child with learning disabilities also can be defined in opposition to those of lower intelligence. However, when this is done, keep in mind that society — you and I — in opposition to buying an automobile, are depriving an immense number of children and their parents of a basic birthright. They are not being given the type of education nor the educational opportunity they deserve. Somehow I am sure that guilt feelings should creep into the thinking of those who deprive. This was an issue which Sam Rabinovitch and I discussed on more than one occasion, and he, like Kirk and I and others, was feeling a growing concern for the injustice which was being done to thousands of children.

TEACHER EDUCATION

As we review some of the major issues related to learning disabilities during the past few years, teacher education comes to the fore quickly. The education of physicians, psychologists, and members of other disciplines is even more recent and is much more incomplete. About 1960 Dr. William Hollister, then of the National Institute for Mental Health (USA) approached me, suggesting that since the United States Office of Education was taking no leadership in the preparation of teachers for what then were being called brain-injured children, would I be interested in making a proposal to NIMH for funds to initiate something along this line. No precedent existed, except for what I had seen Lehtinen do under Strauss' and Werner's supervision and my own theory of what had to be done to counter what we were then calling perceptual pathology in these children. Nevertheless, we moved ahead and prepared such a project.

NIMH made available nearly one-half million dollars, which supported the Syracuse University project for five years, a project which was essentially successful in all respects. Forty-seven teachers were intensively prepared to deal with these children; many of them are still working in the field, now mostly in positions of direction, teacher education, or supervision. Consider, however, that by 1965, essentially one university in North America was attempting to prepare teachers for thousands of children. We at Syracuse accepted into this program twelve teachers per year! Gradually other universities began their own programs, but the early ones, in contrast to the Syracuse program, were limited to short summer session programs. The records are full of instances where a classroom teacher went to a college or university for a three or possibly a six-week program, was taught by non-prepared or ill-prepared professors, and then returned to her school district as the district's consultant in the education of brain-injured children, or by whatsoever other name the children were then called. Learning disabilities as a professional term was not yet commonly utilized, and it was grossly and poorly served.

The preparation of educators, whether classroom teachers or university professors, in the field of learning disabilities had no precedents. To the contrary, teachers of the blind, the mentally retarded, the deaf, and to a lesser extent, the crippled child had been prepared for nearly 100 years. There was a body of research, a methodology, and a corps of well-prepared professors in a few select colleges and universities. Learning disabilities did not have this resource or past history. There was little in the literature to guide those who were attempting to assist. Hence, most of those in colleges, for lack of better things, resorted to remediation — remedial reading, remedial arithmetic, beginning writing, and the like. One cannot remediate a vacuum, and obviously the remedial approach did not, nor does it now, work with these learning disabled children. Sufficient material has been written about the methodology which does appear effective, so that it will not be repeated here. Suffice to say that a structured developmental program of a multisensory nature is required, one which begins with the child at the most primitive level at which that child can produce repetitively a success experience. Regardless of chronological age, the clinical teacher must ascertain this lowest level of success, and build on that. When this is done, optimal results will be obtained. Other components of a successful program are required also, of course.

It is easy to see from these few examples that it is time to review this field, and the Quebec Association for Children with Learning Disabilities is to be complimented on selecting this as a theme for its fifth annual conference. The status of the field at present, as a result of the factors we have already discussed, is characterized by confusion; confusion so wide-spread that there are those who have given up and have deserted the field. At its worst it is epitomized by some who say that there is no such thing as a learning disabled child. However, in my considered opinion the truth will out. If it doesn't, then I, Sam Rabinovitch, William Gaddes, Margie Golick, Sam Kirk, and others who could be mentioned, have been dealing with thousands of figments of our imaginations in the form of children, disembodied souls, or child-ghosts. Bites, scratches, and black and blue marks, however, attest to me that these ghosts are exceedingly physical and realistic, and when one of them calls in desperation, "Dr. C. come here, come here quick. Hold me; I'm going to explode," I know he is not disembodied or a figment of my imagination. He is real. He's a kid I like, and he's in a terrible need of help and that quickly.

A TIME TO ACT

We have had enough pseudo authorities in this field. We have had enough so-called experts. We have had too little basic data with which to work. It is time to act. What do we see as the areas into which we must move and move with alacrity? First, we must train leadership; I have said this before many times.

It is essential that we have prepared for action a corps of outstanding college professors whose primary area of training is in the field of what I will refer to as *neuroeducation*. I do not want to invent a new term; we have enough of these. But I do mean to state that educators of children with perceptual processing deficits must have a background in neurophysiology as well as in instruction and educational methodology in order to effect a proper psychoeducational match between the child's deficits and educational achievement levels. While it is understandable, it is by this date inexcuseable that most of the college professors in the field of learning disabilities are not primarily trained for their positions, or if they are they have been prepared by a previous generation of faculty members who, because of history, are themselves essentially self-prepared. A quality corps of teachers of children will not flow from these sources. Governments have resources so that within a two- to three-year period a group of well-prepared people could be turned out, and within a decade the problem would essentially be solved. Until this happens, the needs of children with learning disabilities, whether caused by neurophysiological dysfunction or environmental or social deprivation and disorganization, will in no way be solved.

Diagnosticians who understand educational practice and small group instruction are also required. Clinical psychology fails in large measure to provide teachers with an appropriate understanding of this issue. School psychology falls far short. There is, however, hope in the ever-growing field of neuropsychology, and it is to this field we turn with the expectation that assistance will be obtained. Canada is fortunate in having some of North America's finest neuropsychologists at Victoria University, Carlton College, University of Windsor, the University of Saskatchewan, and some other centers of learning. Interestingly, each of these people are members of the select International Academy for Research in Learning Disabilities, about which I shall speak in a moment. Sam Rabinovitch, had he lived, would have been a member of this Academy. Although Sam did not call himself a neuropsychologist and the Academy encompasses more than this single discipline, Sam knew his neurology. He was able to approach children essentially with a total knowledge of their needs and their characteristics. He was able to make a differential diagnosis with ease, and thus deal with children in terms of their basic eccentricities. Once upon a time he and I were talking, and he said to me half joking, "Have you ever experienced what kids really go through?" My response then was "No." During the past year, however, I was very ill with infectious hepatitis. Upon my return home from the hospital, I was ensconced in a chair in our living room. It was just prior to Christmas. As I looked out across the room, I was staggered by the number of distractions before me — miscellaneous things on a coffee table, design in a chair fabric, pictures on the far wall, Christmas decorations for the arriving grandchildren, and a variety of other of the usual objets d'art in the room. The stereo with soft music was playing. My wife was talking. All of a sudden I knew what visually and perceptually handicapped children went through every day. My illness had affected the nervous system. I was hyperactive to stimuli, and I cried to my wife either to move me or to strip the room of everything which could be moved and to turn off the stereo. The moment this was completed I could relax, and for the next ten months this non-stimulating, highly structured environment became my therapeutic milieu. I could answer "yes" to Sam at this point. I know personally the terrible trauma which children go through daily in an environment which does not cater to their needs. This needs much more research, but it is a characteristic of the educational regimen which we have advocated for forty years, and which we know works clinically. From personal experience, I know it is an essential element in their education. The neuropsychologist can assist us in quickly ascertaining these perculiar characteristics of the children, and thus assist educators to more quickly adapt programming to child need.

To this point we have stressed with urgency the need for powerful, well-prepared and oriented leaders, professors, and teachers of these children. Jean Renoir, in another setting, expresses my concern for educational giants. In the biography which he wrote, *Renoir, My Father,* he speaks of the materials out of which long-lasting things are made. He writes

> One day I heard my father tell a group of friends who included Vollard the art dealer and Gagnet the collector, "Since the days of the cathedrals we have had but one sculptor. Sculptor is hard. You can still find a few painters and bucketsfull of writers and musicians, but to be a sculptor you have to be a saint, and to have the strength to escape the snare of cleverness . . . and also not to fall into the trap of the would-be rustic. . . . Since Chartres there has been only one sculptor, in my view, and that is Degas. Those who worked on cathedrals . . . succeeded in giving us an idea of eternity. That was the great preoccupation of their time."

It is enough to say that in 1980 we need in the field of learning disabilities a thousand Degases to give us strength to give our children the power to elude traps, to substitute superficial cleverness with honest knowledge and understanding, and to avoid the trap of the cute rustic which belies their underlying shallowness.

Environmental and Social Disorganization

A few moments ago we referred to learning disabled children whose etiology derived from environmental and social disorganization as opposed to neurophysiological dysfunction. The inclusion of the former group into the field of learning disabilities, a group never considered by those who originally investigated this problem, has been one of the major issues causing confusion and chaos in the field. Interestingly enough this group of children, particularly at the younger ages, often illustrates the same perceptual processing problems as do those with a definite diagnosis of central nervous system dysfunction (Cruickshank, Morse, and Johns 1980). It is this group of children and youth which has given rise to two significant problems. First, their inclusion in the definition of learning disabilities has confused educators, for obviously there is no definitive neurological dysfunction. Secondly, these children often come from a single social class and economic order. As such, they are prone to delinquency from the point of society generally. It is my considered opinion that this group is the primary one causing the so-called "link" between learning disability and delinquency. I do not believe that there is a general link between these two factors, and I thoroughly question the statements to this effect which have been made in public so far. What came first, the social pattern which could lead to delinquency or learning disability which resulted in delinquency? We do not have the answer to this question, but I suspect the former rather than the latter if learning disability is accurately defined. The statements which are being made regarding the relationship between delinquency and learning disability are not new. In the 1930s, Professor Clifford R. Shaw, one of the great sociologists of his day, wrote and had published by the University of Chicago Press three fascinating books (among others), namely, *The Jackroller* (1930), *The Natural History of a Delinquent Career* (1931), and *Brothers in Crime* (1938). As he described the boys about whom he wrote, they would today be called learning disabled. However, the total focus was on the social climate which produced the delinquency, not on the neurophysiological issues we face in learning disability. This is an issue on which we as a profession must act in the immediate future and solve before our children get a worse name and reputation than they already have among school people. I do not believe there is validity in the phrase "the link between delinquency and learning disability. Now we must act.

Drugs and Medication

I have often spoken of my concern about the effects of medications on the unborn fetus taken by women during pregnancy. We have very little data on the effect of either drugs administered via prescription or of those purchased without prescription over the counter. One of the speakers at this conference, Dr. Yvonne Brackbill, and her associates, has done considerable research on this problem. Unfortunately, their data are still in the bowels of the computor at the National Institutes of Health in Washington, D.C., with little hope of getting access to them soon. However, be that as it may, we do know clinically that both heroin and methadone have serious effects on the fetus, effects which result in brain injury, mental retardation, and other central nervous system problems which are not remissible. If the placenta is not effective in protecting the fetus from these drugs, as it is not with alcohol, it is quite likely that it likewise does not protect the fragile human organism from the dozens of sleeping tablets, uppers and downers, and related pills and capsules which anyone can purchase regularly without prescription at any supermarket or drugstore. Here is a place to both review and to act with legislation which protects the unborn. During my recent lengthy illness, I watched television a great deal of the time to pass the hours away. To amuse myself, I kept track of advertisements which could have either an appeal to children or an impact on children. During one week, between 10:00 A.M. and 10:00 P.M., Monday through Sunday, inclusive, I counted an average of thirty-six advertisements per day for drugs for headaches, insomnia, and drowsiness when driving. These advertisements came at prime time in the evenings, and during the soap opera times in the afternoon and mornings when a future mother in discomfort might well be watching the shows. I did not watch early Saturday mornings when programs are devoted to children, because I, too, was under medication to sleep, although not for pregnancy! It is my further considered opinion in the light of what we know about heroin and other hard drugs and their impact on the fetus, that we may indeed be creating a generation of brain-injured or learning disabled children through the use of so-called "normal" medications. Hopefully, NIH will release the Brackbill data soon. In the meantime, her statements before the appropriate committee of the United States Senate are on public record and can be obtained by writing to the Chairman of the Senate Committee on Health, U.S. Senate, Washington, D.C. — or better still talking with Dr. Brackbill here at this conference!

Conclusion

Research in All Areas

Research in all areas related to learning disabilities is needed and essential before we can truly say we are meeting the needs of these children. We have mentioned the need of drug research. Two other developments are under way which may have long-term related effects.

The Association for Children with Learning Disabilities (USA) has created a Scientific Study Committee. This committee is assisting in the formulation of a long-term statement of research needs and is composed of leading scientists with research backgrounds. There is little question, but that this group will move with all due deliberate speed to motivate scientists, the U.S. government, and organizations to formulate projects, obtain funding, and to initiate research of significance to our purposes. This group is actively underway meeting again effectively just two weeks ago. Canadian representation is included on the Scientific Study Committee.

A second group I have already mentioned has a different purpose or set of purposes and must move a bit slower. I speak of the International Academy for Research in Learning Disabilities (IARLD). The Quebec Association has invited six members of the Academy from North America to address various sections of this Fifth Annual Meeting and we were pleased to be able to accept. A seventh Academy Fellow from Belgium is also present, and is participating in your meetings.

The International Academy for Research in Learning Disabilities is comprised of scientists, world-wide, voluntarily banded together concerned with the advancement of knowledge in the field of learning disabilities. The academy represents a professional, international, interdisciplinary consortium of scientists.

Members of the International Academy believe that research and theory reflecting many points of view and fields of endeavor are appropriate to the pursuit of this academic society, and adopt a leadership role in the development of a focus to and the parameters of the field of learning disability.

In general, the members of the academy recognize learning disabilities to be related to neurophysiological and neuropsychological deficits, which, in turn, are indigenous to the function or malfunction of the neurological and neuropsychological systems of the human organism. The neurophysiological development of the human organism, its maldevelopment resulting in perceptual processing deficits, and the subsequent impact of these factors on learning and adjustment form the scope of interest to members of the Academy.

The affairs of the International Academy reside in the Executive Committee and the Academy Council. The Executive Committee is composed of elected officers consisting of a President (USA), two Vice-Presidents (Argentina and The Netherlands), a Secretary (Canada), a Treasurer (USA), and the immediate past President. The Academy Council, consisting of ten Academic Fellows, is elected to assist the members of the Executive Committee in the administration and operation of the academy. Not more than one Academy Council member will be elected to the Council from the same country at the same time, hence, ten countries will be represented on the Academy Council at all times.

The officers of the academy shall be elected for a term of four years and may not be re-elected. Initially, members of the Academy Council will be elected for two-, three-, and four-year terms, and, with the exception of those elected or appointed for four-year terms, and, may be re-elected. All Academic Fellows will be eligible to vote with respect to the election of officers and Academic Council members.

Between formal meetings of the Academy, the Council will encourage members in a variety of activities; i.e.,

> to engage in research and writing in the field of learning disabilities; to share their writings as well as pre-publication ideas with others of the Academy through the exchange of papers, reprints, correspondence, books, and other media forms; to encourage and stimulate the international exchange of students in the area of learning disabilities between countries and facili-

ties; to address itself to and provide appropriate pressures to be exerted on governments to foster research and training in the areas of learning disabilities;

The Academy may

foster the establishment of a clearinghouse of information in the areas of learning disabilities; engage, through its members, in research and appropriate training activities; undertake surveys of the development of the field of learning disabilities and bring to the attention of its members and governments those problems on which major attention should be directed; provide, every four years, a review of the literature in the several areas of learning disabilities highlighting new developments in the several fields of learning disabilities, stimulating promising research, and emphasizing new theoretical concepts; publish, as needed, a professional journal, research, newsletter, monograph, or other forms of professional stimulation of the field; engage in contracts with governments, research agencies, publication houses, or with individuals in achieving its professional goals.

In this Memorial Address to the late Sam Rabinovitch we have stressed a number of serious problems facing the field of learning disabilities. There are others which could be mentioned, but there is a limit to the extent to which emotionally we can constantly deal with the negative. There are positives in this statement as well, chief among them the advent of the Scientific Study Committee and the International Academy for Research in Learning Disabilities, the latter composed of 150 of the world's outstanding leadership in many disciplines directly or indirectly concerned with the complex problems of learning disabilities. This group currently represents persons from approximately thirty countries. But as one looks back over the last two or three decades, one sees much of a positive nature, and it is on this tone which I wish to end this presentation.

In 1939 the first conference on learning disabilities, then called brain-injury, was held at what is now called Eastern Michigan University in Ypsilanti, Michigan. Eight persons attended, including four who were making presentations. Today the Quebec Association conference is typical of the group which can be assembled almost any place, from Quebec to Australia; from Australia to Japan; from Japan to Great Britain; from Great Britain to any one of the fifty states in the United States. From a local group made up of a few researchers in a single residential school, a world-wide concern has developed within our lifetimes. This is progress.

While not everyone agrees with the definition of the problem or even its existence, the more intellectually mature are of one mind, and with more and more persons there is a cohesiveness as to terminology, definition, etiology, diagnosis, and treatment regimens. This is progress when one considers the fact that most of the many thousands of concerned individuals have received a minimum of formal training or no training at all.

We have learned to make differential diagnosis between and among children and thus are able to provide more adequately for their individual needs. We can isolate audio, visuo, tactuo, and other sensory perceptual processing deficits in children of any intellectual disability level. While we may not yet be able to isolate all the neurophysiological components in each disabled child, we can make sufficiently accurate diagnoses to permit education to go forth and positive social adjustment to develop. It is interesting to me too, in the light of what we have said about low levels of intelligence and learning disabilities, that the California Association for Neurologically and Educationally Handicapped, for example, has removed their cut-off I.Q. point of 90, so that as of today no designated figure exists, and that organization is moving to attempt to meet the total intellectual spectrum of learning disabilities, as we have advocated for so long. Other states are doing the same, and that is progress.

The concept of structure in its fullest sense is being accepted as an essential in the educational scene, both in school and in the home for these children. Structure is a complicated concept, and includes environmental structure, spatial structure, adult-pupil structure, structured program, and structured teaching materials. A few years ago permissiveness was the keystone in the minds of many educators; today, and always in the opinion of some well-oriented educators, structure in the best sense of the word and as a tool of instruction is being seen as essential in meeting these children's needs. This is progress.

Once upon a time there were two books in print concerning the education of these children, just twenty years ago. Now there is so much printed material, some excellent, some exceedingly naive and poor, that one has to be very selective in utilizing it. I guess this is progress.

I cannot say that any national government has taken a *bona fide* leadership role with respect to the learning disabled individual. Some few have made attempts. But these attempts are only as good as is the level of sophistication and understanding on the part of the civil servants involved, and that has not been uniformly high. However, some governments at least do accept the fact that they have a role, and this is progress.

As we look to the present and the future, there are many unmet needs, all of which we will not identify at this time. Suffice to say there are two needs current which must be addressed, and which are not adequately handled. The adolescent youth with learning disabilities is not yet understood by even a small fraction of secondary school personnel. Programs for these youths are practically non-existent except in a few terribly expensive private schools. This challenge and responsibility must receive the attention of parents and government officials, and a crash program must be undertaken to meet those youths who are now of secondary school age and the ever-increasing number of children in elementary schools who, within a few years, will be of an age to demand admission to middle and upper schools. There is no reason why this program should not be set in place, and it could be achieved in a very short time if a decision to do so were made.

Finally, and related to the needs of the adolescent, let us not overlook the young adult who also may need guidance and special training to fit into society. I have just completed an intensive follow-up of a relatively large group of boys with whom I worked fifteen–seventeen years ago when they were seven to nine years of age. While all but one of these young men has "made it" without police records, all of them could have profited more if adequate counseling, guidance, and prevocational training had been provided them in the secondary school. Some have entered and completed the university, but with a great effort. I am looking forward to receiving a young man next fall into the doctoral program of the University who can neither read or write, but whose baccalaureate degree from an excellent university was awarded *magna cum laude*. With two of my associates, we have just published a book dealing with the struggles of learning disabled youth from adolescence toward adulthood. It is indeed a struggle, and we can do much to lessen this extraordinary effort if we move into an action program now.

To me, Sam Rabinovitch epitomized the leadership we need so desperately in the field of learning disabilities. He was a man with imagination, with technological skills, with an emotional concern for his fellow men, and with an understanding of the anatomical, psychological, neurophysiological, and educational characteristics of those with whom he worked. He possessed an empathy into the problems of childhood, adolescence, and adult-hood, alike. This man could and did offer a better life for those with learning disabilities. He worked quietly, never asking for accolades. He was a man of Canada of whom Canadians can be forever proud. I had the privilege of serving with him on numerous committees of an international nature. I never left a contact with Dr. Rabinovitch except with the knowledge that I had learned and that I had been in the presence of one with whom it was possible to empathize: me with him and him with me. This is the foundation for intellectual progress out of which programmatic advances are made. It is the stage whereon the shadows of Dante's "dark wood" fade and become clear in the light of clinical examination, and the "straight way" is found for children, youth, and their families.

REFERENCES

Cruickshank, W. M.; F. A. Bentzen; F. Ratzeberg; and M. Tannhauser. *A Teaching Method for Brain-Injured and Hyperactive Children*. Syracuse: Syracuse University Press, 1961.

Cruickshank, W. M.; W. C. Morse; and J. Johns, *Learning Disabilities: The Struggle from Adolescence toward Adulthood*. Syracuse: Syracuse University Press, 1980.

Kephart, N. C. *The Slow Learner in the Classroom*. 2nd ed. Columbus: Merrill, 1971.

Renoir, Jean. *Renoir, My Father*. Boston: Little-Brown, 1962.

Shaw, C. F. *The Jackroller*. Chicago: University of Chicago Press, 1930.

Shaw, C. F. *The Natural History of a Delinquent Career*. Chicago: University of Chicago Press, 1931.

Shaw, C. F. *Brothers in Crime*. Chicago: University of Chicago Press, 1938.

Wiederholt, L., "Historical Perspectives on the Education of the Learning Disabled." In *The Second Review of Special Education,* edited by L. Mann and D. A. Sabatino. Philadelphia: JSE Press, 1974.

BIBLIOGRAPHY FOR
WILLIAM M. CRUICKSHANK
1966–81

Cruickshank, W. M., ed. *The Teacher of Brain-Injured Children: A Discussion of the Bases for Competency.* Syracuse: Syracuse University Press, 1966.

Cruickshank, W. M. "An Introductory Overview." In Cruickshank, W. M., ed., *The Teacher of Brain-Injured Children: A Discussion of the Bases for Competency.* Syracuse: Syracuse University Press, 1966.

Cruickshank, W. M. "A Summary." In Cruickshank, W. M., ed., *The Teacher of Brain-Injured Children: A Discussion of the Bases for Competency.* Syracuse: Syracuse University Press, 1966.

Cruickshank, W. M. "Obligations and Expectancies of the Disabled Person in the Educational Process." In Syracuse University School of Social Work, *The Academic Advisement of Disabled Students.* Syracuse: Syracuse University, 1966.

Cruickshank, W. M. *The Brain-Injured Child in Home, School, and Community.* Syracuse: Syracuse University Press, 1967.
Translations and other editions of *The Brain-Injured Child in Home, School, and Community:*

a. J. Valk, trans., *Buitenbeentjes.* Rotterdam, The Netherlands: Lemniscatt, 1970.

b. R. Valasco Fernandez, trans., *El nino con dano cerebral: en la escuela, en la hogar, y en la comunidad.* Mexico City, Mexico: Editorial Trillas, 1971.

c. (British Edition) *The brain-injured child in home, school, and community.* London: Pitman Medical, 1971.

d. E. Reinartz, trans., *Schwierige kinder in schule und elternhaus.* Berlin-Charlottenburg, W. Germany: Carl Marhold Verlagsbunchhandlung, 1973.

e. I. Ryuji, trans., Japanese translation through Charles E. Tuttle Company, Inc., Tokyo, 1974.

f. Talking Book Edition, American Foundation for the Blind, 1976.

g. Designated by the Behavioral Science Book Service as a selection of the month for September 1979.

Cruickshank, W. M. "Hyperactive Children: Their Needs and Curriculum. The Teaching-Learning Process in Educating Emotionally Disturbed Children." Syracuse: Syracuse University Division of Special Education and Rehabilitation, 1967.

Cruickshank, W. M. "Psychopathology and Implications for Educating Brain-Injured Children." In *Educational Implications of Psychopathology for Brain-Injured Children*. Cambridge, Mass.: Leslie College Graduate School of Education, 1967.

Cruickshank, W. M. "Translating Program Objectives into Action—Interagency Cooperation." Paper presented at Institute to Advance Interagency Comprehensive Planning for the Mentally Retarded, November 27–December 1, 1967, Hickory Corners, Michigan. Institute sponsored by Michigan Department of Education and the State Interagency Cadre on Mental Retardation.

Cruickshank, W. M.; J. B. Junkala; J. L. Paul. *The Preparation of Teachers of Brain-Injured Children*. Syracuse: Syracuse University Press, 1968.

Cruickshank, W. M.; J. L. Paul; and J. B. Junkala. *Misfits in the Public Schools*. Syracuse: Syracuse University Press, 1969.

Cruickshank, W. M. "Foreword." In S. Rappaport, *Public Education for Children with Brain Dysfunction*. Syracuse: Syracuse University Press, 1969.

Cruickshank, W. M. "Reflections on Learning Disabilities." In *Meeting Total Needs of Learning Disabled Children: A Forward Look*. Philadelphia: Association for Children with Learning Disabilities, 1970.

Cruickshank, W. M. "An Interdisciplinary Model for Manpower Development for Mental Retardation." In *The Challenge of Mental Retardation in the Community. Proceedings of the first Annual Spring Conference of the ISMR, Ann Arbor, Michigan, May 15–16, 1970*. Ann Arbor: University of Michigan—ISMRRD, 1970.

Cruickshank, W. M., and H. C. Quay. "Learning and Physical Environment: The Necessity for Research and Research Designing." *Exceptional Children* 37 (1970): 261–68.

Cruickshank, W. M. "Rehabilitation Toward a Broader Spectrum." *Psychological Aspects of Disability,* 17 (1970): 149–58.

Cruickshank, W. M.; E. D. Marshall and M. A. Hurley. *Foundations for Mathematics*. Boston: Teaching Resources Corporation, 1971.
Unit I: "Concepts for Sets and Curves," teacher's guide and materials.
Unit II: "Exploring Sets," teacher's guide and materials.

Unit III: "Motor Development: Lines and Planes," teacher's guide and materials.

Unit IV: "Comparing Sets and Numbers," teacher's guide and materials.

Cruickshank, W. M.; F. P. Connor; and H. Rusalem. "Psychological Considerations with Crippled Children." In Cruickshank, W. M., ed., *Psychology of Exceptional Children and Youth,* 3rd rev. ed. Englewood Cliffs, N.J.: Prentice-Hall, 1971. Also in Spanish edition.

Cruickshank, W. M., and J. L. Paul. "The Psychological Characteristics of Brain-Injured Children." In Cruickshank, W. M., ed., *Psychology of Exceptional Children and Youth,* 3rd rev. ed. Englewood Cliffs, N.J.: Prentice-Hall, 1971; retitled "The Psychological Characteristics of Children with Learning Disabilities in *Psychology of exceptional children and youth* (4th revised edition), 1980. Also in Spanish edition.

Cruickshank, W. M. "Comments on the Scope and Training of Support Personnel in Michigan." In Hallahan, D. P., ed. *Guidelines for the Preparation of Support Personnel.* Ann Arbor: University of Michigan – ISMRRD, 1971.

Cruickshank, W. M. "The Brain-Injured Child: Educational Considerations." In Teaching Resources Corporation, *Approaches to Learning Readiness.* Boston: Teaching Resources Corporation, 1971.

Cruickshank, W. M. "Comments on 'Benefit-Cost Analysis' by William B. Neenan." In J. S. Cohen *et al.,* eds., *Benefit-Cost Analysis for Mental Retardation Programs.* Ann Arbor: University of Michigan – ISMRRD, 1971.

Cruickshank, W. M. "Special Education, the Community and Constitutional Issues." In D. L. Walker and D. P. Howard, eds., *Special Education Instrument of Change in Education for the 70's.* Selected papers from the University of Virginia lecture series, 1970–71. Charlottesville, Va.: University of Virginia, 1971.

Cruickshank, W. M. "Mental Retardation: An Overview." In N. S. Springer, ed., *Proceedings of a Conference on Nutrition and Mental Retardation.* Ann Arbor: University of Michigan – ISMRRD, 1972.

Cruickshank, W. M. "Some Issues Facing the Field of Learning Disability." *Journal of Learning Disabilities* 5 (1972): 380–88.

Cruickshank, W. M. "The Interdisciplinary Model for Manpower Development for Mental Retardation." *Indian Journal of Mental Retardation* 5 (1972): 44–57.

Cruickshank, W. M. "The Right Not to be Labelled." In R. M. Segal, ed., *Advocacy for the Legal and Human Rights of the Mentally Retarded.* Ann Arbor: University of Michigan – ISMRRD, 1972.

Cruickshank, W. M., and D. P. Hallahan. "Alfred A. Strauss: Pioneer in Learning Disabilities." *Exceptional Children* 39 (1973): 321–27.

Cruickshank, W. M. and D. P. Hallahan. *Psychoeducational Foundations of Learning Disabilities.* Englewood Cliffs, N.J.: Prentice-Hall, 1973. German translation by E. Reinhardt, *Lernstorungen BZW. Lernbehinderung.* Munich: GmbH, 1979.

Tijdschrift voor Orthopedagogiek (The Netherlands) 2, 10 (1972): 259–94, is devoted to comments by W. M. Cruickshank and discussions of his writings.

Cruickshank, W. M. "Foreword." In J. Kauffman and C. Lewis, eds., *Teaching Children with Behavior Disorders.* Columbus: Charles Merrill, 1974.

Cruickshank, W. M. "Foreword." In A. J. Ayres, *The Development of Sensory and Integrative Theory and Practice: A Collection of the Works of A. Jean Ayres.* Dubuque, Iowa: Kendall/Hunt, 1974.

Cruickshank, W. M. "The False Hope of Integration." *The Slow Learning Child* (Australia) 21 (1974): 67–83. Also in *The Association of Special Education Teachers Journal* (New South Wales, Australia) 3 (1976): 10–17.

Cruickshank, W. M. "Learning Disabilities: A Charter for Excellence." In S. A. Kirk and J. McCarthy, eds., *Learning Disabilities: Selected ACLD Papers.* New York: Houghton-Mifflin, 1975.

Cruickshank, W. M.; J. Wepman; C. Deutsch; C. Strother; and A. Morency. "Learning Disabilities." In N. Hobbs, ed., *Issues in the Classification of Children,* Vol. 1. San Francisco: Jossey-Bass, 1974.

Cruickshank, W. M., and D. P. Hallahan, eds. *Perceptual and Learning Disabilities in Children.* Vol. 1: Psychoeducational Procedures; Vol. 2: Research and Theory. Syracuse: Syracuse University Press, 1975. American Medical Writers Association Award, 1975.

Cruickshank, W. M. "The Psychoeducational Match." In W. M. Cruickshank and D. P. Hallahan, eds., *Perceptual and Learning Disabilities in Children,* Vol. 1. Syracuse: Syracuse University Press, 1975.

Cruickshank, W. M. "The Learning Environment." In W. M. Cruickshank and D. P. Hallahan, eds., *Perceptual and Learning Disabilities in Children,* Vol. 1. Syracuse: Syracuse University Press, 1975.

Cruickshank, W. M. "Perceptual and Learning Disability: A Definition and Projection — An Editorial." *Educational Leadership* 32 (1975): 499–503. Digested in *The Educational Digest* 41 (1975): 31–33.

Cruickshank, W. M., ed. *Cerebral Palsy: A Developmental Disability,* 3rd rev. ed. Syracuse: Syracuse University Press, 1976.

Cruickshank, W. M. "The Problem and Its Scope." In W. M. Cruickshank, ed., *Cerebral Palsy: A Developmental Disability,* 3rd rev. ed. Syracuse: Syracuse University Press, 1976.

Cruickshank, W. M.; D. P. Hallahan; and H. V. Bice. "The Evaluation of Intelligence." In W. M. Cruickshank, ed., *Cerebral Palsy: A Developmental Disability,* 3rd rev. ed. Syracuse, Syracuse University Press, 1976.

Cruickshank, W. M.; D. P. Hallahan; and H. V. Bice. "Personality and Behavioral Characteristics." In W. M. Cruickshank, ed., *Cerebral Palsy: A Developmental Disability,* 3rd rev. ed. Syracuse: Syracuse University Press, 1976.

Cruickshank, W. M. "Educational Planning." In W. M. Cruickshank, ed. *Cerebral Palsy: A Developmental Disability,* 3rd rev. ed. Syracuse: Syracuse University Press, 1976.

Cruickshank, W. M. "William M. Cruickshank." In J. Kauffman and D. Hallahan, eds., *Teaching Children with Learning Disabilities: Personal Perspectives.* Columbus: Charles Merrill, 1976.

Cruickshank, W. M. "Foreword." In D. A. Sanders ed., *Auditory Perception of Speech.* Englewood Cliffs, N.J.: Prentice-Hall, 1976.

Cruickshank, W. M. "Problems in the Education of Children with Learning Difficulties and Some Practical Solutions." *The Exceptional Child* 23 (1976): 146-59.

Cruickshank, W. M. "Myths and Realities in Learning Disabilities." *Journal of Learning Disabilities* 10 (1977): 51-58.

Cruickshank, W. M. Review of *Minimal Cerebral Dysfunction* (by Gross and Wilson). *Journal of Learning Disabilities* 10 (1977): 125-27.

Cruickshank, W. M. "Foreword." In J. L. Paul, G. R. Neufeld, and J. W. Pelosi, eds., *Child Advocacy within the System.* Syracuse: Syracuse University Press, 1977.

Cruickshank, W. M. "Foreword." In A. J. Pappanikou and J. L. Paul, eds., *Mainstreaming Emotionally Disturbed Children.* Syracuse: Syracuse University Press, 1977.

Cruickshank, W. M.; J. L. Paul; and Turnbull, A. P. *Mainstreaming: A Practical Guide.* Syracuse: Syracuse University Press, 1977. Paperback edition published by Schocken Books, 1979.

Cruickshank, W. M. *Learning Disabilities in Home, School, and Community.* Syracuse: Syracuse University Press, 1977. Japanese translation through Scott Meredith Literary Agency, Tokyo, Japan, 1980.

Cruickshank, W. M. "Least Restrictive Placement: Administrative Wishful Thinking." *Journal of Learning Disabilities* 10 (1977): 193-94.

Cruickshank, W. M. "Integration: A Conceptual Model." In T. Nordin and B. Sjovall, eds., *Individualism Och Samhorighet.* Lund, Sweden: Bokforlaget, 1977. Reprinted *Journal of Learning Disabilities* 10 (1977).

Cruickshank, W. M. "When Winter Comes, Can Spring . . ?" *The Exceptional Child* (Australia) 25 (1978): 3-25.

Cruickshank, W. M. "Adolescence and Learning Disabilities: A Time Between." In E. Polak, ed., *Learning Disabilities: Information Please.* Montreal: Quebec Association for Children with Learning Disabilities, 1978. French edition titled *Adolescence et troubles d'apprentissage: Une epoque de la vie.*

Cruickshank, W. M. "Learning Disabilities: Perceptual or other?" *Tijdschrift voor Orthopedagogiek* (The Netherlands) 9 (1978): 421-31. English version on *ACLD Newsbriefs* 125 (1979) 7-10.

Cruickshank, W. M. "Learning Disabilities and the Special School." In *Starpoint: A shining place.* Fort Worth, Tex.: Texas Christian University Press, 1978.

Cruickshank, W. M. "Foreword." In G. P. Markel and J. Greenbaum, *Parents are to be Seen and Heard: Assertiveness and Educational Planning for Handicapped Children.* San Luis Obispo, Ca.: Impact, 1979.

Cruickshank, W. M., and L. J. Lewandowski. "Physical Handicaps." In W. C. Morse, ed., *Humanistic Teaching for Exceptional Children.* Syracuse: Syracuse University Press, 1979.

Cruickshank, W. M., and L. J. Lewandowski. "Cerebral Palsy." In W. C. Morse, ed., *Humanistic Teaching for Exceptional Children.* Syracuse: Syracuse University Press, 1979.

Cruickshank, W. M. "Learning Disabilities: Definitional Statement." In E. Polak, ed., *Issues and Initiatives in Learning Disabilities.* Ottawa: Canadian Association for Children with Learning Disabilities, 1979.

Cruickshank, W. M., and L. J. Lewandowski. "Psychological Development of Crippled Children." In W. M. Cruickshank, ed., *Psychology of Exceptional Children and Youth,* 4th rev. ed. Englewood Cliffs, N.J.: Prentice-Hall, 1980.

Cruickshank, W. M.; W. C. Morse; and J. Johns, *Learning Disabilities: The Struggle from Adolescence toward Adulthood.* Syracuse: Syracuse University Press, 1980.

Cruickshank, W. M., ed., *Approaches to Learning: Vol. 1, The Best of ACLD.* Syracuse: Syracuse University Press, 1980.

Cruickshank, W. M., with V. J. Glennon. "Teaching Mathematics to Children and Youth with Perceptual and Cognitive Processing Deficits." In *The Mathematical Education of Exceptional Children and Youth.* Reston, Va.: National Council of Teachers of Mathematics, 1980, Chapter 4.

Cruickshank, W. M., and A. S. Silver, eds. *Bridges to Tomorrow. Vol. 2, The Best of ACLD.* Syracuse: Syracuse University Press, 1981.

CONTENTS TO VOLUME 1

279

CONCEPTS IN LEARNING DISABILITIES

Selected Writings, Volume 2

was composed in 10-point Compugraphic Times Roman and leaded two points
by Metricomp Studios;
with display type in Foundry Lydian and Lydian Cursive by J. M. Bundscho, Inc.;
printed by sheet-fed offset on 50-pound acid-free Warren Antique Cream paper,
Smyth-sewn and bound over 80-point binder's boards in Columbia Bayside Linen,
by Maple-Vail Book Manufacturing Group, Inc.;
and published by

SYRACUSE UNIVERSITY PRESS

Syracuse, New York 13210